PERSONAL COMPUTING

Jim Huffman

PERSONAL COMPUTING

RESTON PUBLISHING COMPANY, INC.
A Prentice-Hall Company
Reston, Virginia

Library of Congress Cataloging in Publication Data

HUFFMAN, JIM.
    Personal computing.

    Bibliography: p.
    Includes index.
    1. Microcomputers. 2. Microprocessors. I. Title.
QA76.5.H773   001.6'4'04   79-722
ISBN 0-8359-5516-8
ISBN 0-8359-5515-X pbk.

Contents

Preface

The purpose of this book is to introduce you to the world of personal computers. If you are already somewhat familiar with these devices, this text will provide some of the background and the details you might have missed. If you are uncertain as to how these fascinating creations operate, you can use this book to fill in the details. This is intended to be a near universal text. However, things are changing so rapidly in the personal computer field that it is hard to cover all the bases. We cover personal computers in terms as general as possible; then, by bringing in specific terms, we are able to apply the general information. In fact, in this text you will not only receive general and applied theory, but you will get the plans for a complete working microcomputer as well. This computer can be built for very low cost and is used as a type of demonstrator to show direct applications of the theories covered in the text.

Of course, you really don't have to build the computer given in this book. You may already have a system and merely need some further enlightenment on its operation. Or perhaps the facts given here will allow you to properly evaluate the system you have been thinking about purchasing.

For whatever reason you may be reading, you are dealing with a fascinating and ever-changing field. You are a pioneer. This is a new frontier as surely as was radio in its infancy. Have you ever wished you were alive in the days when men in their basements and garages strained to hear voices over crystal sets and pioneered radio and television broadcasting? You have a second chance.

The future is yours. Only you will be able to discover how you will be able to mate this new technology to the needs of today and tomorrow. Personal computers have come of age. They are real and they are impacting on society. But, by their very names, they will find their greatest application as we learn to apply them in our own personal situations. I cannot tell you (and you cannot tell me) what your most important application will be.

Each person's needs and demands are his own, and it is best for everyone if we gain an understanding of our personal computing system so we can devise our own interpersonal relationship. If all this sounds like you are about to enter a science-fiction–like world where you will "invent" your own little cybernetic pal, it is. If we are to understand and interrelate in a world of rapidly changing technology, we must understand what we are doing and come to grips with the reality of it all. This book is indeed about your first crude cyborg: your personal computer system.

PERSONAL COMPUTING

Computer Systems

Man's first computer was his fingers (and perhaps his toes). Sadly, he could only add and subtract with this computer. This computer remembered the last count as long as he didn't get a cramp or make a fist. In 1946 the first totally electronic digital computer, ENIAC (for Electronic Numerical Integrator And Calculator) was developed at the University of Pennsylvania. It used miles of wire and 18,000 vacuum tubes; it failed every few hours and put out enormous volumes of heat using 150 kilowatts. Compared to today's computers it was too slow at 300 multiplications per second and far too expensive. Furthermore, ENIAC, in its 40-by-20-foot room, and all its grandchildren for years to come were giant devices that gulped in a tremendous volume of data, juggled it around in their insides, and spat out the results of their manipulations on ultra-expensive high speed printers and other machinery that would give your local auto mechanics nightmares. All this whirring, buzzing, and blinking gave us the tremendous age of the computer, and these computers cost the people who bought them a lot of money.

Not only were the first computers costly, they were big and bulky and demanded a lot of care just to keep things running. Since these computers were so big, bulky, and expensive, they came to be used almost exclusively by the big industrial companies. Most computers even had to have their own special rooms with private air conditioning because of the tremendous amount of heat generated by all the vacuum tubes. But despite the drawbacks, a binary digital computer made possible feats of data processing and problem solving that had previously been impossible.

Through the succeeding generations of computers, speed was the main factor to consider, since all the processing was being done in simple binary on/off conditions. More speed meant simply that more money had to be spent in developing a more sophisticated technology. As it cost more to develop this new computer technology, the companies that were in the forefront had to make more profit. They charged whatever the market would bear in order to have the money left over to come up with new technologies. Thus, already high-priced computers became even higher priced. Yet somewhere in the back of most of these designers' minds was the dream of the day when people could afford their own personal computers. That dream must have seemed a million years from fulfillment.

The technology race continued. Only the big companies were the customers of the computer companies. Only the biggest corporations could afford the outlandish prices they had to pay to get the latest electronic "brains." Because of the demands the big corporations made of the computer manufacturers, technology leaned toward pleasing the "bigs." Computer salespeople adapted their sales techniques to the bigs. Peripheral or add-on equipment manufacturers were building products geared to the big corporations.

Since the bigs had many employees, they wanted printers that could print paychecks faster. They wanted storage devices, like tapes, that were fast and would hold vast amounts of data. They wanted faster terminals with capabilities for easier operation. The bigs also wanted software, or computer programs, that allowed ease of operation by unskilled people. None of these motives were the same ones the pioneer "computer hobbyists" would have in later years. But the technologies that made computers and their peripherals faster would also end up making them cheaper and more sophisticated. As computer users, or prospective users, we owe a lot to the pioneers, the big corporations who demanded technology from manufacturers without much regard to cost.

But, despite our debt to them, we also have much to "unlearn." For instance, the computer salesman with his classical approach to selling a computer by talking about its speed, amount of memory, etc., is going to take a back seat in the personal computer market. He will be replaced by the marketer who explains how pretty the box will look on the kitchen cupboard. In fact, the personal computer salesman may not even mention that the computer is a computer. He may not want to scare the potential customer with thoughts of some giant electronic brain with whirring tapes and card readers. Instead of crowing about the amount of memory or the speed, the future salesman will say, "Here is such-and-such company's black box. For only $299.95, it will balance your checkbook in fifty seconds. It will remember up to three hundred checks at a time, too."

Education is going to have to conform to the "new rules of personal computing," too. Most instructors came up through the traditional computing ranks. They are entering the educational field with approaches and backgrounds relevant to the "bigs." No one is saying that all instruction is outdated or that all instructors are using outdated and outmoded ideas. It is just that it is a very human characteristic to resist change. Personal computing education is going to have to become super flexible because the world of personal computers is a world of rapid change. The personal computer is being nearly revolutionized by new developments almost daily. College and technical school instructors are going to have to ride the tide of change. Of course, for many, the first change will be the biggest. That change for them will be the change to thinking of a personal computer instead of a classical computer.

It is most people's guess that education normally is at least a few years behind technology. With few exceptions, most schools not specializing in technical education, yet offering computer-type curriculums will have the hardest time changing. Keep in mind that we are talking about personal computers here and we are looking to the day when everyone in a household will have his own computer. Thus, the teaching of the interrelationship of the personal computer to the individual will be as important at a liberal arts college as at a technical school. So-called "old school" computer educators are likely to take the classical computer approach to teaching personal computers. This text is intended to impress on you that this approach doesn't fit the personal computer system. Typically, in today's educational environment, a computer is better if it is faster and bigger (in other words, more powerful). This is not necessarily true in personal computing. In fact, most experts agree that cost alone will become the major factor in considering a personal computing system. All agree that there is an attractive cost area of less than $1,000 that will make ownership of a personal computer an affordable reality. A cost of $500 (today's dollars) or below will practically insure the personal computer's success as a major consumer product like the TV and the calculator.

It is cost that has kept the average person from computers up to this point. Even the cost of programming will continue to keep away the student. Not that the student of personal computing will have a problem with costs, it is just that his instructor remembers that only a few years ago (when the instructor was receiving his education) computer time was very expensive. Computer time is the time the computer uses to perform the operations you command it to do. While the bits and bytes are handled by the electronic hardware, they are arranged by programming the computer using changeable commands. These commands are called "software" since they are changeable and are written out on paper before being entered in the computer. With really big computers, running some software can cost as much in computer time as a small personal computer system now costs.

Because of this cost situation, computer programming has assumed a classical approach, too. Programmers were faced with some unique situations that have influenced and will continue to influence their approach to writing software for computers. Some knowledge of classical hardware and software is necessary to an understanding of this situation and how to deal with it.

HARDWARE

The electronic digital computer was different from the older analog computers in that it used and stored data in two simple states (thus the name "binary"). Analog computers, on the other hand, were widely used by the military in such things as radar systems and other control areas where some function such as following a target with an antenna had to be performed. In the analog computer, if storage had to be performed, it was done with a capacitor. The capacitor worked according to its property of energy storage—if a certain analog level were to be remembered, it was fed to a capacitor where it set the charge on the capacitor. Operational amplifiers were developed to provide the functions performed by the analog computer. For instance, multiplying by "N" was performed by running the analog signal through an amplifier with a known gain of "N" times. You could even add by introducing a DC voltage and letting the analog signal ride the DC level. Subtracting simply meant adding a negative voltage. To invert, you used a common cathode amplifier (like a common emitter) with a gain of one. To perform integration and differentiation, you would use RC networks with your amplifier system.

Figure 1–1 shows a simple mathematical function performed by an analog computer. You can see how the operational amplifiers provide outputs. Although the data was hard to interpret, you could perform analysis against time by using an oscilloscope or you could perform so-called steady-state, or signal-less, analysis by looking at meters connected to the output of the last operational amplifier. The system was, of course, prone to error. It was hard to reproduce exact operating conditions from day to day. The kind of operational amplifiers that could retain their characteristics were very, very expensive. Nevertheless, for a time there were no alternatives except to carry out calculations by hand. Sometimes hand calculations were faster than setting up the functions on an analog computer and running the programs. Certainly one would not "go to the computer" for an answer to a simple question. These systems were good only for problems involving many

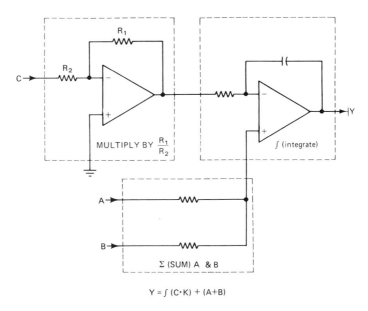

$$Y = \int (C \cdot K) + (A+B)$$

FIGURE 1–1. Simple math function running on a very simple analog computer. The result Y is controlled mathematically by the other functions as they are set up in the operational amplifiers.

operations, or "iterations" as they are called, varying only certain conditions.

Digital computers, on the other hand, offered new alternatives to the involved setup time and the general expense of analog computers. Digital computers reduced everything to a series of yes/no decisions. Electronically, these yes/no decisions could be duplicated by on and off. Since there were only two states for the stages of the computer, they were called "binary computers." Even though it may seem somewhat crude to try to reduce operations to binary, the relative speed at which the electronic circuits could operate allowed the computer to make its yes/no evaluations many times in a second. Though a critical problem with a lot of steps might take a few minutes or even hours to run, it still became practical to solve complex problems within hours—problems that previously would have taken an entire staff of mathematicians days or weeks to solve. The electronic circuits didn't make mistakes either, as long as they were working correctly and as long as the problem was entered correctly.

As far as making the machines work correctly, it was much easier to duplicate circuits where tubes were either conducting or shut off. Expensive operational amplifiers with their complicated schemes to

eliminate drift errors, etc., were no longer needed. Remembering something in "digital" was easier, too. Instead of a capacitor that was
constantly losing its charge, memory could be performed by an electronic circuit known as a "flip-flop" that would stay either "flipped" or
"flopped" depending on the conditions of its input, as long as the power
to the circuit was on. Figure 1–2 shows a flip-flop circuit.

When the voltage of input 1 is positive, it causes the tube to
saturate. The output of the saturated tube goes negative (its output drops
toward zero volts), and this more negative signal causes tube 2 to cut off.
The positive voltage output from cutoff tube 2 now holds tube 1 in
saturation even though the signal that caused all the flipping and
flopping to happen in the first place has long since gone away. Thus, the
memory action. Now, if another positive input comes along to input 1,
nothing will happen to the flip-flop. But if a positive voltage comes along
on the input 2 side of the flip-flop, tube 2 will turn on and tube 1 will turn
off. Tube 1 will hold tube 2 on and the negative output of tube 2 will hold
tube 1 off. Our flip-flop "flipped" before, now it has "flopped." It will
again retain this state until acted upon by the proper input signal to flip
it back. The flip-flop holds its previous conditions or state until another
input makes it change state.

Even if you are moving things around at a very high rate of speed,

FIGURE 1–2. Functional drawing of the circuit for a flip-flop. When one of the tube
conducts, the other is cut off. The tubes then stay in that state until an input comes in
to the flip-flop to change its state.

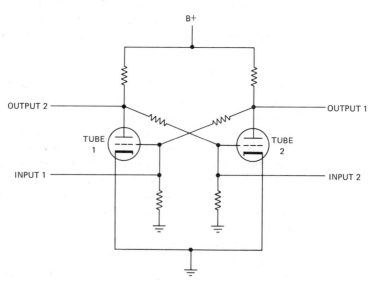

running a lot of binary signals around in a computer can be a little slow. As soon as you start moving a large quantity of data within the machine, you spend a lot of time with simple on/off circuit conditions. Therefore, the on/off states of "bits" are arranged in parallel so that actually the machine is performing operations on many bits at the same time. This is the configuration of the bits within the machine. The computer is configured with a bit, byte, and word structure. As already explained, a bit is an on/off state. When many of these bits are used together at the same time they create a machine "word."

Words are the tools that make sense to the computer. A word is an arrangement of data bits such as that shown in Figure 1–3 which is acted upon all at once by the computer. Note that a word may further be broken into a "byte" (like bite), which is the smallest part of the computer's word that can contain a complete character. There is a standard code for data characters called the "American Standard Code for Information Interchange," ASCII (Asky) for short. All alphabetical and numerical characters are represented by either 7 or 9 bits. The complete ASCII code is given in the appendix at the back of this book. One of the bits of the ASCII code is a parity bit, or a bit that helps in error correction when transmitting ASCII. The computer can drop the parity bit internally. The typical byte will be 6 or 8 bits, rather than 7 or 9.

Thus, we may find the internal structure of a given computer to be configured as a 32-bit word with four 8-bit bytes. A typical "8-bit" microcomputer has an 8-bit byte, but also an 8-bit word. There is only one character per word in this device.

Now, if we are to store meaningful information in our computer, we must have one flip-flop per bit. For a 32-bit computer you would have 32 flip-flops just to store one data word! What's more, to move data from one place to another in the computer, you will have to have 32 interconnecting wires with a common ground. These wires are usually arranged to feed bus wires from one point to another inside the computer. Thus, we find the use of the terms "data bus" and "address bus" in the computer. The data bus is what is in the computer, or the

FIGURE 1–3.   Thirty-two-bit computer "word," showing "bit," "byte," and word structure.

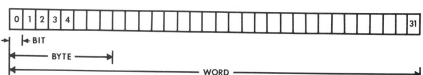

contents. The address bus tells where the data is located. It is like a map. You can tell right now that there is a lot of wiring and other circuitry involved in hooking together all the internal pieces of the computer. If for no other reason, early computers were doomed to be expensive.

Figure 1-4 shows some peripherals along with the computer (processor) as the hardware in the typical large computer center. Peripherals are devices that serve the computer, such as card readers, tape units, printers, etc.

Figure 1-5 shows the internal parts of a typical computer in its "classical" configuration. All computers contain five fundamental circuits: input, output, processing, storage, and control. The circuits make up the computer hardware. The circuits perform the processes called for in the instructions (the computer software).

The input and output circuits move data to and from the computer. The Input/Output (I/O) data signals may be serial (a bit at a time), parallel (several bits at once), or a combination of both. The processing circuits, sometimes called the "arithmetic (ə·rith′mə·tik) circuits," perform operations on a computer datum. The arithmetic operations can range

FIGURE 1−4. Typical peripherals in a large computer center. Although the computer itself makes up the "brains" of the operation, the peripherals offer interconnections to the outside world.

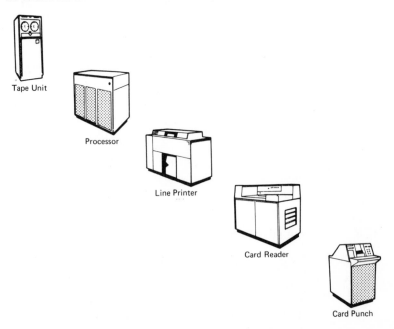

Tape Unit

Processor

Line Printer

Card Reader

Card Punch

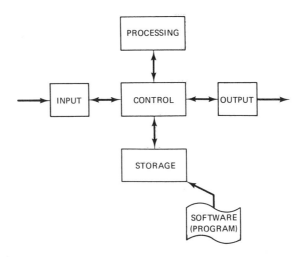

FIGURE 1–5.   The "classical" binary computer configured in
five different parts. Note that without the software programs,
the hardware can perform no useful function.

from AND or OR, to MULTIPLY or DIVIDE, depending on the complexity of the computer. Other operations provide for moving data, while still others control the sequence of operation. The storage circuits in the computer provide the capability for storing data and/or instructions. The control circuits actually manage input, output, storage, and processes. The control circuits decode the program (software) from the storage circuit and send various "enables" to other computer circuits. Ultimately, all operations are controlled by the computer program.

All computers are just variations of the parts and pieces shown in the diagram. Each of the pieces can be simple or complex. If these five hardware areas are not present, the equipment is not called a computer. It may be a *piece* of a computer or may even perform a part of the functions of a computer, but unless it has the five parts in some form or another, it is not a computer.

Although the computer must contain five basic areas, some of the areas may be combined. For instance, a computer must have input circuits and output circuits. (This is how both the data and the program that controls the operations get into the computer in the first place, and how useful information gets from the computer to the operator.) The input and output circuits can be thought of together. When you consider both, they are combined and called the "input/output circuits," or I/O circuits for short.

A simple version of a computer may be shown abbreviated. Although all five parts are present, we combine the Control and Processing (or arithmetic) to become an ALCU or Arithmetic Logic and Control Unit. Another common name for this circuit is the "CPU" or Central Processing Unit.

Logical decisions take place in the CPU (ALCU). The logical functions include the familiar "OR" function wherein a bit-by-bit comparison of two data is carried on, and if either "A" or "B" is a logic one, the computer output is a logic one. The AND functions are also performed in the CPU. If "A" and "B" are both ones, the output is a logic one. Of course, our computer will "AND" and "OR" its bits several bits at a time by using a parallel arrangement of gates hooked to the bus. (Remember, the computer uses words or bytes.) At any rate, the CPU will also allow any number of other commands to be performed depending on the complexity of the computer itself. In microprocessors, the processing and control circuits are considered one area and are sometimes called the MPU for "Micro" Processing Unit instead of CPU.

Figure 1-6 is a drawing of the arithmetic circuits from a minicomputer. The circuits are simplified to make their operation clearer. Two inputs may enter this arithmetic circuit; the storage register input and the main memory input. The two inputs are 16-bit (two 8-bit bytes) data words. Control for the arithmetic section comes from the control inputs shown in Figure 1-6. When the program elects to ADD the two signals, the control input enables the SUM circuit. The serial data signals enter the arithmetic section and are added, bit by bit. (In some computers the data signals enter the SUM circuit in parallel.) The SUM circuit output feeds an OR circuit. All other OR inputs are disabled so the OR output is identical to the SUM output. Thus the DATA OUT signal is the sum of the contents of the main memory and the storage register. Operation of the other circuits is similar. Control signals enable the OR, AND, OR (EXCLUSIVE OR), and MUL/DIV circuits. Thus the output of the arithmetic section is a data signal upon which the program command has been "executed." Data from the arithmetic section is usually stored in the computer's memory at the completion of the process.

The memory section of the computer provides storage of data from the arithmetic section or input section. The data storage may be temporary as in the case of storing data from the arithmetic section. Storage may be permanent, as in the case of the stored program. The storage can also be unalterable as in the read only memory. Two types of memories are widely used in computers. These are solid state (including Read Only Memory, ROM) and magnetic, such as bubble and core. Tape, card, and disc memories are usually limited to use in peripherals as an extension of the computer's storage. Memories can provide main

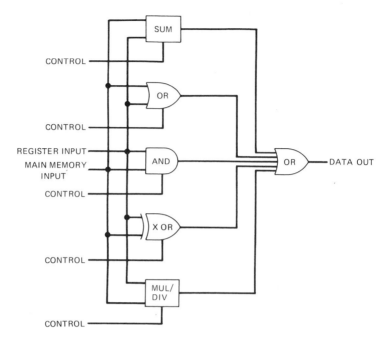

FIGURE 1–6. Arithmetic circuit. It is through these circuits that the signals within the computer are routed to modify the data in the manner that is specified in the computer's program. Control word decoding circuits supply the "control" signals, which in turn allow memory and register data to combine to supply the modified Data Out.

storage as shown in Figure 1–5, or can provide secondary storage. An example of a secondary storage memory is the buffer associated with the input/output circuits. The buffer memory is like a bucket; it catches the bits from a peripheral and waits to pour them into the computer when it has collected a bucketful.

The use of medium- and large-scale integration techniques has led to the use of solid-state memories. The solid-state memory is normally faster than the other types. The simplest solid-state memory is the shift register. One shift register memory uses a string of flip-flops in series. Each flip-flop remembers what happened to it, then transfers its data to its neighbor shifting the data through. Data enters or exits in serial, parallel, or both, depending on configuration. The data is stored until it is cleared or replaced with new data. Word-long shift register memories are called "word storage positions" or word buffers or accumulators. The control circuits enable a certain word storage position, or register, as called out in the program. The data is then stored in or read from the storage position in the memory.

Another type of solid-state memory stores the programs permanently. This permanent storage memory is called a "read only" memory. Read only memories are being used to store fixed subroutines in some large computers and are used most commonly in personal computers. The program calls for subroutine (such as $\sqrt{x}$). The read only memory is enabled, and the computer operates under control of the pre-programmed read only memory until the square root is found, then the program returns to the main memory. One type of solid-state ROM is the Metal-Oxide-Semiconductor (MOS) device which provides large amounts of bits per square inch of storage. MOS devices store the program in the capacitance between a reverse-biased PN junction. The manufacturer supplies the ROM with the specified program built in. When a ROM is needed, a program is written and debugged on a simulator. Then the program is supplied to the memory manufacturer. A variation of the ROM is the Programmable ROM, or PROM, which is user programmable. There are even Erasable PROMs, EPROMs, which are erased by exposure to ultraviolet light. Electrically Alterable PROMs, EAPROMs, work like EPROMs except the erasing can be done electrically.

The core memory is widely used in large computers. Cores are cheap, reliable, and easily obtained, but not normally as small or as fast as solid-state memories. Core memories basically consist of a matrix of magnetic cores. The cores are addressed by selecting X and Y coordinates. The X and Y lines are pulsed and the cores selected are magnetized. Cores magnetized in one direction equal a logic 1 and cores magnetized in the opposite direction equal logic 0.

Figure 1–7 shows a simple core memory. The currents in the X and Y lines are called the "half-select currents." Two times the current flowing in either the X or Y lines is required to saturate a core. With half the select current in each of the X and Y lines, only the cores that appear at the intersection of the X and Y lines will be saturated. All the X and Y lines feed all core planes as shown in Figure 1–7. There will be one core plane per bit in a machine word. A specified X and Y address will find the intersection of the same core position in each plane. The two half-currents (X and Y) will switch the core in each plane to logic 1. Note that for any one X and Y drive line, the same position in all three core planes will store logic 1. The inhibit signal causes the selected core to store logic 0.

The Inhibit Input is a half-current drive signal. When the bit to be stored is a logic 0, the Inhibit Loop for that bit (core plane) of the word is energized. The half-current inhibit drive is opposite the X and Y "write currents" so the core does not switch. Thus an inhibit input causes storage of a logic 0 when a logic 0 is present in the data signal.

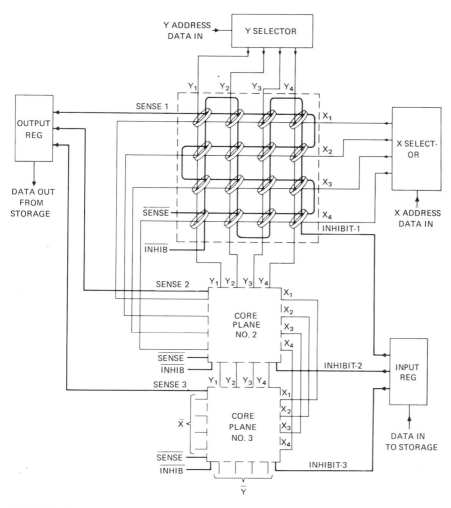

FIGURE 1–7. Computer core memory. This memory is made up of tiny magnetic cores that are switched and magnetized by various drive currents to hold data for the computer. Since the storage is magnetic, it is called non-volatile memory. It remains when power is removed.

To read from the cores, the X and Y read addresses are chosen and a half-current in each (opposite direction of the read current) switches the addressed cores in each plane to logic 0. If the core is presently a logic 1, the sense line for that core plane will feel an output pulse. If the core is at logic 0 there will be no output. Output depends on the magnetic properties of the core. The smaller the core, the more critically temperature affects its magnetic properties. Temperature-controlled power supplies usually supply current drive for core memories when temperature changes are extreme.

Drive currents switch the core during a read from core. The read action causes the core to switch to logic 0 and the stored data changes. This is called a "destructive read" because the stored data is lost. To compensate, the computer rewrites the data back into core while the X and Y addresses remain the same. Core memories have this "write after read" cycle to keep data from being lost. Core memories are called "random access" memories because the X and Y address can be selected at random.

Figure 1–8 is a simplified drawing of typical control circuits. The circuits shown are again based on circuits from a minicomputer. The circuits control fewer functions than in a more complex computer. This minicomputer uses a ROM to store the program. The mini also uses solid-state RAM (Random Access Memory) called the "accessible memory" and a two-word storage register called the "accumulator."

The hub of the control circuits is the instruction decoder. Instruction inputs from the ROM enter the Instruction Decoder and become commands to the computer's gating circuits. The gating circuits are: the Accumulator Input Selector, Accessible Memory or Accumulator Output Selector, Arithmetic Input Selector, Input and Output Control circuits, and the Clock Generator. All the gating circuits are similar to the gating circuits in the arithmetic section of the computer. That is, the instruction decoder supplies the enabling signals, and gating circuits route the selected data to the respective circuit in the computer.

The instruction decoder consists of two major portions. They are the Instruction Storage Register and the Instruction Decoder Circuits. Figure 1–8 shows the instruction decode circuits and the circuits involved in an instruction "execute." The circuits have been simplified from the actual circuits in the computer to make the operation clearer. As the figure shows, the instructions from the ROM enter the instruction storage register. The read action takes place during the minicomputer's "instruction read cycle." During the instruction read cycle, the instruction decoder circuits decode the contents of the word. This enables the operations to be performed during the "instruction execute cycle." The instruction word from the ROM has been simplified to fifteen data bits. The structure of the instruction word serves as an example to show the reader the function of the circuits in the instruction decoder. This instruction is only one of many instructions in the computer's repertoire (list of possible instructions). The bits 1 through 4 of the instruction word provide control for the address of the data storage register in the accessible memory. Bits 5 through 9 of the word control the Peripheral Address and the Rotata/Bit Select signals. Bits 10 and 11 control the

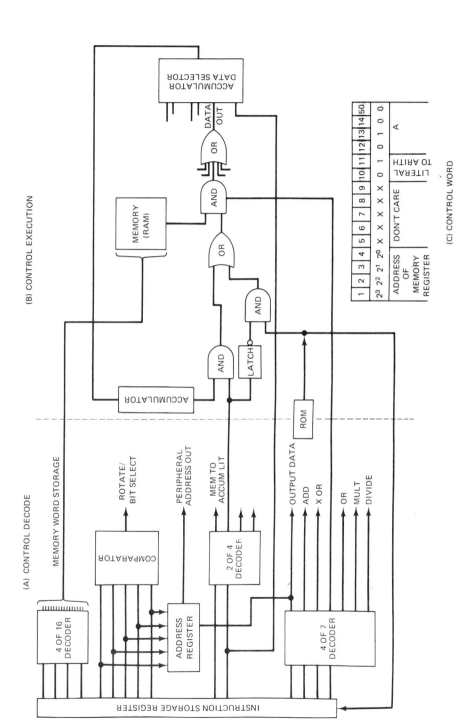

FIGURE 1–8. Instruction word decoding and control circuits in a typical computer. This is how the instruction (control) word is broken down within the computer. The figure also shows (B) the place where the control instruction is executed. (C) is a typical control word.

accumulator, accessible memory, and the literal word (from the ROM). Bits 12 through 15 of the instruction word control the operation to be performed on the selected data signal. (A literal is actually a data word, but not an instruction. An example of a literal would be a constant "K" that must be added to another number to arrive at an answer for a specific problem.)

The instruction word shown in Figure 1-8(c) controls the operations depicted in the "Typical Instruction Execute" portion of the figure. During the instruction read cycle, the instruction from the ROM enters the instruction storage register. The register applies its outputs to the various decoders. The first four bits of the word select a register in the memory. In the example shown, the first four bits might be 1001 (binary 9). In this case, register 9 in the memory is enabled.

Bits 5 through 9 of the word provide no control in the sample instruction word, so their condition is ignored. Bits 10 and 11 cause an output from the 1 of 4 decoder at the line marked 0–1. This means that either a literal from the ROM or data from the accumulator will enter the arithmetic section of the computer. The arithmetic section is now ready to accept the literal output from the ROM through the latch, AND gate, and the OR gate. Bit 11 of the instruction is a logic 1. This enables the Accumulator Data Selector to receive the data from the arithmetic section.

Finally, the process to be performed on the data is determined by bits 12 through 15 of the instruction word via the 1 of 7 decoder. Reference to the instruction word shows that the equivalent binary code of the last four bits is a "4." This enables the fourth output from the 1 of 7 decoder: the AND command. The AND command enables an AND gate in the arithmetic section. Now the instruction read cycle is complete and the instruction execute cycle begins.

During the instruction execute cycle, the instruction is carried out on the selected data signals. With the instruction word shown in Figure 1–8, the execution will take place as follows: the timing circuits generate a clock signal and the ROM and the main memory start to output serial data. Both output signals are combined in an AND gate in the arithmetic section so the DATA OUT signal is routed by the accumulator data selector to the accumulator. Since the accumulator clock is also present, the ANDed data fills the accumulator. At the end of the instruction execution cycle, the accumulator contains the logical AND of memory register 9 and the literal. The computer recycles to the instruction read cycle again and new instruction is read into the instruction decode circuits. (Typically, after the instruction we just processed, the next instruction might be "Store Accumulator in Register 9." Thus register 9 would contain the modified data signal.) Thus the control circuits enable the operation of the other circuits within the computer. Each operation is carried out step by step by an instruction. A set of instructions which provides a specific function is called a "program" or a "routine."

Thus, a minimum computer system may be broken into three main areas which consist of a total of five functions. By combining functions we still have CPU, memory, and I/O. Oh yes, don't forget the software. Somewhere in our computer we will have to have some software in order to tell the CPU what and when to perform I/O, when and where to store data, and when and what to perform in the way of math and logical operations.

SOFTWARE

Even though I fear overuse of the following phrase, it is important to discuss it because, literally, "the computer is nothing without software." In other words, there will have to be commands in memory that will execute in the CPU in some order prescribed by the program writer or programmer.

Keep in mind the computer is a machine and the programmer is a human—another man/machine relationship. The man must think logically in order to use the machine. Man must know everything there is to know about the machine to operate it most effectively. Each machine has its own rules. For instance, when turned on the computer must go somewhere and "fetch" the first instruction. If the computer will proceed in some manner from start up or reset, we can write a series of orderly instructions which are the program. We can even instruct our computer to break its normal pattern of sequential operation and go to another instruction wherever we wish to send it, to fetch data from memory, to put data in memory, or to start a new sequence of programs, sometimes called a "subroutine." (These are apart from the main routine, performing some function that is essential to the main routine.) Upon finishing the subroutine, we can command the computer to return to where it was and begin processing where it left off.

By using so-called "conditional branches" to another area of the program we can set up conditions for jumping to a new program. For instance, if we get an input on I/O circuit #1, we want to add the number that is on the input (or I/O port) so our program says, "Test port 1 and branch (if there is an input) to 3000." This means that no matter where our program is in memory it will start executing the instructions at memory position 3000 if an input comes in on port 1. We actually take a mass of electronic hardware and tell the control circuits how to hook them up to perform some function. Whether the function is that of calculating the orbital velocity of a satellite, or simply printing on a typewriter, everything that goes on in the computer is controlled by the program. The program is written by a programmer, just as the hardware is designed by a circuit designer. The programmer writes his program by knowing what the system needs to do and by knowing how the computer can perform this task. At least in theory, the programmer works in two stages. Stage one is determining the job to be done. Stage two is applying the job to the specific computer that will perform it. First, a flow chart is written to describe the job. The performance of the task is accomplished by applying the steps on the flow chart to the instructions in the computer's repertoire.

In the history of the computer the software story goes somewhat like the story of the hardware. Only the large corporations could afford the computers in the first place and they needed big programs to handle needs for thousands of employees. These software tasks were phenomenal and usually had to be done in a hurry by the programmer in order to satisfy a large customer, hungry for what the computer could offer his company in the form of data processing. Programming tasks were organized so that groups of programmers worked together. Obviously, it was important for all the programs to fit together, so complicated rules were formulated for the programmers on a project. These rules were devised by the manufacturer to allow all the little programs written by individual programmers to fit into the overall requirements of the system. Soon there were industry-wide standards of programming so that one programmer could be replaced with another who had nothing to do with the original programming but who would have to be able to modify or customize some feature of a program for a new customer. Still, there was the problem of nonstandard computers. No one manufacturer duplicated the system of another and thus a software "ADD" command on one machine might be a logical "OR" command on another. On the machine level, in machine language programming, the program would be very much a function of the hardware.

Since computers are essentially dumb, the first programmers had to write programs in machine language. Later, programs would be written on other computers which would cross-translate into another computer's language so writing programs would be a little easier. Software was written for one machine that made it emulate the other computer's instruction set. Then, by telling the familiar computer what to do, we could develop software for the new computer.

The flow chart, the programmer's schematic diagram, is an expression of the task to be performed. Figure 1–9 shows a portion of a flow chart. This program is part of an "executive routine." The executive routine controls basic computer system operation. In fact, in some computers the executive routine is called the "operating system" or OS.

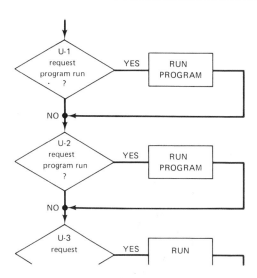

FIGURE 1–9. Software Polling routine diagrammed out in flowchart form. Here there are three or more terminals connected to the computer. The system is asking if each of the units wishes to run its program and then is going on or running the program, depending on the terminal.

The program in Figure 1–9 is simple. The programmer asks (shown by a diamond-shaped "decision block") if Unit 1 requires to run a program. If the answer is "Yes," the program runs. If the answer is "No," the computer jumps to the next decision block and asks if Unit 2 has a program to run. The process continues so that after the last unit is serviced the first unit is serviced again.

The example shown is, of course, very basic. Computer software is often as complicated as the hardware that performs the instructions. Basically, software organization is similar to hardware. There is "system" with "programs" that make it up. Each program contains routines which allow the performance of the program. Routines are sometimes made up of subroutines which allow the accomplishment of the routines. The programs, routines, and subroutines are combined by the programmers to make a functioning system.

Let's look at the evolution of programming. First task, get something into the computer. We are talking about I/O routines that allow you to put data into the computer in the first place. Just think, you would not be able to load the program into the computer until you wrote a program that would accept data at a port. Once you get data into the port, you can put the program into the computer via a peripheral such as a card reader or tape. The program that allows another program to be entered is called a "bootstrap program." The bootstrap has to be entered into the computer by going into the area of memory that the computer would start at on "reset" or "power on." This, of course, would depend on the manufacturer; many computers start up at memory location 0. You must jam the bootstrap into the memory without the help of the computer's CPU. A device with a bunch of lights and toggle switches called a "front panel" was devised for this purpose. The front panel allows you to load by hand by arranging a series of switches and pushing a load button which institutes the jamming. It is this front panel which is the scary part of the computer. This is where we see flashing lights and banks of complicated looking switches. A front panel can be handy for troubleshooting, but its principal purpose is to start the computer by hand loading bootstrap programs. A simpler method is to put the bootstrap on ROM.

Obviously, once you are past the hurdle of bootstrapping in the program, you can do whatever you want. The bootstrap and other similar machine language programs are direct applications programs.

After the simple bootstrap programs came the loader programs that allowed data from, for instance, a magnetic tape unit to load in a more complex program. You might load in a debug program which allows you to troubleshoot your way through the programs you write. Debug programs allow you to inspect selected memory positions, insert characters, punch cards or paper tape to save programs, read cards or paper tape, and do other things, such as entering points in the program called "breakpoints." Breakpoints are instructions that stop the normal flow of the program and allow the state of registers and other electronic circuits to be inspected with a cathode ray tube (CRT) or other type terminal. A terminal is a peripheral that terminates the computer to a human. On the CRT screen you see letters and numbers in the machine language. These numbers and letters will mean little to the nonprogrammer but will be of immense value to the person doing the debugging.

Even the simpler debug programs became more sophisticated.

The next level of programming was probably developed more to allow another more familiar computer to aid in writing the basic routines for a new computer than anything else. This is the assembly language level. In the assembler, instead of using the logic ones and zeros of machine language, the programmer uses mnemonic (nee-mon´-ic) symbols for its functions. The translation from mnemonic to machine language is performed by the computer instead of the human programmer. By relying on the computer we make fewer mistakes. Mnemonics are easier to memorize than a string of numbers. Assemblers are the programs that perform the assembly into machine language within the computer being programmed, and cross-assemblers perform assembly by simulating the instruction set of another computer. The assembler also has commands or "assembler directives," as they are called, that cause the assembly program to perform such things as listing out on a terminal or a printer.

The next language level demands some very specific standards. A program called an "interpreter" resides in memory along with your program. If you use an interpreter and tell the computer to add 6 and 6 and print the results on a terminal, the interpreter will analyze your input and decode each entry a piece at a time. If you make an illegal command, the interpreter will give you an error message in some readable form. If you write a legal command, it will interpret each entry. The interpreter knows when to print the results when you give it a specific command such as a Carriage Return. The interpreter uses a buffer, or short memory storage area, so it interprets on a line-by-line basis. Also, you can put multiple-line programs in memory and the program will sequentially interpret and execute, line by line, until you change the sequence. Interpreters are important because they allow programming in some high level language that is easy for humans to use.

BASIC (Beginners' All-Purpose Symbolic Interchange Code) is a simple language that is easy to understand and BASIC interpreters are common. A command to print a letter "A" in basic is simply—PRINT "A." In assembly language in a 6800 microcomputer that would be:

```
10 NAM print routine (assembler directive)
20 ORG 0 (assembler directive tells where to start)
30 Start LDAA#'A
40 JMP print
50 End
```

The print in line 40 is the name of a subroutine that will cause whatever is in register A to print on the CRT. We will not show the print subroutine here because we will assume it is part of the I/O software package. In machine language using a hexidecimal number system, our program would look like this:

```
86 41
7E E1D1
```

Written in binary (as the machine sees it):

```
10001010
01000001
01111101
11010001
11000001
```

Note the compactness of the hexidecimal listing. Note the efficiency of the machine language. While it is efficient, machine language is certainly tougher to use than the BASIC interpreter's simple command— PRINT "A."

To get the ease of programming in a high level language like BASIC and the efficiency of the machine language, programmers devised the Compiler. We might have a BASIC Compiler which uses the simple BASIC commands, and then we go through an assembly step where we interpret the program only once and convert it to its equivalent machine code. Thus the machine itself would reduce the simple statement— PRINT "A" to:

    86 41
    7E E1D1

The compiler is faster than an interpreter, too, because you don't have to pause to interpret each command. Some compilers use an RTP or Run Time Package that contains all the math and I/O subroutines, although that means the RTP must be present like an interpreter when the program is in the computer. The RTP is usually much smaller than an interpreter and it is a lot faster since its subroutines are being called by the main program only when needed. The compiler is the faster performer and it combines the ease of use of the high level language.

Depending on the high level language used and its standards, you will have to learn how to talk to the computer. In one language, such as BASIC, you add two numbers, A & B, by using A + B. Still another language might use AB+, or AB= (the plus sign is assumed). In fact, you may write your own high level language some day, and only you know what operators you will designate to use.

The high level languages have one great advantage. Any program written in FORTRAN (for FORmula TRANslation), for example, will theoretically operate on any manufacturer's machine that has a FORTRAN interpreter or compiler. In real life this is not always true because of some differences in what is actually provided in a given machine, but nearly always with minor modifications, a BASIC program is a BASIC program and it will run on any machine capable of running BASIC.

This chapter has been the background or foundation for the whole book. Terms like *compilers, assemblers, bytes,* and *literals* are software words. Hardware terms include *flip-flop, register, RAM,* and so on. Keep in mind the makeup of the classic big computers and the kinds of backgrounds big computer users have. Personal computer systems are like the bigs in basic functions, but they differ at the applications level. Hardware and software are so closely interrelated in the microcomputer that it is nearly impossible to understand one without the other.

The Progression to Personal Computer Systems

The hardware end of computing was revolutionized with the introduction of the transistor in the mid to late 1950s. Even though the first transistors were crude by today's standards, they suddenly allowed the monstrous computers of the earlier age to shrink their energy needs. The first transistorized computer was built in 1960. There was no heat-generating filament within the transistor, and this one feature meant that computers needed less special treatment, such as air conditioning. The filtered, even temperature air was still used, but now primarily to preserve the magnetic tapes and discs in good condition. Transistors also allowed more computer power to be built in the same area because they occupied less space.

Technology advanced—men learned new and better ways to make transistors. They became more reliable and were able to work at higher frequencies. The higher frequencies held the promise of these transistorized computers processing data at speeds heretofore unachievable with tube-type technology. Packaging transistor circuitry took great strides with the progression of printed circuit technology. Printed circuits were now being fabricated that had more than just the traditional wiring on one or both sides. Multilayer PC boards allowed new smaller circuit packaging. This also allowed higher speed switching inside the circuits. Transistors were switching very fast now. Even though the electrical signals were traveling around in the computer at nearly the speed of light, there were literally miles of interconnecting wires and it was the delays encountered in the miles of interconnections that became the major deterrent to higher operating speed.

Smaller meant faster. It became important to make sure circuit functions were performed by as small a circuit as possible. Packaging became a technology. Eventually, even though transistors were already tiny, designers began to worry about the relatively large packages that protected the silicon and germanium "chips" that were performing the transistors' function. Since much of the space in the package was just that—space—designers were wondering about the practicality of changing the packaging. It was possible to use only the transistor chips without a package, then to weld tiny leads to the chips and mount them in a package that put chips, painted-on resistors, and printed-on capacitors all on a common base of ceramic known as a "substrate."

. The technology of painting, or silk screening on resistive paints, was known since the days of the early AC-DC five-tube radios. Sometimes simple resistor capacitor (RC) circuits were put together that way and then dipped in a potting compound. The same held for these early, thick film circuits using so-called active components (transistors), as well as the passive components such as resistors and capacitors. By using thick film (and later thin film) technology one could put a whole flip-flop or even several flip-flops in a tiny package that would occupy perhaps one-fourth the space of equivalent discrete components. Figure 2–1 shows the relative progression in size of a given circuit all the way from tube type to present day IC's. By modularizing the circuits like this, higher speeds were not only possible, but extremely practical. Also, significant size reduction was possible.

It was this size reduction that made the dream of a truly small computer come true. Before the dream could be realized though, a new

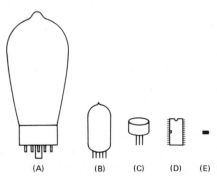

(A)   (B)   (C)   (D)   (E)

FIGURE 2–1. Progression in compactness of electronic circuits is shown here, from the old-fashioned electron tube (A) to the miniature tube (B) to the transistor (C). Next came the multi-function IC "bug" shown (relative size) at (D), and, last, the actual IC "chip" (relative size) at (E). This tiny chip contains hundreds and hundreds of circuit components that replace the functions of hundreds of equivalent electron tubes.

technology would be born. The Integrated Circuit would come out of the lab and into the world. Multitransistor chips were already practical where the technology of fabricating a transistor allowed fabrication of several transistors all possessing the same basic characteristic, all on the same semiconductor chip (silicon or germanium). Now, it was possible to duplicate not only the transistor, but a resistor by using a straight piece of silicon as an interconnection between the two transistors. With the new technology came fabrication of a whole circuit such as a flip-flop, complete with all its previously external components integrated into a complete semiconductor chip. These new "integrated" circuits were called "IC's" for short.

The first, early 1960 IC's contained a single circuit, such as a logic gate or a flip-flop, made up of transistors and resistors. These were called "RTL" for Resistor-Transistor Logic IC's. First offered by Fairchild and Texas Instruments, RTL was challenged as a key technology in 1962. To a great degree, RTL was overshadowed by its baby brother, DTL.

Diode Transistor Logic (DTL) was a big step upward. It promised more speed because it eliminated the RC time constants simulated when switching on and off in the junction capacitance of the transistors. Signetics and Fairchild vied for the championship in DTL IC's. Fairchild's now famous 930 series was a little less sensitive but showed good noise immunity.

It was Sylvania that first introduced TTL (T^2L) or Transistor Transistor Logic. It was called "SUHL" for Sylvania Ultra High Speed Logic. This was the forerunner of today's TTL. Meanwhile both Fairchild and Signetics could see the handwriting on the wall and were working on their own versions of T^2L. It was the now famous TI 5400 series T^2L that really set the standard. Introduced in 1964, it would be "the" logic system for decades to come. Computers could now be put together using IC's. The IC would become a sophisticated part of the big machines. Computers would also become smaller and cheaper and would move us one step closer to the age of personal computing.

Because of the speed offerings IC's were being rapidly pressed into service in the big mainframes. Huge multimillion dollar computers were made obsolete almost overnight. The IC versions were faster and that gave them the power to provide even more computational power. Early on, the IC's had been extremely expensive and it was once again large-scale buying by major corporations that caused even more technological advancement.

Motorola broke the speed barrier with 1 nanosecond (1 milli-microsecond) MECL, for Motorola Emitter Coupled Logic. Speed was the emphasis. Process more and move it around faster was the order of the day. Emitter-coupled logic used transistor switches that didn't saturate or cut off. Thus switching times were cut enormously. There was no need for a very large junction capacitance to have to charge and discharge all the time in order to switch. The only problem was the 60 ma dissipation per gate. It took about five gates to make a flip-flop. ECL promised to put the heat back in the computer room, so most designers opted for TTL, and mixed in ECL at critical places.

In 1968 RCA introduced a family called "CMOS," Complementary Metal-Oxide-Semiconductor. It used the same basic technology as field effect transistors, or FETS. The metal oxide formed an insulating layer which gave very high input impedances and much lower power consumption. It obviously meant slower speeds too, but for requirements where current drain was to be minimized it was great. CMOS debuted under the name of "CD 4000 COS/MOS." It was the MOS technology with its high density that would allow the microprocessor IC of today. CMOS technology today still favors the 4000 series. But the emphasis is now on BMOS or Buffered CMOS. It uses high powered output stages for speed and for compatability in driving TTL type logic. Most other CMOS does not have enough power output to be able to drive regular TTL. It is this buffered technology that allows the one chip computer to interface to standard "off the shelf" IC's to make a personal computer system complete. After all it will not be possible for you to have a personal computer system unless you can talk to the outside world via terminals, teletypes, printers, and the myriad of other external or peripheral devices.

By 1972 the super fast switching diode, the Schottky (pronounced "shot key"), was added to the TTL IC so that it would clamp the input and output excursions and provide a path to discharge the internal junction capacitances that slowed down the operation of the TTL circuit. S-TTL challenged ECL for capturing the high speed end of things and dissipated a lot less power to get some impressive speeds. Both ECL and Schottky were developed to appease the computer industries' need for high speed logic.

Currently, the emphasis in IC's is in the area of low-powered TTL with built-in Schottky diode clamps. Here we have a logic family that is comparable to standard TTL and which consumes much less power. In fact the speed of LS-TTL is around the same as standard TTL, but the power consumption is one-fifth that of standard TTL. This satisfies demands by computer people for less power consumption and thus less heat when you get a cabinet full of IC's. At the same time, the speed is fast enough to make the LS attractive except for the most demanding applications.

Minicomputers and miniskirts were brought to prominence

around the same time (early 1960s) as popular IC's. Pioneer efforts in minicomputer development systems sales went to a handful of small companies. These companies went to market to get a fragment of the dollars available to the "bigs," but they thought to make up the difference in volume. And they did. Even today, there is a sufficient minicomputer market to go around. The minis were not as powerful as the bigs by any means, but with the development of peripherals more appropriate for mini users, they would soon become a formidable contender to the bigs. As IC's came along, the minis, with their main objectives of lower cost and smaller size than the bigs, found market niches to fill that they surely never dreamed about.

Currently, minis are used "on site" to process data that may be fed to the "bigs" in a distributed processing system. They also are used as industrial control centers, serving as the brains to huge electrically controlled machines. The last time you bought a plane ticket, chances are it was confirmed and reserved via a minicomputer. But the minis sometimes would not just control machines or act as so-called "smart terminals" to a larger computer. No, as the software for the minis developed, the minis were used for small business accounting.

Minis made it possible to set up a computer system for one to two hundred thousand dollars and unlocked the doors for medium-sized and smaller businesses to have on-site computers. Businessmen had known for years the value those big computers provided the big companies. Not only did they make bookkeeping more efficient and less expensive, the big computers held the keys to analysis of where the business stood at any time so the businessmen could make proper decisions on where (and when) to move in the future. Now that minicomputers made systems available for the smaller businesses, those businesses could see the promise of saving the same time and money on accounting and could see the potential for increasing profits that could be applied to growth in the areas to which the new-found data centers would point them. In short, even though the minis were too expensive for the general public, thay would pay for themselves many times over in a medium-sized business operation that could afford to pay for them initially.

Mini peripherals were not far away from the minicomputer. Hard discs that were used in big computer centers were shrunken slightly and slowed down a bit, and they became minicomputer storage peripherals. Floppy discs that used the whirling magnetic disc spinning in a cardboard holder like a record jacket were to become common minicomputer peripherals. Low cost terminals that depended on the minicomputer itself for some of the output chores were developed. Buffers were taken out of printers, and technology was borrowed to produce lower cost versions of the printers used in computer centers. Teletype devices were interfaced to the minicomputer and the mini wasted a little of its own time servicing the peripherals directly. The bigs would have thought servicing any but the highest speed peripherals in real time to be a waste. But for a minicomputer being used in a business, the owner would hardly note the slight time delays inherent in these systems. Big computers were usually serving so many users that people who had used computers were fairly accustomed to slow response times anyway. To them, the mini reacted like any computer they had ever used at any other time.

As MSI (medium scale integration, 12 to 100 gates per chip) took hold, it paved the way for much improvement in size reduction of minicomputers and at the same time performance of the machines was reaching a point where they would compete with the bigs. More and more functions could be built into their smaller and smaller packages, and speed of the actual processor could be improved so much that now minis could replace many bigger computers with no noticeable problems. And minis were still considerably less expensive than the bigs, even though the IC had brought down prices of computers across the board. Minis with the proper peripherals were going in systems for $50,000 and up. More and more businesses were able to afford their own computers.

To date, progress in minicomputers has been phenomenal. Some manufacturers are offering complete minimal computer systems using minis that start around $12,000. Part of the reason for this repricing is competition from microcomputers, but another reason is that the same technical improvements that are heralding the age of the microcomputer—digital watches and digital calculators—are contributing to the improvement.

Truly the minicomputer was the second step, but the transistor was the first step in moving from the cumbersome age of the giant ENIAC toward the day when the personal computer would become a reality. Some sacrifices in computing power would have to be made, but as microcomputers developed, they were able to take over many of the tasks along with the mini, and now we find these hybrid systems performing with all the apparent speed and power of the bigs.

One final technological breakthrough clinched the microcomputer's becoming a practical reality. That was the introduction of LSI or Large Scale Integrated circuits. Now chip densities made it possible to put many different functions in a chip. In fact, it soon became possible to put an entire CPU on a chip. Originally, what was on the one chip was the MPU. But they required support chips to make them into functioning computers. One had to add memory and I/O to have a complete computer. As technology marched on, it was not too long until an entire computer with limited I/O memory and the MPU would be combined on one chip, and thus truly was born the one-chip computer.

Even before the one-chip computer actually became a reality the hardy old electronics experimenter had created his own personal computing systems and was working away at the machines that would become the forerunners of the personal computer systems of the future. In the next chapter we will discuss in detail some of the microprocessor chips that stand at the forefront of the personal computer systems of today and which will undoubtedly be the basis upon which systems of the future are built.

The Microprocessor, Heart of the Personal Computer

The birth of LSI technology outlined in the previous chapter brought with it the possibility of putting a whole CPU or even a computer on a single integrated circuit chip. Already there are several one-chip micro-computers, each containing the five basic parts of a computer mentioned earlier. There are also a vast number of two-chip microcomputer systems available at this writing. In fact, one company, National Semiconductor, predicts a complete mainframe computer on a single chip in the very near future. This "mainframe on a chip" would mean that the equivalent of the famous IBM 370 computer could be built in a package the size of a typewriter. That package could contain the computer, memory, some tape or disc storage, a typewriter keyboard, and a CRT (Cathode Ray Tube) display.

Already, one can make a computer equivalent to the IBM 370/158 and put the whole thing in a 19-inch rack. Experts project by the year 1985, LSI device manufacturing techniques will have improved a hundredfold. This means that the IBM 370 mainframe on a chip will undoubtedly become a reality.

Since we are most concerned with the realities of personal computers, we must dwell on what is presently on hand, rather than what is going to happen. Simply stated, however, both the concept of what is real and what is in the future and the present state of the art are constantly and rapidly changing. We shall attempt to cover the most practical base while leaving the update on the most current events to the magazines and technical journals.

Once you have mastered the basic principles described in the text, you would do well to keep current by reading as many pertinent publications as possible along the way. In looking at the various existing microprocessors it is good to mix a little recent history with a great deal of present day and a smattering of tomorrow. We shall cover mostly the most popular micros at present. The 8-bit machines are showing that they are around to stay in the mainstream of microcomputer applications, so we will concentrate on the 8-bit devices. Because of the recent Heathkit adventure into the field of personal computers and the impact that should have, we will cover the Heathkit choice for a 16-bit machine, the LSI-11. It is thought by some that the 16-bit micros that emulate their bigger brothers, the minicomputers, will have the biggest impact on the field. These processors are supposedly more likely personal computer candidates because of the voluminous amount of software that is already available for the mini counterpart. Also, the design of the chips is oriented toward number crunching more than control, as in the 8-bit machines.

The early microprocessor systems would be limited in byte size mostly by packaging constraints and the state of the art in chip fabrication. Thus, the earliest recognized microprocessor chip, the Intel Corporations's 4004, would be a 4-bit/byte word micro with a limited command repertoire. The first generation Intel 4004, 8008, Fairchild PPS-25, Rockwell PPS-4 and PPS-8, and National IMP used PMOS (P-channel MOS) technology to achieve the chip density that made the microprocessors practical in the first place. The second generation chips, like the Intel 8080, Motorola 6800, and the Fairchild F-8, used the more sophisticated and expensive N channel process. This gave them faster speed without compromising chip density. Already, one company, RCA, is well into production of a CMOS (Complementary MOS, P- and N-type channels intermixed) which is several times an improvement in power consumption over its first and second generation predecessors. However, despite the problems of being a pioneer, the Intel 4004 made a splash in the industry.

Even with its limited architecture and small command repertoire, the Intel 4004 held out the promise of revolutionizing computers with its 4001 ROM and 4002 RAM, introduced in 1971. And, it had no trouble in living up to everyone's expectations. The 4004 was out to change the face of the entire electronics industry. In fact, because of the monstrous impact of the microprocessor on industry, it was not until some time later that the microcomputer as such was to become a reality. The occasional exceptions were the engineers and technicians who had worked with these wonder chips in some controller applications at work and had seen the potential for them in some application other than an industrial controller. Many times the early microprocessor IC's were purchased at relatively high cost and were integrated into a hobby computer system. For the common man, however, even the typical electronics experimenter, the microcomputer was not yet a possibility.

Although they had limitations, the early 4-bit MPU's were still computer-like in that they could perform completely programmable functions just like the giant computers and the minis. Here the controlling was done by one chip instead of a whole group of circuits. The hardware for an application could be developed so that only the software needed to be changed to allow use of the IC in various different products. Indeed, the first microprocessor (UP) applications were as *μP* industrial controllers. This is an application where the microprocessor controlled the actions of some machine, like an injection molding machine, or the like. On the home front, the same basic circuit that was controlling a washing machine was also controlling a microwave oven. The changes or differences were essentially taken care of in the software. For the manufacturer, this meant lower parts inventory. That, in turn, meant less expense for the company and higher profits. Products would be easier to service because trouble-shooting aids or diagnostics could be programmed right into the unit. Either the factory could hook up the UP with test gear, or the UP would have built-in software routines that could tell the user what was wrong. The manufacturers were saving money in the development of new products, too. Basically, all the equipment they manufactured was using the same circuits with the software serving as the key. Computers were even helping to write their own programs too. Cross-assemblers were being used to write programs on dissimilar computers. The microprocessor was revolutionizing equipment design.

The microprocessor would revolutionize what was demanded of the user, too. In the day of the reign of the bigs and even the minis, there were hardware-oriented engineers and software-oriented programmers. Indeed, the customary rivalries even existed between the two groups, with each harboring some kind of professional jealousy of the other, manifesting itself in comments by the engineers. Engineers claimed the programmers would have nothing to work with were it not for the extraordinary capabilities designed into the computers by the engineers.

The expected counterargument from the programmers was essentially that without good programs the poor machines would, despite all the nifty circuits, merely sit and win prizes for "best decorated boat anchor" and the like. Of course, both were right. Engineers were providing the most sophisticated hardware ever known to man, and programmers were almost artistically draining the highest possible performance out of those circuits. The problem is that neither of the two rival groups knew much about the other's field. Oh, most engineers had a knowledge of the limited use of Fortran (for FORmula TRANslation) computer language. But, believe it or not, programmers were seldom more familiar with the hardware than occasionally being able to hook up a new printer that came in, as long as the instructions were very, very clear. While engineers talked transistors and active circuits, programmers talked linking loaders and macros. The microcomputer changed this divided relationship between hardware and software. The engineer found himself designing a complete computer system now, not just some obscure part of the whole larger system. Now the engineer would become acutely aware of the software that was about to play such an active role in the functioning of his new circuit. A lot of engineers were at a loss, and when they called on the programmers for help, the programmers found themselves talking in binary and gates, instead of some super-sophisticated operating system that allowed them to develop programs and debug their software by using established methods. In the beginning, the engineers did a lot of programming and the programmers learned a lot about the hardware so they could come up with cross-assemblers for the UPs.

It took an interesting sort of person to work with the first microprocessors. The software and hardware were so closely related that a thorough knowledge of both was needed. The man who rose to become his company's microspecialist was most probably the engineer who was "technician oriented." In fact, sometimes the technician who worked for the engineer in putting things together would end up emerging as his company's specialist. In the early stages all microprocessor people were self-taught because books didn't even exist to tell them what they needed to do. These early pioneers would become the authors of the books that would soon teach others about the units. For the time, someone who had become interested in the micros would have to read about everything that was happening and try to keep up with the rapid development of the microprocessor. This meant that programmers were excluded from the early race to determine which of the two groups would reign supreme as the early experts in the field. Even though the interested programmer might have a greater-than-normal knowledge of the hardware, he would still have to wait for further developments to create the whole microcomputer for him to work with and get to know.

This situation was sad in a way, because it caused a serious shortage of good software right in the middle of a hardware explosion, but now all is beginning to come into balance.

Even though the microcomputer contains the five parts of the classic computer, some of the parts are usually on one chip while the rest of the parts are on other chips. In the big computer and the minicomputer, the registers that work with the CPU are located in the computer's main core area, although they may be working with the CPU as if they were somehow internal to the CPU proper. Some of these registers may be used as data accumulators and are called "accumulator registers." It is possible to move these registers around in main memory, or "core," so that you can make the CPU think it has a number of accumulators with different contents. Many times a computer is faked out by special hardware circuits that effectively move core addresses around and simulate movable memory. These systems are called "virtual memory systems." This is also one method for time-sharing of the CPU between different programs simultaneously.

Microprocessors, on the other hand, generally have internal accumulator registers. This poses a unique problem for the UP programmer because some of the tricks that are used on the bigger computers will not work on micros. Because of the structure, the hardware and the software are very closely interrelated and that is why the programmer has to learn the hardware and the hardware engineer has to learn about the software. **2058655**

The marketplace has settled somewhat and it appears that industry is now rather reluctant to bring out a new UP family and the newer chips that are coming out now use established software. Either they are more powerful versions of existing systems, or they are UP chips that use the same basic machine language instruction sets as some popular minicomputers.

At this writing there are at least a dozen popular micro chips available. We have chosen one, the Motorola-designed 6800, to cover in depth. The 6800 is an excellent tutorial chip because its internal structure and software are easily learned. It is already used by many technical schools and home study courses to teach microprocessors. It's easy-to-understand programming scheme makes machine level programming much easier than a lot of other chips. Also, the chip is already the basis for several inexpensive home computer systems, and both Fortran and BASIC high level languages are available. Before we look specifically at the internal structure of the 6800, we should have a closer look at some of the other most popular UP chips.

Although the 4004 (circa 1971) and 8008 are no longer popular, they were the first 4- and 8-bit chips and we will have a look at the modernized version of the 4004 to give a basis for our chip-to-chip comparison.

The 4004/4040 is shown internally in Figure 3–1. The starred parts are actually in the latest updated version of the 4004, the 4040. You can see that the microprocessor IC has its own CPU and memory circuits right on the chip. The original 4004 did not have the memory. Neither version contains its own I/O circuit; however, it does contain a control bus which allows you to select which one of several add-on chips you use within the program. The address bus and the data bus share the same wires. The IC is controlled by time multiplexing; that is, the CPU knows that at one time the bus contains an address in memory and during the next time, data related to the previous address. Multiplexing address and data like this is common in IC's where there are not enough pins to allow each bus line to have its own separate terminating pin.

Software for the 4040 is made up of fifty-nine instructions. Instruction cycle time is 8 microseconds (Usec or US). That means any memory you use must be capable of reacting to an address and putting out correct data within 8 Usec. In practical memories, speeds of .5 US, or 500 nanoseconds (NS, or Nsec) are common for solid-state memory circuits. Interrupting can be done easily in the 4040, for the IC has automatic saving.

In a UP, an interrupt is a signal that comes in from the outside and causes the computer to interrupt what it is doing and go elsewhere in the program to perform an operation. At the end of the interrupt routine, the computer has to be able to go back to the original program and continue where it left off. Of course, since you are interrupting the normal flow of the program, you will have to restore all the registers in the UP so that when the old routine starts back up, it will not even know it had been stopped. In some UP's all the vectoring, or jumping, to the interrupt routine and the saving of the data has to be done externally, either by additional hardware or by software in the interrupt routine. As mentioned before, the 4040 automatically vectors or directs the program to the interrupt routine and automatically saves the contents of the registers within the IC. That means the status of the program, such as where the program was when the interrupt occurred and what was in the accumulator and other registers, is stored in memory till the interrupt routine is finished.

The 8080 is probably, at least for the time being, the most popular UP chip. It is the chip used in the famous Altair 8800 from MITS. It was the Altair that became the first widely available personal computer for the hobbyist. Figure 3–2 shows the internal structure of the 8080. There is a 16-bit PC (Program Counter), a 16-bit SP (Stack Pointer), and other

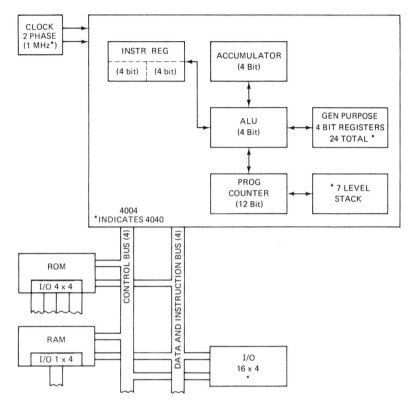

FIGURE 3–1. Outline and specifications for the 4004/4040. The 4040 is merely an updated and improved version of the 4004. All references to the 4040 are marked with asterisks.

Software: 59 instructions (*in the 4040 include the 4004). Data manipulation instructions—arithmetic and shift, BCD arithmetic via BCD correction, *logicals, *compare. Data movement instructions—uses GP registers as pointers to reach memory, takes several steps, GP registers can be reached directly, has immediate and indirect mode, 1/0 is on memory chips, 1/0 addresses share memory addresses. Program manipulation instructions—conditional branch, skip on zero, *seven nested subroutine levels, *software interrupt disable, *automatic saving and vectoring of interrupts. Program status manipulation—can test status with a conditional branch instruction.

Hardware: PMOS LSI family of custom parts. Power required 15 vdc. 4040 is 24-pin package.

Improvements over 4004: Improvements include interrupt, single-step operation, option for lower power standby mode, new memory and I/O and clock devices.

Software support: MAC40 Cross-assembler and INTERP/40 cross-simulator on minicomputers and for timeshare. Program library has over 50 programs. No high-level languages available or planned.

Hardware support: Designer's kit is available and Intellect 4/Mod 4 development system containing resident monitor and peripheral interfaces.

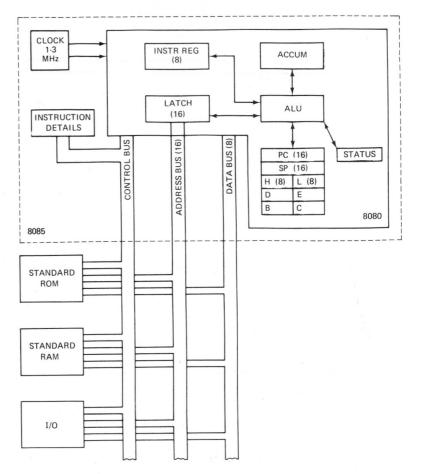

FIGURE 3–2. Outline and specifications for the 8080 and the 8085 microprocessor chips. The 8085 includes the clock for the 8080 and uses the same address multiplexing scheme.

Software: 78 basic instructions, 2 Usec typical execute time, three 16-bit pointer-type registers allow efficient addressing up to 65K bytes. Data manipulation instructions—arithmetic, logic, BCD arithmetic, double precision operations (instructions stick two bytes together as one 16-bit word). Data movement instructions—has three pairs of general purpose registers to address low- and high-order bits of 16-bit addresses, can do multiple indexing with these registers, but takes additional steps over those used by classical index register. Program manipulation instructions—stack pointer for interrupts, SP also allows pop/push of data into a stack, unlimited subroutine nesting, general purpose registers can be incremented/decremented, multiple interrupts, bus controls allow DMA. Program status manipulation instructions—software access to status register.

Hardware: NMOS, 2-phase clock, requires plus and minus 5 and plus 12. High speed (A versions—4MHZ 8080A, 5MHZ 8085) available. 8085 needs only plus 5 volts.

Differences between 8080 and 8085: The 8085 incorporates, has clock. Also has less stringent memory-access requirements, but multiplexes lower address byte on data bus so may need external address latch in some applications.

Software support: PL/M (programming language [micro]), relocating macro-assembler and text editor (both resident), library of over 200 programs—BASIC, Fortran, Micro-Forth.

Hardware support: A wide range of support from the many chip suppliers; Intel offers ICE-85 emulator, SDK-85, and UPP-855, all for the 8085. Myriads of development systems available, including use as the most popular hobbyist chip in use today.

internal registers. As in other UP's, the program counter keeps track of which memory location is being accessed for the instruction. The SP is a register that is set up to point at an area of memory that contains some valuable data, such as the contents of the accumulator or other register during an interrupt. The stack pointer can be incremented or decremented to allow it to point at a different memory slot where data can be saved or read. This means the register contents may be pushed onto or popped off the stack, which in turn may be designated to be in any area in memory. In this manner, the 8080 structure is like its bigger computer brothers. Because you use external memory for the stack, you can "nest" subroutines.

Nesting occurs when a subroutine or interrupt can push the contents of registers on the stack and then that interrupt or subroutine can call another subroutine (again exercising the stack). In other words, if you are executing a program and an interrupt occurs, your program will finish the current instruction, push all necessary data onto the stack, automatically incrementing or decrementing the SP each time, and start the interrupt routine. If another interrupt occurs in the middle of the interrupt routine, the same thing happens except that this time the new interrupt routine is nested in the old routine. Because your external memory and the stack are almost unlimited in size, the processor is said to allow what is commonly called "unlimited subroutine nesting."

The 8080 also contains four registers arranged as two 8-bit registers in series. These registers are used by the programmer as places where data may be stored temporarily. Six of these byte-long registers are used as working registers, that is, they are accessible to the programmer. The chip has various addressing modes that allow for easier, more efficient programming. Some of the seventy-eight instructions allow for moving data between the accumulator and the six working registers. And, the way the working registers are arranged, the data may be in 8-bit bytes or in whole 16-bit portions at once. This allows some sophisticated address manipulations. In software there are many cross-assemblers available to run on the most popular bigs and minis. There are Fortran, BASIC, and other high level languages available for the 8080.

The most powerful of the UP chips (8-bit ones, that is) is the 6502. Many people may argue that the Z–80 discussed later is the most powerful 8-bit unit, but test after test running so-called "benchmark" programs show the 6502 the victor in speed of processing. Benchmarks are tests that are written to accomplish a given task in the most efficient programming possible for evaluating computer systems. Although a computer may have fast execution times, its instruction set may not lend itself to efficient programming, and it will run more slowly than a theoretically slower machine in a benchmark run.

The 6502 is shown in Figure 3–3. It has a pair of index registers (both 8-bit) that may be used to point to areas of memory. It also has an accumulator. The 6502 uses "pipeline" architecture, that is, while it is processing an instruction in the CPU, it is accessing the next one out in memory. This is typical in minis and big computers, but rare in microcomputers. That means when running at 2 MHz, the 6502 can throughput (get an instruction from memory and execute it) at the same speed as the 8080 running at 4 MHz (although 8080's don't run at 4 MHz anyway).

In addition the 6502 has thirteen different addressing modes and fifty-seven instructions. This makes it powerful in benchmark testing and a powerful choice in microprocessors. At this writing, the 6502 is not as popular as the 8080 or even the 6800, but it is growing in popularity because of its speed and efficiency coupled with the ease of programming. Programming for the 6502 is very similar to the 6800 although not fully compatible. The available software includes BASIC Interpreters, a Fortran Compiler, and a cross-assembler for DEC minis (DEC is a trademark of Digital Equipment Corporation).

The Z–80 (Figure 3–4) is considered by some to be the most powerful of all the 8-bit machines and it may well be ahead of most. It certainly is designed to overpower the 8080 as it is software compatible with the 8080 and responds to the entire 8080 instruction set, plus it adds fifty additional instructions uniquely its own. It also has special registers that control refresh when using dynamic RAM's in its memory system. Dynamic RAM's store data in integrated capacitors on the chip and these capacitors have to be refreshed with their charge occasionally. The Z–80 has the refresh circuitry built right on the chip.

The Z–80 will run at 4 or more MHz so it is speed compatible, instruction for instruction, with the 6502. Note that it duplicated the six working registers in the 8080 plus adds six more. This gives it quite a bit more power than the 8080. It also has two accumulators and can do some things all the others fail to do. For instance, it can rotate bits and shift bits around out in memory. Many of the other UPs have to have the data in an accumulator or other internal register to perform such functions. In this respect, the Z–80 is much more like a bigger computer than any of the others. BASIC, Cobol, and Fortran, as well as PL/Z (patterned after IBM's Programming Language One, PL/1) are available as high level languages for the Z–80.

The 6800/6802 is shown in Figure 3–5. It is the 6802, an updated version of the 6800, that we will use as our personal computer. We will probably refer to the 6802 as the 6800 out of habit if nothing else.

There are two accumulators in the 6800, an SP and a 16-bit Index Register. The instruction set is actually copied from the Digital Equip-

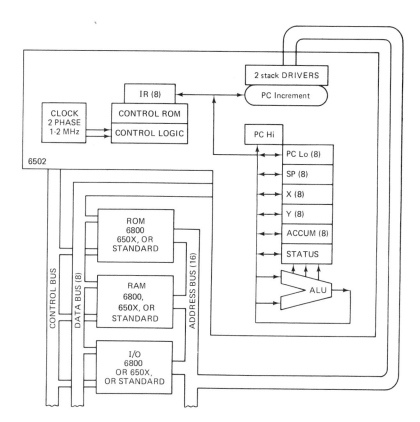

FIGURE 3-3.   Outline and specifications for the 6502 microprocessor. Other versions are controller-type models with lower pin counts and thus cheaper packages.

Software: 57 instructions, 13 powerful addressing modes, typical instructions execute in 2.5 Usec, pipeline architecture.   Data manipulation instructions—arithmetic, logical, decimal mode; can operate direct on memory space which can be RAM or I/O.   Data movement instructions—true indexed addressing, short-form addressing to zero page, two sophisticated indirect addressed and indirect indexed instructions for tables.   Program manipulation instructions—conditional branches with signed relative address, non-maskable and maskable interrupts, stack pointer for interrupts.   Program status manipulation instruction—push and pull status register from stack, set and clear carry, decimal mode, and interrupt bits, external access to one status bit for peripheral handshaking.

Hardware: NMOS, plus 5 volt 4MHZ max clock rate.

Differences between models: 6502 and 6512 are 40-pin with 16-bit addresses. 6503 and 6513 have NMI and IRQ interrupts and address only 4K. 6504 and 6514 have IRQ only and address 8K. 6506 and 6515 have single interrupt address 4K and bring out memory-ready pin.

Software support: Mini-based cross-assembler, debugger, text editor, assembler, BASIC on ROM and assembler on ROM, Fortran compiler, cross-emulator and BASIC.

Hardware support: KIM-1 pc board-type development system, Rockwell system, 6502-type systems can develop software for the family of controller chips. Will interface 6800 family of peripheral parts.

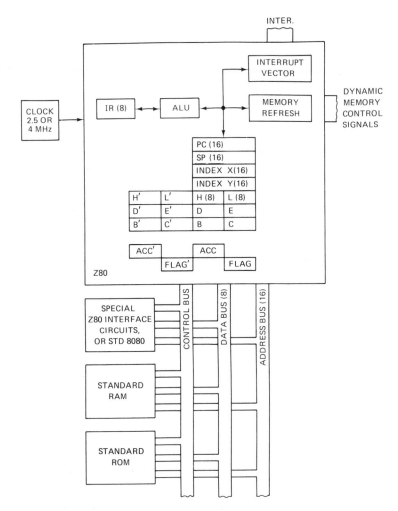

FIGURE 3–4. Outline and specifications for the Z-80 computer.

Software: 50 additional instructions over the totally compatible 8080, many more registers than the 8080, two banks of GP registers allow fast response, dynamic memory refresh circuit, vectored interrupt. Data manipulation instructions—arithmetic, logicals, 16-bit BCD add and subtract, nine different shift and rotate commands outs in any memory location, can set and reset and test any bit in any register or memory location. Data movement instructions—8- or 16-bit register or memory loads, two true index registers, memory-block-oriented move and search commands. Program manipulation instructions—uses stack in RAM, relative jumps, 3 types of selectable responses to interrupts (vector priority). Program status manipulation instructions—seven flag bits can be stored and tested.

Hardware: NMOS, static, single-phase clock, plus 5, TTL compatible I/O, auto refresh dynamic RAMS.

Software support: Macro-assembler, relocatable assembler, linking loader, file maintenance disc operating programs, BASIC, COBOL, Fortran, and PL/Z.

Hardware support: evaluation boards to development systems with discs. Emulators available. Also popular in hobbyist systems because of compatability with 8080.

ment Corp's famous PDP–11 minicomputer, and it is as accurate as is possible with an 8-bit machine. There are a total of seventy-two instructions and seven different addressing modes. This is a powerful combination for the 6800 and, consequently, it has a BASIC Interpreter and Compiler, Fortran Compiler, and cross-compiler available. We will consider the 6800 in much greater depth in the next chapters, but it is presented here for an introduction and comparison.

The 16-bit LSI–11 microprocessor is one of the minicomputer simulators. The LSI–11 actually can run PDP–11 programs as is. It has a similar instruction set and even runs at a speed sufficient to rival many PDP–11 configurations. The PDP–11 which is one of the most powerful and popular minis on the market is the product of Digital Equipment Corp., as is the LSI–11. The LSI–11 would have to be considered more of a one-board computer than as a chip-oriented machine like the other micros. It takes many support chips to make up an LSI–11 microcomputer. The most fascinating part of the makeup of the LSI–11 is the fact that it is microprogrammed. That is, the instruction words that the LSI–11 recognizes can be changed via programming.

Microprogramming could be the subject of a book in itself, but a little background should suffice for some basic understanding of the LSI–11. Many bigs and minis use microprogramming, as do some of the micros already mentioned. In the micros, the "micro-code," as it is called, is not accessible to the programming personnel. The chip manufacturer builds in the microcode at the time the chip is made. In the minis and the bigs, at least some of the microcode is available to the programmer whereby a simple program (micro program) within the CPU structure allows one to change the instruction or write a new one. For instance, in the 6800 (and in hexadecimal) a command to compare the A accumulator and the B accumulator is 11 and its mnemonic is CBA. The command CBA in assembler language is interpreted to be an 11 in machine language.

Were the 6800 microprogrammable (meaning you have access to the code), you could change the CBA instruction to a 12, 22, or any other code that suited your fancy. In this way your new 6800 computer code could perhaps be altered to simulate the code of the RRR–000 computer. Futhermore, you could also take the CBA instruction and change what it does in the processor. For instance, the real CBA instruction subtracts the B accumulator from the A accumulator (without changing either one) and uses the result of the subtraction to determine whether or not the two accumulators are equal. You could change the microcode to perform the same phantom subtraction, but this time modify the contents of ACCB (accumulator B) to contain the results of the subtrac-

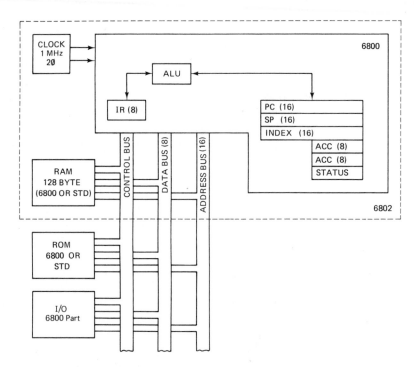

FIGURE 3–5.   6800 and 6802 microprocessor chips. This chip, in the form of 6802, is the one that is used in the text to fabricate a personal computer system.

Software: copied from the PDP-11, 72 instructions, 7 addressing modes, executes instructions in 2.5 Usec, faster versions are available.   Data manipulation instructions— arithmetic, logical, two accumulators with appropriate instructions.   Data movement instructions—first-page limited addressing for speed, relative addressing allows data relocation.   Program manipulation instructions—has PDP-11 branches and conditional branches, unlimited subroutine nesting via stack, achieves functionally vectored interrupt via software.   Program status manipulation instructions—storing and testing status register.

Hardware: NMOS 40-pin package, plus 5 only, 6802 requires a low-cost crystal running at 4 times clock (4MHZ).

Differences between models: 6802 has memory on chip (may be disabled), with power down data retention on first 32 bytes; 6802 requires a crystal with its on-chip clock.

Software support: cross-assembler timeshare and mini's, interactive simulator, editor, macroassembler, DOS (Disc Operating System), popular MIKBUG debug, PL / M, Fortran, BASIC interpreter and Compiler, over 65 programs in library.

Hardware support: various systems available, especially EXORCISOR, and evaluation MOD / 2, peripheral chips being added constantly to the family of parts.

tion. You can see how by microprogramming, you can change the whole operation of the microcomputer.

Because the LSI-11 is microprogrammable, it is reasonable to expect that, given access to the microcode, you could write instructions that would allow the LSI-11 to simulate another minicomputer rather than the PDP-11. The microinstructions for the LSI-11 are stored in a ROM called MICROM. Each microinstruction is actually 22-bits wide. The six extra bits are used for controlling other functions. One is used to latch a subroutine return address, one invokes the programmed translations, while the other four bits drive TTL compatible signals that are used for special control functions within the microcomputer associated with the microprocessor. It is obvious from this that the LSI-11 is far from a one-chip micro, but then its power is vastly greater than its one- and two-chip contemporaries.

All the PDP-11 software will virtually run on the LSI-11. Of course, one must remember that certain system differences within a microcomputer using the LSI-11 microprocessor might mean you would have to modify the software slightly to resolve address conflicts. But on the whole, the LSI-11 can run the Fortran compilers, cross-assemblers for micros, BASIC interpreters and compilers, debuggers, etc., that are now running on the PDP-11's everywhere.

You can use a system like the LSI-11/03 to insure compatability of programs since these systems, sold by DEC, are totally address compatible. Note that the DEC LSI-11 is what is used in the Heathkit H-11 computer system. The H-11 micro is software compatible with the DEC PDP-11/03. The LSI-11/03 is compatible with all the DEC peripherals, too. This means there are hard discs, Decwriters, and a myriad of other accessories available for the unit.

By no means have we even tried to cover all the available microprocessor chips in this chapter. Because there are so many available and because there are so many new chips coming into the marketplace on an almost daily basis, we can't realistically even try. It is not the purpose of this book to contain all available data. We are going to show you how to put together a personal computer system, how to evaluate one that is on the market, and/or how to use your system or others. We are also trying to give you the kind of background that will better prepare you to cope with what is coming in the near and distant future. As you should know by now, a microprocessor does not make a computer. The next chapter covers the interconnection of the microprocessor into a microprocessor system, complete with peripherals.

4

The Personal Computer System

No one really knows the exact date the first personal computer system went into action. We are safe in speculating that students at the University of Pennsylvania must have used ENIAC for solving some of their homework problems or for playing some simple games. Therefore, we can consider that the first personal computing system was the first computer developed in early 1951.

The personal computer that we know today came into public view in December 1974. The reaction to the advent of the home computer was extraordinary. Hundreds of new computer manufacturing companies sprang up, each with the dream that the personal computer had literally come of age and that his company was destined to become the IBM of personal computing. Although there was indeed a market for the personal computing devices, the companies may have been a bit hasty in the evaluation of the immediate market potential. Hobby computerists were limited in number, and many of the retail stores that catered to hobbyists went broke, along with some manufacturers. But, for each one who failed, two succeeded by picking some specialized area where a microprocessor could be applied to solve some special problem.

Emphasis in personal computing shifted to the small business user who could afford the $5,000 or more it took to put together a useful system with the necessary accessories. The hobbyist became mainly the technology pioneer developing the things that would ultimately make an under $500 system with peripherals a reality. Presently, Commodore and Radio Shack are making personal computer systems which retail around the $500 range with CRT readouts and tape cassette hookups for storage of data and programs. Now with Heathkit entering the field with both the 8080-based H8 and the LSI-11 Model H11, covering both the business and personal fields, we are destined to see price reductions in the peripheral area which will make the extremely low cost a reality. It is the low cost factor that is the key to mass appeal. The age of personal computer systems for you has arrived because you are reading this book. The field is just not quite ready for prime time television ads. It will be soon. Here is how it started:

The headline on the cover of the January 1975 issue of *Popular Electronics* magazine read "Project Breakthrough! World's First Minicomputer Kit to Rival Commercial Models . . . 'Altair 8800'." Although the headline was really describing a microcomputer, as was later pointed out in the text of the article, the important thing was not the misuse of terminology, it was that personal computing had reached the average electronics experimenter. Although months before (July 1974), rival *Radio Electronics* had carried an article on how to build an 8008-based computer, the Mark 8, it didn't cause the sensation that the Altair caused. It would not be long until that personal computer would find its way into the homes of people not quite so super-technically inclined. The importance of having a mass appeal electronics magazine publicizing a personal computer system cannot be overstated. "P.E.," as it is called, claims to reach a greater number of readers than any other magazine in the electronics field, and the articles are more "mass oriented" (though obviously slanted toward the person in electronics).

As early as 1966 the Amateur Computer Society, headquartered in New York, had fifty members nationwide. Some very highly technically oriented individuals were building their own computers from scratch.

By the time MITS introduced the Altair 8800, the 4004, and 8008, UP chips were going strong. Less than six months after the advent of the MITS Altair 8800 computer, two hundred people showed up to form the SCCS: Southern California Computer Society, probably the first computer club largely organized around the personal computer. Today these personal computer users' clubs thrive in all parts of the country. Membership in these clubs and microcomputer magazine subscription indicate that there are several tens of thousands of personal computer systems owners in the U.S. and foreign countries at this time.

By Christmas 1975, MITS was offering its Altair computer with such handy little peripherals as an octal (Base 8) numbering system, data terminal, printer, floppy disc system, and terminal, along with the 8800 computer. There were also a variety of memory cards and I/O cards and some software, such as 4K (occupied only 4,000 bytes) BASIC, 8K

BASIC, and an Extended BASIC that worked with the disc. These were all interpreters. The bus structure in the Altair computer was a 100-pin system using printed circuit board edge connectors. That is where the male end of the connector is etched right onto the PC board. And the connector fits on this edge connector to allow the computer's bus to link all the boards in the system. Because the Altair bus was the first, many accessory boards were made for it. By the time other systems came out, they would find it smart to offer Altair bus compatibility. The Altair bus has come to be known as the "S–100 (for Standard-100) bus." A lot more software was floating around the country for the 8080 microprocessor too, so it saw its way into almost all the new systems from other manufacturers.

There were a lot of other small computers coming along during the six months after the introduction of the Altair, but perhaps none made as lasting an impression as the advent of Southwest Technical Productions Corporation's little 6800. This one was really different. First of all, it dared used the Motorola 6800 UP chip and not the 8080. Secondly, it was not even Altair bus compatible. The SWTPC 6800 was cheaper, too. The connector system used to hook up the 50-pin bus was much more rugged and reliable than the Altair 100-pin bus. Furthermore, the bus wires themselves were fatter traces on a printed circuit board and that meant lower noise. The biggest difference was that the SWT machine had no front panel switches and lights. It relied on a built-in ROM to start the computer running from power on. The now famous Mikbug ROM from Motorola gave the user instant operation with a terminal without loading in any kind of bootstrap on front panel switches. And the debug commands right in the ROM allowed you to inspect memory and change whatever was necessary. Again, all from power on and from a terminal. The I/O software was really in firmware.

Early Southwest Tech ads apologized for not giving the builder anything to brag about. He hadn't had to spend months troubleshooting a newly assembled kit. His had worked right away according to their claims and they were supposedly sorry for taking away his chance to make a big hit at the computer club by telling how he was able to get his system running.

The SWTPC was a very low cost system, and this appealed to many users. But there were no high level languages when the 6800 first came out, so 6800 users started banging away in machine language. That helped 6800 users know their machines. Today most 6800 users are a little more technically inclined than the 8080 users who got spoiled by having BASIC for a long time.

There were other companies, too. The now defunct Sphere Corporation sold a lot of orders for the microcomputer they offered. For some unknown reason, they could not supply demand and put too much strain on their new company. After about two years, it folded. There were still many other personal computer system manufacturers offering products for both the so-called "SS-50" and the "S-100" bus. Now there are 6502, RCA 1802 low current CMOS systems, and Z-80 systems on the market. And they exist in every conceivable form, too—not just the S-100 or SS-50 buses. We shall cover some of the main microcomputer peripherals in understandable detail, then we shall go in depth into the 6800 UP family.

One of the accessories easiest to use and manufacture for a personal computer system is the software, but it is not always the easiest to develop. There may be more money involved in coming up with the programming for a micro than for the computer components themselves. It is not uncommon to buy an off-the-shelf (already put together) system from someone and then take literally months to develop the software. And the high level languages that are available for a given UP chip may not work because of the unique way a system is wired together. The basic wiring of the micro can change addresses within the system and make it machine incompatible. It is impossible to buy 6800 BASIC and run it as is on every 6800-based computer system.

For instance, in the SWTPC 6800 microcomputer, the I/O addresses are at memory location 8000 (Hex). Another 6800 system, the Midwest Scientific Instrument's System, uses I/O at highest memory addresses (F000). Therefore, it is impossible to run SWTPC software (without modification) on the MSI computer and vice versa, even though they are both 6800 based. Because of the differing instruction sets, it is also impossible for you to run 8080 software on the 6800. Although it is possible to run 8080 software on a Z-80 (assuming memory I/O locations are the same), it is not necessarily possible to run Z-80 on an 8080 because of the additional instructions one or more of which is likely to have been used in the Z-80 program.

Because of the discrepancies between systems, much software that was made available to the user of the chip by the chip manufacturer would have to be seriously modified in order to work on a microcomputer manufacturer's machine. Since modification of software was a sizeable task, it was some significant time after the advent of the personal computer from MITS (the Altair 8800) that good software came into being. It is likely that manufacturers started to work on the software and the hardware together, but because programming a micro was new—even to the seasoned programmer—it took longer for the programs to develop than the hardware.

One of the earliest languages developed for the 8080 was a language called "Tiny BASIC." It was published in a computer hobbyist newsletter called "Dr Dobbs Journal of Computer Calisthenics and

Orthodontia." Most of the builders of the MITS personal computer took some time to get the things up and running so they were just about ready when the Tiny BASIC appeared. Tiny BASIC was a limited form of ANSI BASIC (American National Standards Institute) which could handle limited arithmetic, and would PRINT letters or "strings" as they are called, but would not take in string (or alphabetical) data as a program input while running. Probably the easiest thing to do with this limited higher level language was to program simple games such as "high-low" or "lunar lander." High-low is a game wherein the computer "thinks up" a random number and tells you whether your guess is too high, too low, or right on. You demonstrate your skill by taking fewer guesses to get the number. Lunar lander is a game that deals with trying to land a simulated spacecraft on the moon without running out of fuel or crashing. In the beginning, those who had worked so hard to put their microcomputers together and get them running found it refreshing and relaxing to play games. The personal computer with high level language found its earliest application in being a toy for its master and owner.

Because of the games applications, as the programs became more powerful, the games became more complex. As mentioned before, MITS had a powerful BASIC Interpreter less than a year after it introduced the Altair 8800 computer in *Popular Electronics*. The people who opted to wait and see and took the less costly route with the 6800 from SWTPC, had a rougher time. BASIC for that machine was longer coming. Since the 6800 was easier to program at the machine language level than was the 8080 anyway, a lot of specialized machine language software was being published for the SWTPC 6800 in the hobbyist publications. Meanwhile the people with Altairs were pumping out BASIC applications programs. Now, nearly every microcomputer system manufacturer offers powerful high level language software for his machine. Various BASICs are floating around with capabilities that make the host microcomputer far outperform the ENIAC of the 1950s.

It is the applications programs that are suffering from a "software void." Applications programs use the programming power of the microcomputer to perform useful functions, such as bookkeeping for a business, maintenance of mailing lists, etc. Literature is quick to tell you that you can have your own personal computer and that the computer is capable of not only balancing your checkbook, but turning on the sprinklers and controlling many other household functions at the same time. While ultimately, these statements will be true, it is a little misleading. It takes applications software and special hardware interfaces to do all this. All that means extra money for the controlling hardware and the software will have to be written if it doesn't already exist (and chances are, it doesn't).

Micros are powerful and capable devices, but you should be aware that they are no panacea at this point in their development and it's a good bet that these other applications are a way down the pike. In reality, it is not really logical from a cost standpoint to use the same microcomputer for controlling a burglar alarm and home heating system and to balance your checkbook, too. The spectacular cost for this programming would be ridiculous when you weigh it against the cost of using a more simple approach: a "dedicated" microprocessor system for controlling physical functions. The programming would be a fraction of the cost, and the microprocessor itself would be relatively inexpensive. The whole thing would probably work better, too, since the dedicated "controller," as it is called, would be just doing the controlling. A microprocessor makes a good controller, but, calling on it to also be a "number cruncher," that is, a heavily math- and general-purpose oriented computer system would be demanding a lot. So as we think of a personal computing system, we are envisioning a system that is capable of magnificent feats, but it is more practical to perform some limited functions and do those well.

Of course, by the time you finish this book you will be able to decide which course you want. If you are interested in model train control, you will build up your microprocessor with a minimum of memory and a lot of control programs and outside-world interfaces that will allow you to control a maximum number of functions with a minimum amount of hassle and do it well. If you are looking for a machine to play Star Trek games you will probably be happy to start with one serial port and hook in a CRT display and a teletype. You will want quite a bit more RAM than a controller would need for storing and executing your program and you would want the capability of using some high level language to make your programming efforts more palatable. If you are motivated to apply microprocessors to some control or general-purpose application that only you have tucked away in the back of your mind, you may be interested in purchasing a development system.

Development systems are provided by the manufacturer of the microprocessor chips and they generally have all kinds of deluxe software, some of which comes free as part of the package. Development systems often contain simulators too. Suppose you are developing that home alarm system controller and you want to use one of the new one-chip microcomputers in it. You would build up the circuit board containing all the controls and outside-world interfaces and write the software in assembly language on the development system CRT. The development system would then "assemble" your program into machine language. Now you plug the simulator into your circuit board in place of the microprocessor IC. You then execute your control program as if you have the microprocessor chip installed and running. Now, if you find out the outside lights come on too late after the sun disappears, you merely go back into your original program by using a program called an "editor" to make the necessary changes. Your development system then reassembles the program into machine language and again simulates the processor chip via the simulator plug-in cable to your circuit board. Programs can be written and changed inexpensively and quickly. If your program has serious "bugs" that keep it from running properly, the simulator will allow the development system to step through your program displaying the results of each step. Single-step mode allows you to perform one operation at a time and then display the results. You tell the system to execute the next program step. Sometimes there is a slow-run mode which allows you to observe signals and control outputs that normally occur too fast to see. All this depends on what you tell your development system to do. Since the development system is also a complete computer, you can do some other exciting things with it.

At least one company offers a development system that has a so-called "emulator" that can impersonate the characteristics of another type of processor. Thus you could build and check out a processor that uses the 8080 IC in a development system, and then try using a 6800. This is the ultimate cross-assembler wherein not only the programs but the circuit itself can be simulated by the host system.

In the line of hardware available for microprocessor personal computing systems, there has been much improvement since the early days of personal computing when the only programs that were being written to interface with the outside world were programs that could blink the lights on the front of an ALTAIR in a preprogrammed sequence. The only early interface was the front panel of the computer itself.

The workhorse of the computer peripheral industry, and one that is extremely popular with hobbyist-type computers, is the famous teletype. These tele "printers" contain their own keyboard so that you have a complete computer terminal with capabilities of transmitting and receiving. The most popular and easy to interface to a micro-processor system is the Model 33 ASR Teletype. New Model 33's cost around $2,000 but used ones can be found for below $1,000. If you purchase a teletype without ASR (Automatic Send Receive) you can lower the price even further. The ASR is a paper tape punch and reader. However, for personal computer systems which use magnetic tape storage, an ASR unit would not be necessary. Because of the extreme popularity of the teletype and the fact that is an industry-wide standard, programs are offered in teletype-compatible punched paper tape. Often the company making software available will use one kind of magnetic tape system, such as the Kansas City Standard, and then offer punched paper tape as an alternative. High speed tape readers, which utilize semiconductor light sensitive pickups to detect the presence of the holes in the punched paper tape, have been offered for microcomputer hobbyists since the days of the Altair 8800. At the present time Heathkit is offering a high speed punch and reader for use with their H8 and H11 computers and all Heathkit programs are supplied in punched paper tape form. There are some disadvantages in trying to store the tapes, such as the fact that they are extremely bulky and—since no matter what the speed of the puncher reader the holes must be a certain distance apart—the more data you have, the longer the tape. This aggravates program storage problems. Nevertheless, because punched paper tapes have been around for years, they have proven their reliability and there's no problem with tape-to-tape standards. Even when a high speed tape reader is used, a tape punching mechanism is still necessary and thus maintains the old faithful Model 33.

It is possible to purchase a Model 33 teletype without the keyboard coding assembly. The printer only teletype is known as an "RO33" or Read Only 33. And when they can be found, they will generally sell for under $400. The printer mechanism for the Model 33 prints on 8½"-wide paper and is capable of printing a total of 72 characters (in a printer this is called a "72-column line"). Because of the electromechanical setup in a printer using a Model 33, however, it is not possible to mechanically backspace. Thus the teletype does not make a good typewriter since you cannot backspace and correct the printed page. When a paper tape punch reader is used, however, it is possible to use the rub-out symbol in conjunction with an actual backspace button on the tape, and thus produce an error-free punched paper tape which can be put on the reader of the teletype to print an error-free page.

While the ruggedness and reliability of the Model 33 teletype has been proven over many years of use, there are some major disadvantages. The primary disadvantage is that the baud rate is fixed at 110 baud. At 110 baud or 10 cps (characters per second), the printout rate is fairly slow. There is no way to modify the electromechanical mechanism to allow the machine to operate at any different speed. This is to be contrasted with the later model teletypes which are available now that will operate at various rates and which use a dot matrix printhead with over-strike capability. These sophisticated machines are quite expensive however, and with a minimum of accessories a good price for a new one would be well over $3,000. Because the new models of teletype are as rugged and reliable as the old ones, one does not find many of the newer model teletypes available on the surplus market. Some day

Teletype Corporation will make such progress in the production of peripherals that it will essentially make obsolete its latest design, and these later model teletypes will find their way into the used and surplus marketplace.

One must be cautioned to be aware that the extremely old teletypes (such as the Model 15) that can be purchased on the surplus market for less than $50, while appearing attractive as computer peripherals on the outside, are not quite so easy to use with the microcomputer.

The ancient teletypes used five-level punched tapes (rather than seven-level ASCII code) and ran at only 60 words per minute. It is the five-level code that causes extreme problems. It is called a "Baudot code," and because it does not have an adequate number of bits to be able to represent the entire ASCII character set, Baudot machines use shift commands prior to the reception of the letters and figures. When the receiving teletype picks up one of these LTRS commands (letters), it mechanically shifts the teletype to make letters. The same holds for figures and punctuation characters. When the teletype receives the FIGS command, it shifts into position electromechanically so that all the characters that follow will be numbers. There is, of course, absolutely nothing wrong with the Model 15 teletype. It's just that interfacing it with a microcomputer system is rather difficult.

The teletype character recognized by the standard Model 33 is a serial data character which consists of seven bits plus parity plus a start and two stop bits. It is transmitted at 110 baud which is just under 10 milliseconds. If you're wondering why the 110-baud figure, quickly add up seven bits plus parity equals eight bits, then three bits making up start and stop make eleven bits total to represent one word. To achieve the 10 cps rate it would be necessary to transmit the character (baud) at 10 times the bit rate. Ten times eleven bits equals 110 baud. Out of the seven bits of data that are transmitted, the least significant bit goes out on the serial data line first. In the standard 20-milliamp current make/break interface that is supplied with the Model 33 teletype, a mark or 1 is a current on condition and a space or off condition corresponding to logic 0 is an open condition. The reason it is dubbed a "20-milliamp loop" is that you are detecting whether or not the 20 milliamps of current is flowing through the circuit. The teletypes can be interconnected so that several can be hooked in series on one loop and fed by a common 20-milliamp power source, and any of the teletypes on the loop will interrupt the loop and transmit to the other machines on the loop. Some automatic identification information built into the teletype keyboard makes use of the "Here Is" key, so that information on the source teletype unit can be transmitted to all the teletypes connected on the loop. In standard computer interface configuration where the teletype is serving as computer I/O, chances are there would not be more than one teletype connected on the loop. The loop in turn would connect to the computer IC circuits. Since the teletype itself does not contain its own 20-milliamp power supply, the 20 milliamps will have to be supplied by the computer I/O circuits.

A widely used interface standard which can be built into the Model 33 teletype and which has become a standard for serial data interconnection on personal computer systems is the RS–232C standard. Rather than using currents, as with the 20-milliamp loop, system RS–232C uses voltage levels with 0 defined as +3 to +9 volts or more and 1 as –3 to –9 volts or less. Now all the peripherals that are interconnected on the same RS–232C serial data line will be connected in parallel. All the peripherals on the RS–232C line may be connected in parallel with the transmitting unit being the one that will supply the logic 1 voltage pulses to the computer or other peripheral.

Low cost terminals were readily available for personal computing systems even before the computers were available. In fact a much earlier issue of *Radio Electronics* magazine carried an article on the "TV Typewriter," as it was called (TVT I Sept. 1973, TVT II Feb. 1975). It was a terminal that utilized a slightly modified TV set for the CRT (cathode ray tube) display. These TV typewriters contain a full alphanumeric keyboard and are capable of displaying up to sixteen lines each containing thirty-two characters. These terminals were low cost items, considering one would have to pay nearly $2,000 for a typical CRT terminal. The TV typewriters caught on instantly for use with personal computer systems.

CRT terminals that interact with computers are limited usually to character displays which can be alphanumeric and special characters, as well as foreign characters. There are also graphics systems available which produce line drawings of objects; some of these are just now becoming practical for the personal computer system.

Figure 4–1 shows a block diagram of a CRT Terminal. Note that the terminal itself is shown with I/O circuits that allow it to interface with any computer which has the capability of interfacing with any other serial terminal, such as a teletype (TTY). Thus the CRT terminal appears to the computer to be a teletype. There are boards which plug into the personal computer system which provide the video output to a simple CRT, but these are usually not called "terminals" because of the dependence on the internal workings of the host computer. Commonly, these are simply called "CRT driver boards." Their advantage is that data is written on the screen almost instantaneously. They invariably use some sort of Direct Memory Access (DMA) system. This means that

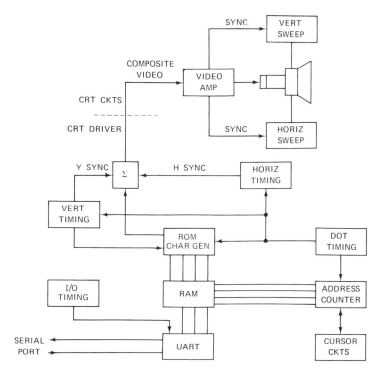

FIGURE 4–1. CRT-terminal block diagram. The CRT terminal is a quite convenient replacement for the TTY terminal. Its only drawback is the fact that it does not provide hard-copy printout. CRT terminals are largely used for editing, and a printer is usually used in conjunction with the system to provide the hard copy.

the display memory is written and read (accessed) directly by the MPU as if it were part of the computer's memory. In some extremely low cost CRT driver interfaces, the computer's memory also serves as the display memory. These systems usually allow you to do such things as generate a multiple cursor. Cursors are lighted up or underlined areas that show you where the next character will be written when you type on the keyboard. Multiple cursors can provide coarse graphics display. To display a line, you merely generate a number of cursors side by side. Circles are actually a series of cursor blocks with the edges touching to arrange a circle. Close inspection of the circle makes the block-type line segments clear but from a distance the circle looks as if it were drawn with a fat pen.

True graphics in a CRT display are given by using vectors to draw straight lines of various lengths on the CRT. By shortening the line, it is theoretically possible to light only the area of the screen created by the size of the electron beam and phosphor dots. This area illuminated only by the width of the modulating electron beam is called a "pixel." A number of pixels are arranged like the block cursors so that they create either a line or a character (as shown in Figure 4-2). Lines of light are swept across the screen of the CRT continuously, but the intensity of the electron beam is kept at such a level that the lines do not cause the phosphor screen to light up. When the timing circuits in the display driver circuits determine that a spot is to be illuminated, the video signal goes positive. Since the CRT is actually like any other electron tube, and the video signal is applied to the grid of the tube, it conducts more when the video signal goes positive. This action lights up the screen creating the dots that will form the lines making up the character. As the electron beam sweeps back at a much higher speed it is cut off (retrace blanking). The next electron beam sweep creates the next row of dots making up

FIGURE 4-2.   CRT screen, showing the scanning action of the electron beam and the composite video signals in relationship to the overall picture.

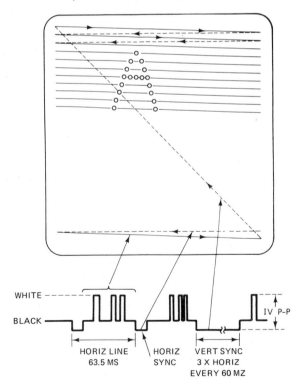

more of the character. Again the retrace is blanked. Blanking occurs at the end of the horizontal line and is called the "Horizontal Sync Period." The CRT driver circuits detect the horizontal sync signal which is a low or even negative voltage, and this sync pulse is used to keep the sweep in sync with the timing circuits. When the sync/blanking signal combines with the video signal and the vertical sync pulse (formed by counting the proper number of horizontal lines), the resultant signal is called the "Composite Video Signal."

Some personal computer systems further use the composite video signal to modulate an rf (radio frequency) carrier signal that is tuned to some unused TV channel. In this way, it is possible to display the output of the personal computer system on a standard home TV set without making any internal modifications to the set itself. CRT displays are relatively inexpensive ways to display a lot of data. A CRT terminal doesn't give hard copy printouts of programs, however, and once the data is off the screen, it is lost forever. Fortunately, there were already some low cost printers being made for minicomputer users; unfortunately, they still cost several hundred dollars.

SWTPC was the first to introduce a limited ability, limited price printer for the user of the microprocessor as a personal computer. It has some limitations; for one, it only prints up to forty characters on a line (forty columns). It uses a dot matrix print head, however, and print quality for the device is pretty good. However, the paper size is limited to a 4½-inch roll and the reliability in the models I have seen leaves a bit to be desired. But for $250, it is a good buy for a home system. The limited column width is not too bad, especially since it will be used primarily for recording program steps anyway, and an instruction seldom takes up even a part of this line length. The little unit will print seventy-five lines per minute and that is a lot faster than a teletype.

The dot matrix printer principle is fairly simple. It works somewhat like the CRT display except that rather than creating the character a line at a time, the characters are created a column at a time. Seven (or more) tiny rods are connected to solenoids which are driven as shown in Figure 4–3 by timing circuitry similar to that in the CRT Display. As the timing circuits dictate, rows of dots are formed at the same time and all proper solenoids are driven for creating the given character in the given column. After five columns are formed, the character is completely shaped and the printer spaces two column times to give the proper space between characters. After printing to the end of the line, the paper is advanced and is moved to the next character starting point plus two "row" spaces to properly space the distance between lines. The left margin (called the "home position" for the print head) is detected by operating a mechanical or optical switch that signals the printer control circuits that a line has been printed and initiates the paper advance.

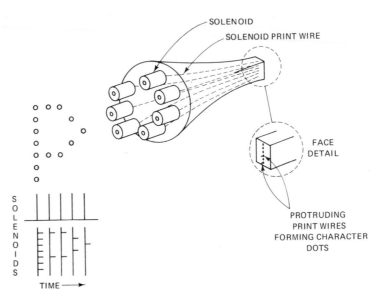

FIGURE 4–3. Drawing of the dot-matrix printhead and timing diagram showing the formation of the letter "P." Similar to the solenoids, the needle printer uses tiny needles, but instead of the solenoids, electrically operated relay-like hammers bang the needles into the ribbon and form the dot-matrix character on the paper.

Because you must print a whole line of data in this type printer, it is called a "line printer." There can be no character at a time printing like you get with a typewriter because the head has to keep moving once it is started. The line can be filled on the left or right with spaces to inhibit printing except in some desired area, but you do not see the characters until a print command sends the print head across the paper in one complete line. Some line printers are capable of striking over a line that has already been printed. Other schemes exist for allowing a shift of the head or the platen (paper roller) to allow use of two-color ribbons for such uses as in cash registers.

The problem of hard copy for a personal computer system is an age-old problem. We have seen how a dot matrix printer setup works—there are some other types of printers (shown in Figure 4–4) which should be mentioned at this point. There are basically two types of printers: impact and nonimpact. Impact printers include cylinder, ball, wheel, dot matrix, daisy wheel, and chain or band type. There are also drum types, although they are used generally in smaller calculator-type units. The nonimpact printers include thermo printers, which cause printing on special thermal sensitive paper; electrostatic printers, which

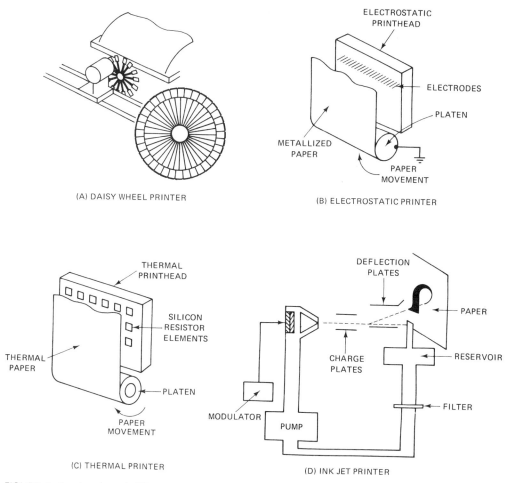

(A) DAISY WHEEL PRINTER

(B) ELECTROSTATIC PRINTER

(C) THERMAL PRINTER

(D) INK JET PRINTER

FIGURE 4–4. A group of different printing mechanisms that may be used now or in the future with personal computer systems. All but (A) are non-impact printers, and the function of each, along with a comparison of systems, is covered in the text.

use special metalized paper; and finally, ink jet printers, which spray a jet of ink using a high voltage deflection system similar to that in a CRT.

The cylinder or ball or wheel printing devices are among the most common impact printing mechanisms. These are the printers that are used in the Model 33 teletype, for instance. In these devices a character-studded rotating ball, cylinder, or print wheel is controlled electromechanically and is either hit by a hammer or directly strikes the ink ribbon or carbon film ribbon creating the impression on the printout paper. There are several advantages to this type of printing: multiple copies are easily produced, the printing is high quality depending on the characters that have been imbedded into the wheel or cylinder, and the cost of this type printing arrangement is relatively inexpensive. These printers use standard paper. Most of the units produce eighty or more columns, and they have easily changed character fonts. On the other hand, because they are electromechanical devices, these printers are usually quite noisy and are extremely slow. They're also mechanically complex and although durable and reliable, when servicing becomes a problem one must generally have some specialized training in how to repair these devices. It is impossible, too, by using this type system to be able to produce graphics on the paper should there ever be a need. And finally, because of the electromechanical setup, carriage control is generally not available. This means, as mentioned in the discussion of the teletype, it's impossible to backspace and print over characters with the TTY-type impact printing mechanism.

Daisy wheel printers mix the best of both worlds, that of a solenoid of the dot matrix printer and the solid character of the impact-type printer. Here the solid characters are contained on a print wheel which has ninety-six spokes. Each character is embossed on a tip of the printwheel. The print hammer or solenoid strikes the desired tip to produce the printed letter. The print head itself looks somewhat like a flower petal or daisy wheel, and electromechanical drivers spin the correct character into firing position for the print hammer to hit. The daisy wheels are easily interchangeable so that fonts can be changed very easily; thus the daisy wheel printer finds itself in word processing applications where art work is to be prepared by the printer itself and where various fonts may be chosen to put together a printed page. For instance, using a daisy wheel printer, along with some sort of editing CRT, one is able to produce an error-free page. By typing in a computer, one can also justify the type on the right hand of the page and subdivide the page into two or more columns. A sheet of specially treated white paper is inserted into the daisy wheel printer carriage mechanism and an absolutely correct page is printed out. On this page, however, where there are to be italicized characters, white spots are left. At the bottom of the page when the camera-ready characters have been printed, the daisy wheel is changed to the italic wheel and again under word processor control, the printer prints short lines of italicized characters which are designed by the word processing machine to precisely fit into the blank spaces left in the printed page. The person preparing the art work cuts out the italicized words and glues them in place on the printed page. You now have a camera-ready piece of art work which is ready to be printed into a format such as this book. A variation of the daisy wheel has been recently introduced by a company which calls their printer a "Spin Writer." It uses the same daisy wheel petal-type arrangement except that the spokes are bent upward so that the print wheel itself is actually a cup shape. This cup-shaped wheel spins in front of the print hammer solenoid the same as in the daisy wheel printer. The spin writer offers the same advantages as the daisy wheel. Of course, the company who sells it claims it has benefits over the daisy wheel printer. At any rate, the advantages for a daisy wheel or a spin wheel-type arrangement are that multiple copies are easily produced and that you can use standard paper. Also, it operates at an incredibly high speed, it is relatively quiet and has excellent print quality. However, its cost ranges from moderate to high, and it requires sophisticated drive electronics to line up the daisy petals. Like other impact printers that use discrete characters, these do not have the graphics capabilities of, say, the dot matrix-type printer.

Most giant computer systems contain one or more chain or band printers because of their exceptionally high print speed. A closed chain or metal band containing multiple sets of characters spins on drive wheels at an oval path behind the printing paper. In front of the paper sits a bank of impact hammers. The printer drives each hammer at precisely the instant that each desired character appears in its impact window. Printing appears on either the front or the back side of the paper depending on the ink source. This type printer has exceptionally high speed, over 1200 lpm (lines per minute), uses standard computer paper, can produce at least 135 columns, and has multiple copy capabilities. However, all the components in the chain or band printer are extremely high cost and mechanically sensitive. Character fonts obviously are difficult to change. The print quality is only fair, graphics are out, and the printers are moderately noisy. However, they are so fast that in a big computer center they are almost a necessity. It is doubtful that chain or band technology will ever reach the personal computer user, but it may be possible that at some point in your personal computing career you will stumble on a surplus chain or band printer at a low enough cost to make it a good addition to your personal computer system.

Of the nonimpact printers there are the spark gap or electrostatic printers. These use a low cost stationary print head but require extensive drive and interface circuitry. However, they are extremely low cost which makes them very appealing to the hobbyist market.

Metalized paper is moved past a row of electrodes. At the precise moment of contact, the entire bank of electrodes fires producing a row of spaced dots. The paper advances one step and another row of dots is printed and this process continues until an entire block of characters has been created. By mounting several print heads side by side it is possible to create a forty-or-eighty-column printer capable of writing an entire line at a time. The advantages are obvious: extremely high speed (some of these units approach chain printers in performance), also low cost. Because of the versatility of using the tiny pin-like electrodes, these printers easily produce virtually any size of style of character and are very quiet in operation. The only mechanism that is moving is the metalized paper. Since the size and style of character are easy to reproduce, so are graphics. Mechanical failures are reduced because of a minimum of moving parts. The disadvantages, on the other hand, aren't nearly as important as the advantages. The major disadvantage is that since it requires special paper, sometimes the print quality can be extremely poor. The units produce a burnt paper smell which is sometimes offensive. The electronics required to drive this type printer are the most sophisticated of all the others. While the unit is unable to make multiple copies, it is able to print fast enough to make several copies in the time in which many printers make one pass at a multiple copy. Another disadvantage is that most of the electrostatic printers that are available on the market at this time use an extremely narrow forty-column width. Nevertheless, electrostatic technology is a sufficient point of change so that electrostatic printers promise to become formidable contenders in personal computer systems' hard copy production.

Another of the nonimpact printers which is extremely popular in small table-top pocket calculators is the thermal printer. These work basically the same way as spark gap printers; however, silicon thermal resistor elements form the segments of the letters. They literally burn characters onto a specially treated paper and because of the extremely low-burn temperature (usually no greater than 100° Centigrade), they can operate fairly fast. The heating elements can be configured as dot matrix or dot row, and these printers because of their quiet operation enjoy varying degrees of popularity. Their cost is low to moderate; the fonts are easily controlled; operation is very quiet. Proper heat sinking of the thermo print head can achieve moderate speeds with high mechanical reliability and fair-to-good print quality. Depending on the print head, they are capable of producing clean graphics. However, the most common thermal print heads are less than forty characters wide, and again they use a special paper. They cannot produce multiple copies. The silicon resistor element sometimes wears unevenly creating uneven characters, and the special paper will not retain character readability in high sunlight. The special paper can also lose characters when exposed to high heat and humidity.

The final nonimpact printer that has been mentioned is the ink jet printer. At least one company has come out with a fairly low cost ink jet printing mechanism. This works on the same principle as in the Millikan oil drop experiment. A charged glob of ink forced from the reservoir flies through the ink injector and then is deflected. By carefully controlling the angle of deflection, the glob of ink can be make to hit the paper in the exact desired position. By using a pulsed rapid injection system and controlled deflection angle, the ink jet printer creates a dot matrix-like character. The entire ink jet mechanism rides along the carriage to produce the desired length.

Basically, an electronic transducer causes a mechanical reaction to squirt an ink drop from a nozzle. The ink drop passes through a charged electrode which causes the ink drop to take on an electrical charge and then past high voltage deflection plates which either repel or attract the charged ink drop. The drops that are not deflected to the paper are caught and then reused through a special reservoir. The advantages of ink jet printers are exceptionally high speed (over 1,200 lpm on some models), the ability to use a wide variety of papers, and extremely quiet operation. Most units produce eighty or more columns, printing quality is good, and graphic fonts are easily produced. The disadvantages at the present time include high cost (although it appears the technology is going to allow a cost reduction). These units, like other nonimpact printers, cannot produce multiple copies. There are certain mechanical reliability problems that come into play because of the complex deflection plate mechanism, too. Also, the injector sometimes clogs but technology will probably come to the rescue there, too.

More than one manufacturer sells a needle printer for under $600. The needle printer works on the same principle as the dot matrix printer except that the dots are formed by banging on the back of some little needles to form the characters. The low cost printers now available give the personal computer user some useful peripherals that help cultivate a further exchange of software. Lower cost printers are in the works now and promise to do even more for personal computer systems.

Lear Siegler was the first, and I suspect will not be the last, to lower the price on one of its beautifully cabineted terminals to less than $1,000. Now the bigs are beginning to see the microcomputer market as viable. The commercial looking ADM–3 terminal (a so-called "dumb" terminal because all it can do is communicate with a computer) brings the sophisticated looks of professional equipment to personal computer peripherals.

Hobbyists and even small business users were demanding bulk memory storage systems. At first, hobbyists wanted to be able to store programs somehow, and punched paper tape was bulky and impractical, for no other reason than the $2,000 plus expense of a teletype tape drive to punch and read. One of the earlier hobbyist computer magazine publishers, *Byte* magazine, sponsored a get-together for personal computer system manufacturers. The group met in Kansas City to try to arrive at a standard for the storage and retrieval of programs for hobbyists. That group came up with a method for storing digital data on standard Phillips cassette tapes by using an external circuit with a standard, moderately priced cassette recorder. The Kansas City Standard is still in wide use today. It allows recording digital data on machines with widely varying tape speeds. This means there can be an interchange of programs via cassette tapes recorded to the Kansas City Standard. Suppliers went right to work providing the interface circuits between the computer and the tape recorder. With the cassette mass storage device you could write a program for your computer, save it on the cassette, and any time thereafter, run the program by loading from the cassette into the computer.

Although the Kansas City Standard is widely used among hobbyists, there are other types of magnetic tape computer storage methods available. The greatest majority of these use standard Phillips-type cassette tapes for data storage. The differences come in how the magnetic fluctuations (for creating logic 1 and logic 0) are stored on the magnetic tape. Special digital recording heads allow the recording of logic 1's and logic 0's directly as digital data. These heads are built for low distortion so that each transition to a logic 1 creates a positive output from the magnetic head. Driver circuits for the magnetic head are interconnected in such a way that a logic 0 is recorded in the opposite direction, thus magnetizing the oxide on the tape in the reverse direction for logic 0. When the tape itself has passed by a pickup head or "read" head, the output pulses are either positive or negative depending on whether a logic 1 or logic 0 was recorded on the tape. This type of recording system is called "phase modulation" and is even used in floppy disc systems. One of the simplest coding systems is called "NRZ1" (Non-Return to Zero, change at logic 1). The recording track is divided into small segments all the same length. For instance, if the recording is made at a bit packing density of 100 BPI (bits per inch), each segment would be 1/100 of an inch or .01 inches long. The read electronics are gated so they only read signals which come shortly before to shortly after the dividing line between segments. In other words we're not interested in the duration of the magnetic field itself, only in the short time periods between each recorded segment. As shown in Figure 4–5, during this transition period if there is a magnetic transition from one direction to another, a pulse will appear in the gate. The presence of a pulse indicates a logic 1 and the absence of a pulse, a logic 0. These recording systems are fine for a fancy digital head data system but what about using an inexpensive audio recorder?

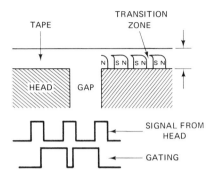

FIGURE 4–5. NRZ1 (non return to Zero, change at 1) recording system. Here you see how the magnetic tape is recorded on and how the timing signal is lined up to occur slightly before the end and slightly before the recorded signal. Any transition from a one to zero will cause an output pulse.

Audio recorders without special heads are very fussy about what they are willing to accept as input signals. They are designed to exactly reproduce whatever signal caused the original recording. Therefore, the audio people attempt to compensate for any nonlinear response in the tape head both on record and playback to make response more or less flat over the entire audio spectrum. While this kind of compensation does affect sine waves, it spreads the harmonic energy in a square wave and generally makes a messy wave form. Figure 4-6 shows what happens if a square wave form is recorded on an audio cassette head. Note the impulse on both the leading and trailing edge of the square wave. Play this back, you get a double impulse, one pair at the leading edge and one at the trailing edge of the original square wave. There is no way to get a square wave back for a square wave in. Another problem is that audio recording systems are recorded with bias and with the tape in less than saturation, or in other words, with fairly low signals. Professional digital recording uses saturation recording methods as we have already mentioned. To overcome all these problems, the low cost digital hobbyist system uses a biased FM carrier to avoid the distortion problems inherent in recording with a low cost audio tape machine. Another problem solved by the Kansas City Standard was to compensate for differing speeds between low cost audio cassette recorders.

Using the Kansas City Standard you simply put a signal on the tape that not only tells you where the 1's and 0's are but also how fast the tape is going. The recovered speed information controls the receive timing

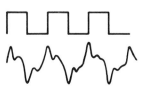

FIGURE 4–6. Square wave applied to audio record head. If one tries to record a square wave with an audio head, the problems mount up. You actually get a spike when the square wave goes high and then another when the square wave goes low. Add to this resonance in the circuit, and you get ringing at some frequency.

circuits. The result is called a "self-clocking" recording method. The Kansas City Standard was also designed especially to operate with a low cost, easily available circuit which changed the serial data (bit follows bit) to parallel data similar to that used in the bus structure of microprocessors. This device was called "UART" for Universal Asynchronous Receiver Transmitter. The UART demanded clock at sixteen times the data rate. This means that it has the opportunity to sample each receive bit sixteen times and allows it to compensate for the line hits and other interference which may disturb the normally clean wave form one might expect to receive.

Using the Kansas City Standard to record a 1, you record sixteen half sine waves of a frequency that is eight times the data rate. For a 0 you record eight half sine waves of a frequency that is four times the data rate. Each half sine wave is switched just before its zero crossing is phased, so that the wave form appears to be continuous as shown in Figure 4–7. If we switched the wave forms anywhere, we might switch one of the analog signals while it was at a high voltage level. If the preceding bit had been at a lower voltage level, it would cause a very fast low-to-high transition similar to a square wave. That would create a pulsed magnetic output on the head as discussed previously. At last, the analog output signals from the interface are reduced in amplitude to

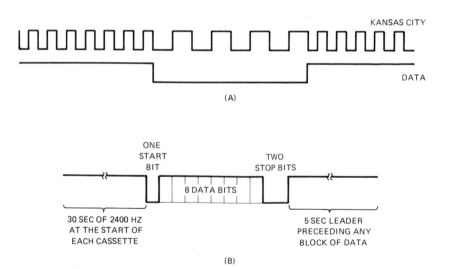

FIGURE 4–7. Kansas City recording standard. Part (A) of the figure shows the actual encoding scheme, while Part (B) gives the leader, start/stop standards, etc. This encoding scheme is very popular with computer hobbyists because it works with inexpensive cassette recorders.

make them compatible with the auxiliary input of a low cost standard cassette recorder.

During playback, signals from the earphone plug on the tape recorder are amplitude limited to minimize tape variations and interference from bias, hum, and other noise. One clock pulse is reconstructed from each zero crossing. The distance between zero crossings is measured and if the distance is too great to be a 1, a 0 output is provided on the data line and a new clock pulse is thrown in for the UART receiver circuitry. Otherwise a logic 1 is provided on the data line and no extra clock pulses are needed.

To compensate for overspeeding which would be caused by recording on a slow tape machine and playing back on a fast one, the characters are output slightly slower holding the character rate down to say 75 or 80 percent of capacity. If overspeeding is present, the maximum rate that would be encountered is still under what a system can accept.

From this, you can see that the Kansas City Standard is extremely tolerant of tape speed differences because it is self-clocking and will tolerate something like a 20 percent variation from normal. This makes it excellent for use in interchanging programs between personal computer users. It must be kept in mind however that we have covered the recording problem only on a bit-by-bit basis, and that these bits must be organized properly in blocks on the tape in order to be used by one system or another.

We will quickly look at an example of one of the most popular hobbyist tape recording formats. It is a format generated by software located in the MIKBUG debugging program written for Motorola 6800 microprocessor. The data record for MIKBUG is divided into frames. The start of each record is denoted by the recording of an S. Next a 1, 0, or 9 indicates the type of record, 0 being a head of record, 1 being a data record, 9 being an end-of-file record. The data record is the one we are concerned with, so the first two recorded characters on the tape will be S1. The S1 is followed by the byte count which tells how many bytes of data follow. After the byte count comes the address where the data bits are to be stored. For instance if the four following bytes were 0000, it would mean that we will start storing the data at location 0000 and will continue until the data record ends, or until we receive an end-of-file record. The end of the data stream is followed by a checksum number. The checksum number is derived by summing the data bits in another register as they are loaded. When the last data bit has been counted, the checksum is then pulled from the other register and stuck on the end of the tape. Whenever a checksum error is detected, it instructs the MIKBUG firmware to cause the data terminal to print a question mark and stop the cassette player or tape reader. The MIKBUG format is written for punched paper tape format, but, as pointed out earlier, the cassette tape replaces paper tape and is more likely to be found in a personal computing system.

Obviously, before tapes can be interchanged from one system to another, the user will have to make sure that his tape data formats are compatible with the data formats on the tape he is trying to read into his system. That is why the use of a standard such as MIKBUG is handy, although there are other standards. In many, data is stored in fixed 128 character blocks. We will not try to go into all the existing standards at this time. It is better that the reader understand principles since specifics are constantly changing. The hobbyist computer publications will be a source of the most current information on tape data formats.

Some years ago, IBM developed a magnetic bulk storage device they called a "diskette." Big magnetic discs spinning at thousands of revolutions per minute had always been popular with the bigs in big computer centers. These "hard discs" as they were known could store millions of bytes of data (megabytes). IBM's so-called "floppy"diskette (because it was flexible, not hard) was used to replace punch card machinery in computer centers. Data from computer terminals were entered on the terminals, edited by the operator, and then saved on diskette. Later the diskettes could be taken to the big computer which would process it, and store the combined data of many diskettes. The bulk data could then be put onto a hard disc or magnetic tape system by the big computer. Then floppies were a natural peripheral for personal computers.

While the floppies were originally not megabyte stores, they were capable of holding over a quarter of a million bytes of data. They turned at only 300 rpm, but the access time was much faster than a cassette recorder/player system. When compared to the 8 or 12 kilobytes of RAM common in many microcomputer systems at the time, the few hundred thousand bytes was indeed mass storage. And, compared to tape, the speed was breathtaking, 240,000 bits per second is not uncommon. Floppy systems are now available that can store (using a non-IBM format) and double the density of the recording up to 800,000 bytes. That is only on one side of the diskette. Since the magnetic oxide coating exists on both sides of the disc anyway, systems are now using a top and bottom head to utilize both sides of the diskette without removing it from the disk drive. By combining dual density and two heads, true megabyte floppies now exist. Since it is common to provide two floppy drives (to make disc-to-disc editing and file changing easier), it is not uncommon to see floppy drives advertised offering two megabyte storage. The cost of these systems gets lower all the time.

At first, single-sided, single-drive IBM format (270,000 byte) disc systems cost better than $3,000. Now you can get a dual drive system with dual heads and double density for less than that. The minifloppy, with storage on the order of just under one-half the standard floppy, is available too, but compromises in its performance at this stage make it best suited for applications where space is at a premium.

A typical floppy disc is shown in Figure 4–8 with accompanying details in the following figures. Basically, six essential signals allow communication with the disc drive. These are done generally by electronics controlling the drive called the "disc controller." For recording, there are two major formats: the IBM or soft-sectored format, where the sectors of the disc are defined as "a function of timing in software," and the hard-sectored disc where built-in timing marks control the data storage areas on the disc. In either system, there will be at least one index hole to provide synchronization by means of an optical pickup arrangement. There will be an output from the light pickup for each revolution of the disc for use in synchronizing the soft-sectored format. There may be sixteen or thirty-two output pulses in a hard-sectored format.

Bit timing in a typical disc system is taken care of on the same track where the data is recorded by using a unique recording method, "FM" or

FIGURE 4–8. Floppy diskette (A) and simplified disc drive mechanics at (B). Diskettes are the mainstay of the sophisticated storage for the personal computer system at this time. Hard-disc systems are being introduced at low cost at this writing, and they hold the hope of super mass storage at fairly low cost. The floppy should never disappear entirely as it is important for easily workable and handleable magnetic storage.

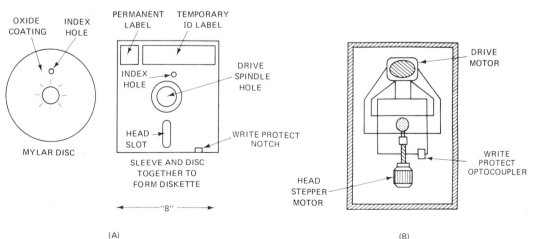

Frequency Modulation, that allows the timing data to be separated as information is read from the disc. If one of the bit cells contains only one switching transition as shown in the figure, then the bit is a logic 0. If there is the customary one bit of timing followed by another bit (data) the data stored on the disc is a logic 1. In this way the logic 1's and 0's representing data are taken from the disc. At the same time the clock that will be used to synchronize the data within the disc drive electronics is removed. In this way the logic 1's and 0's representing the data are taken from the disc at a time dependent on the clock generated by the disc itself. This means you can transfer a disc encoded on one drive to another drive that may be running faster or slower than the original disc drive without errors.

Typical specifications for a floppy disc would be: 77 tracks per diskette; 16 hard sectors per track; 256 bytes per sector; 315,392 bytes per diskette; 3,200 bits per inch (BPI) recording density (6,400 BPI for double density); and such speed and performance specifications as 360 RPM rotational speed; 8 millisecond track-to-track access time; 8 millisecond settling time (the time it takes the head to settle once it is engaged against the diskette); 40 millisecond engage time; 10 millisecond sector read/write time; 250 millisecond average access time; and the possibility of using a dual head system, wherein one head reads and writes data from the top of the disc while the other head reads and writes data on the bottom of the disc.

The disc media itself consists of a round platter of mylar coated on one or both sides with an oxide recording surface. The read/record head is similar to those used in tape recorders (except with characteristics that allow it to record digital rather than audio). The plastic platter is inserted into a low friction envelope that protects it from external damage, dust, etc. There is a head slot provided in the envelope, cut long and narrow so the disc drive head can move across the surface of the disc and read and record data from the system. The envelope also has holes that allow the light generator/pickup assembly to shine through the index holes in the plastic platter to provide synchronizing drive pulses. The index holes on the envelope and on the drive are offset to keep the disc from being inserted in the wrong direction. As is the case with cassette tape recorders, a built-in write/protect is available on the envelope which keeps the user from being able to accidentally write data on a disc which has valuable programs that must be protected.

Two sizes of disc and disc drive are available. The standard size floppy disc is eight inches on a side, with the minifloppy using a diskette that is only 5¼ inches. On both the standard and minifloppy, the first track is labeled "track 00" and is located at the outside of the disc. The last track is located on the inside. Minifloppies generally only use thirty-five tracks total.

The sector recording format in the typical hard-sectored floppy disc will go something like that shown in the figures with the sector pulse first, then a preamble, then a sync signal, then track ID data, followed by sector ID data, followed by 256 data bytes (128 data bytes, if 32 sector holes are used), followed by checksum bytes, followed by a postamble. At the end of the postamble the next sector pulse occurs. At the beginning of each sector, thirty-two bytes of 00 are written to allow the electronic circuits in the disc controller to get themselves into synchronization after the head has moved to a new sector area. Following the preamble, one byte of FF (in hexidecimal representing eight logic 1 bits in a row) is written to serve as a synchronization word for the data which is to follow. Next, track and sector identification information, which is dependent on the location determined by the controlling electronics and software, is included. The 256 data bytes given in this example would be any form of data that is to be stored on the diskette. As each data byte is written onto the controller, a two-byte (four-digit hexidecimal) checksum is computed by simply adding the equivalent numbers created by the data. This checksum is then stored in the checksum area and followed by the postamble which covers the remainder of the sector with logic 0's. During read-back operations, the track and sector information read from the diskette is compared with the requested track and sector to insure the proper sector is selected. In addition, as data is read from the controller, a new checksum is computed and compared with the checksum recorded on the diskette. If the two values do not agree then a checksum error has been detected. The software controlling the disc (usually called "disc driver software") would generally reread the disc several times when a checksum error occurs. Rereading would compensate for any temporary problems which might have caused the read error on the diskette. If the checksum problem is not able to be resolved, the software will flag the operator indicating to him that a checksum error has occurred and generally telling the user what track and sector are involved.

Any temporary error encountered in reading data from a disc is usually called a "soft error" and is usually corrected by simply rereading or moving the head back and forth once. If this operation doesn't correct the error, the error is decided to be a hard error which results in unrecoverable data. There are basically three types of error: Write, Read, and Seek. With the Write errors you use a Write Check Procedure where the drive reads the data again after recording during the next disc revolution. Normally, if this process shows an error you simply Write the data again. If after some predetermined number of tries (generally ten) the data is still written incorrectly, you must consider the track or sector damaged and unusable.

Read errors have already been mentioned; they too divide further into soft and hard varieties. Seek errors result when the head has not reached correct track. Seek errors can be verified by reading track and sector ID data at the beginning of the track. Whenever such an error occurs, you move the head back to track 00 and start all over again. Again after so many tries, one will generate a seek error message telling the operator that an error exists on the diskette which cannot be cleared by simply rereading data. The checksum error detection is called "CRC," or Cyclic Redundancy Checking. The controller electronics will generally provide at least six essential signals to allow communication with the disc drive.

First, Motor On. This signal also turns the motor off. You allow one second after activation when turning the motor on and deactivate the drive after two seconds or ten revolutions whenever no further commands are issued. This saves wear and tear on the disc drive motor. Some floppy disc drives for personal computing systems allow the disc drive motor to run all the time. This means the plastic platter is turning within the protective envelope at all times. Even though the envelope is designed to be a low friction affair, there will still be wear on the oxide coating of the platter. The motor on signal merely minimizes this wear.

The second signal needed to drive a floppy disc system properly is the Direction Select signal. This signal sets the direction in which the head will move. Third, the Step Signal moves the head one track toward the disc's center or away from it. Fourth, Write Gate. When this line goes active a write operation is enabled. When it goes inactive a read occurs. If the diskette envelope write/protect hole is open, this signal will have no effect. The fifth required signal is Track 00. This indicates that the head has reached the outside track of the diskette and will move no further outward even if an additional step command is issued. Finally, the Index/Sector signal results whenever the drive detects an index hole (or a sector hole in the case of hard sectoring).

Typically the operating sequence would go something like this: the Disc Controller activates the Drive Select (usually controllers oversee more than one unit so it enables whichever drive has been selected for access). Then the controller sets the Direction Select which latches the head's direction of movement; as a result the head will move either toward the disc's center or toward the outer part of the disc. The write gate would first go inactive so that no writing would occur during head movement. The controller then pulses the step line until the head reaches the desired track. At this point the write gate may be enabled and data pulsed in on the data line or the write gate may remain disabled and data can be read out on the data line. The controller electronics will interface the head with the outside world so that the data from the source will be properly encoded as it is recorded, or decoded as it is read from the diskette.

A Microprocessor Chip Family and Support Chips

This chapter will present the specific family of integrated circuits that represent the M6800 family from Motorola. This includes the 6800 microprocessor chip, the 6802 microprocessor chip (which is the specific one we shall use in creating our own personal computer system), the 6810 RAM, 6820 parallel interface adapter, 6830 ROM, and 6850 ACIA (Asynchronous Communications Interface Adapter). Each of these family members will be described in enough detail to allow you to use this chapter of the book as a reference when expanding the basic personal computer. Other family members including the 6843 floppy disc controller IC, and the 6845 CRT controller will be looked at, as well as some other members of the M6800 family that may be encountered in your further studies of microcomputers.

Some nonfamily member support chips will be presented in detail here. These, like the family members, are presented both for background into the operation of the personal computer, as well as to show circuit operation for future system growth. Again, this part of the book will serve as an invaluable reference for system troubleshooting or expansion.

Armed with the basic knowledge of the microprocessor and support IC's contained herein, you will be able to make more intelligent evaluations of systems that you may be considering putting into your computer system. You will also be able to refer to this area for information in troubleshooting and programming your personal computer should you build the system in the next chapter, or, should you decide to obtain a commercially available unit that uses the 6800.

Understanding the ins and outs of the 6800 microprocessor will help you understand the 8080 and similar chips as you study them further. Also significant is the very close similarity between the structure of the 6502 and the 6800. Both the software and hardware configurations of the 680X and 650X and families are pretty similar though not identical. One last feature is the similarity of the 6800 instruction set with that of the PDP-11 minicomputer. The more you know about the 6800, the easier it will be for you to understand the functions of minicomputers.

This chapter is fairly weighty technically, so it is laid out so you can grow with the chapter as you grow in technical knowledge about the actions and reactions within the personal computer system. The first paragraphs on each IC are fairly easy to understand and will provide novice level introductions. The next few paragraphs dealing with a given IC will go deeper. As the descriptions continue, they become more and more technical in nature, till finally they end up with the engineering specifications and parameters.

To use this chapter, read the sections as far as you can with relative ease. Go through each section of the chapter and do the same. When the chapter is all finished, you may choose to read on, or go back and reread. After reading the next few chapters of the book you will be able to come back to this chapter and read with more understanding. When you have read the book and are working with your personal computer system, you will probably be able to read right through the heavier technical material.

Obviously some readers will skim through the whole write-up with ease the first time, but unless you already have some microcomputer background or are familiar with computer hardware in general, you will likely find at least some parts that will need rereading.

SECTION I.
M6800 FAMILY:

General

You have already been introduced to the 6800 chip itself in previous chapters, so you should be familiar with its basic makeup. This chapter will go more extensively into the chip.

The M6800 family of parts has been designed to set the standard for microcomputer system architectures. Family designers tried to minimize the number of components and support packages required to make the microprocessor system. The 6800 microprocessor IC was designed with the total system in mind. Since the designers knew a microcomputer using the microprocessor would have to have some form of memory, the family RAM and ROM were planned. The designer solved the need for outside world interface with the PIA or ACIA. Both the PIA and the ACIA appear to the microprocessor as simple memory locations on the address and data bus. Either interface is completely programmable at the bus, and all the information about signals coming in and going out of these peripheral parts is available on the microprocessor's bus. The M6800 family is designed with what is called a "bus-oriented" architecture.

A bus-oriented architecture accomplishes several things within the microcomputer: it simplifies the interface between memory and peripheral parts and it eliminates the use for special I/O instructions. Because of this simplification system throughput is faster.

By using N–channel MOS technology the VGG power supply required by most MOS designs has been eliminated and only one +5 volt power supply is required. Because of the use of the single supply, TTL circuits can share the same power supply with the members of the family. Because of buffers designed into the output circuits, each chip can directly drive the TTL IC's signal lines, too. The minimum system using the 6800 microprocessor would be the MC6800 microprocessor chip, MCM6810A 128-by-8-bit RAM and the MCM6830A 1024-by-8-bit ROM. Generally one would use either the MC6820 PIA, which is merely a parallel output port, or the MC6850 ACIA, which is a serial output port. For a complete system, system program resides in the ROM, system variables are stored in RAM, and system I/O is accomplished through either the PIA or ACIA.

In using the 6802 microprocessor in place of the 6800, one eliminates the need for special clock circuits and the 6810 128-x-8-bit RAM, as there is a 128-x-8-bit RAM and clock circuit built on the chip of the 6802. Except for a few unnecessary pins and a couple of functions that have been added, the 6802 is identical to the 6800 microprocessor.

SECTION II. 6800 MICRO-PROCESSOR

Hardware

Figure 5–1 shows the 6800 microprocessor and its input and output structure. The processor is bidirectional. That is, data out of the processor chip and data into the processor chip come in on the same shared data bus line. The processor itself controls the 16-bit address bus in its entirety except during operation using direct memory access (DMA), in which some peripheral device may disconnect the 6800 microprocessor from the address line and supply its own address on the address bus. For clarity, we will consider that the address will originate in the microprocessor chip. Depending on the interconnection capacitance between lines, the processor is capable of directly interfacing

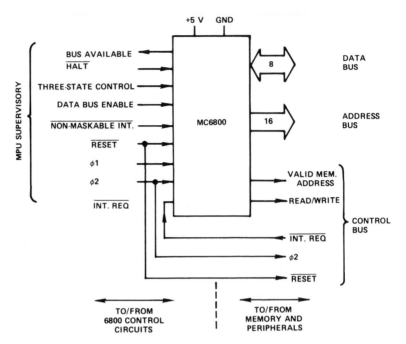

FIGURE 5–1.   Input/output structure of the 6800 microprocessor. Block diagram showing the I/O and control structure of the 6800. (Courtesy of Motorola, Inc., Semiconductor Group)

eight peripheral ports and one TTL load on the same bus with a 1-MHz minor cycle clock rate. For systems requiring additional peripheral parts, the data bus and address buses can all be extended through the use of buffers which will be explained later on in this chapter. A brief review of the processor's internal structure is in order (refer to Figure 5-2.

The 6800 has two 8-bit accumulators which are used to hold operands and results from the ALU. The 16-bit index register stores memory addresses for the index mode of memory addressing. This register more or less points to a specific area in memory and memory addresses are referenced to this pointer. The stack pointer is a 2-byte or 16-bit register containing the address of the next available location in an external stack. This stack memory is in any designated RAM location. The stack pointer itself is initialized sometime during power-up sequence. It is possible then to merely push data onto the stack for temporary storage without any memory address worries. When the data is pulled from the stack it will be re-stored as original. During this time the programmer has had to give no regard to specific memory address

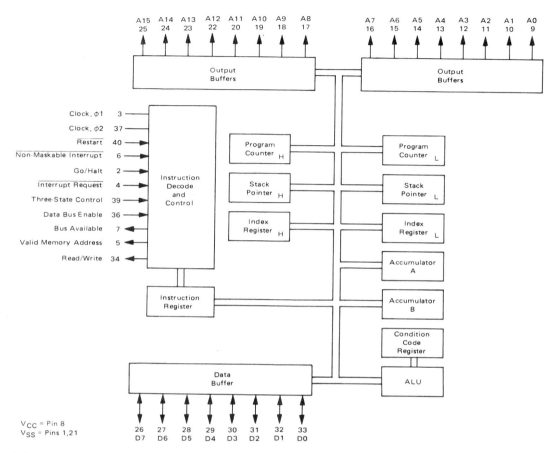

FIGURE 5-2. Expanded block diagram of the 6800 microprocessor. This figure shows the internal structure of the 6800, along with the pinouts. (Courtesy of Motorola, Inc., Semiconductor Group)

where the data was temporarily stored, since that was automatically taken care of by the stack pointer.

The program counter is a 16-bit register which contains the program address. At power on, the program counter outputs memory location FFFE (from this point on we'll always talk in hexidecimal), and the data bus will output a byte which will amount to half a memory address. During the next timing cycle the program counter will be advanced to FFFF. The data bus collects the next eight bits of the hard-wired vector address. It is the total accumulated address that the processor jumps to and starts to run a program.

A Condition Code Register or "flag" register contains six bits of codes. The condition codes indicate the result of an operation in the

ALU. The six bits are: -(n), 0(z), overflow (v), carry from bit 7 (c), and half-carry from bit 3 (h). These bits of a code are used as testable conditions for any conditional instruction that takes place in the microprocessor. The sixth bit is bit 4 of the condition code—the interrupt mask bit (i). The unused bits of the condition code register (bits 6 and 7) are always 1's. If we ask the microprocessor to check a particular number against another and branch if the two numbers are equal, the microprocessor subtracts one number from the other and checks the z bit in the condition code register to decide whether or not it should branch to the address we conditionally commanded it to go to.

The minimum instruction execution time in the 6800 is two microseconds. As seen in the figure, processor control lines include reset, which automatically restarts the processor, initializing all its internal registers and setting the program counter to FFFE. There is a Not NMI line (nonmaskable interrupt) which is a signal input capable of interrupting the processor in the middle of an instruction and causing it to go to some specified address and perform another instruction. The nonmaskable feature merely means that the processor cannot override the interrupt command. Once NMI occurs, the processor must go through the interrupt routine and carry it to its finish. The Halt control line stops the operation of the processor until it receives a specific enable to continue. This is not like the NMI in that the halt line merely stops the processor from executing any more of its instructions. When the Halt line is restored, the processor will continue to execute the instructions in the program. From this you can see the Halt line could be used by a device seeking to "borrow" the address and data bus to perform a DMA. The BA line is the Bus Available line and indicates to some peripheral device that the address bus is available or that there is not a valid address on the address bus. This line is handy for peripheral devices that use the principle of processor cycle stealing, wherein they wait until the processor is not using the address line and then go use it for their own DMA. The TSC line is the Three-State Control line. Whenever TSC is a logic 1, the address bus and all other necessary lines are placed in a high impedance state that tends to relate to a short DMA application. The DBE line is the data bus enable which again is used during DMA to allow the data bus to be used either by the 6800 microprocessor or the peripheral seeking DMA. Of course some of these signals will not be used if the processor system is not going to use DMA.

The other signal lines are bus control lines rather than processor control lines. These include the reset line since it will be used not only to reset the processor but to reset other things on the bus such as PIA's or ACIA's. The Ø1 and Ø2 data clock signals are used internally in the 6800 microprocessor to control the sequence of events that goes on. The Ø2 clock is used by some of the peripheral chips that comprise the microcomputer system. The IRQ line is a maskable interrupt similar in function to NMI, except that by masking the I bit in the condition code register, we are able to control whether or not the microprocessor is influenced by the IRQ interrupt. The VMA line is sent out from the 6800 processor to allow the decoding circuits and the peripheral chips to know that a Valid Memory Address is on the address bus. The address bus may be jumping around prior to the time the VMA occurs, but when the VMA does occur, the decoding circuits know for sure that the processor has a legitimate address present on the 16-bit address bus. The R/W (read/write) signal is used by peripheral chips to tell when the processor is putting data on the 8-bit data bus or when the processor is trying to read data on the 8-bit data bus. Here's an example of how the VMA R/W and 8-bit data and 16-bit address bus would work together.

Upon reset the program counter points to FFFE then VMA would go high and all the devices on the 16-bit address bus would take a look at the address present. (FFFE would be the address of ROM.) Meanwhile, the processor would signal all the peripheral devices that it wished to read data from location FFFE by putting the R/W signal high. When the ROM decoded FFFE it might output an 01 and internally store it in its circuits. During the next 01/02 clock cycle, the 16-bit address line would become FFFF, R/W would be a 1, and at some point VMA would indicate that the 16-bit address was valid. At that point all the peripheral devices on the address bus would decode the address. Again, the address would point to a place in ROM and the data stored at that location in ROM might be a 00. The processor would then take the 00 in through the 8-bit data bus, and it would now have a complete address at which to start executing the first step of your computer program, Address 0100.

At this point operation of the computer is purely logical. The address bus in going to become 0100 during the next clock cycle. The VMA signal is going to indicate that there is a valid address on the address bus, and the R/W line is going to go high because the processor knows that the very first instruction of your own program is located at memory location 0100 and the processor must go and fetch that instruction in order to interpret what that instruction is. From this point, the data bus will contain the first instruction of the program and that instruction will control the bus control signals and all other signals via the processor's instruction repertoire.

The microprocessor input/output is actually broken into three groups as previously discussed. The bus interface line, the bus control lines, and the processor control line. The bus interface lines are both the 8-bit data bus and the 16-bit address bus. Each of these three groups will be discussed at this point in more detail, and reference should be made to Figure 5–2, the expanded block diagram. Microprocessor address bus lines A0–A15 are contained on sixteen pins of the microprocessor IC and are used for the address bus. These outputs are three-state drivers. That means they may be a logic 1, a logic 0, or an open circuit (high impedance). The 6800 MPU may be used in DMA applications by putting TSC in its high state, forcing the address bus and R/W lines to go into the three-state mode. The data bus lines D0–D7 are contained on eight of the MPU's forty pins and are bidirectional, transferring data to and from the peripheral devices. The three-state drivers on the data bus line can be put into three-state mode by forcing DBE low. The R/W line normally controls the direction of data flow on the data bus. Should the data bus be heavily loaded and need some type of tristate, bidirectional bus transceivers (integrated circuits which are capable of tristate operation and which are bidirectional, allowing data to be either transmitted in or out), the R/W line will be the line that is used to control the direction of data flow within the transceivers. The bus control lines include the microprocessor clock inputs phase 1 and phase 2 (Ø1, Ø2). Two pins are used for a two-phase nonoverlapping clock. A third clock, the E enable, which is in phase with Ø2, is needed to transfer data to peripherals. It is gained in essence in the normal system by strapping Ø2 to E. Data transfers to the processor are made during the Ø2 time. The Ø2 clock is also tied to the DBE line which enables the data bus output buffers. A previously unmentioned member of the M6800 family, the MC6871A clock circuit, provides Ø1 and Ø2 signals which meet all the MPU drive requirements. For instance, the capacity of drive requirements for the E enable line for this system is 90 picofarad, 60 picofarad for peripheral E input capacitance, and 30 picofarad for interconnections. The MC6871A clock circuit also provides a TTL compatible E enable output (Ø2 TTL) which leads Ø2 by approximately one TTL driver circuit stage delay. Since data bus drivers go into their three-state mode with the trailing edge of Ø2 and E, this allows for sufficient hold time, nearly 300 nanoseconds. In systems having TTL loads on the data bus, E can be tied to DBE. Variations between E and Ø2 do not affect the processor or peripheral data bus hold time requirements, providing the trailing edge of E occurs after the trailing edge of Ø2.

The microprocessor IRQ line is a level-sensitive input which requests that an interrupt sequence be generated within the machine when IRQ is low. The normal sequence of operation is that on receipt of an IRQ the processor waits until it completes the current instruction that is being executed before it recognizes the request. At that time if the interrupt mask bit in the condition code register is not set, the machine begins the interrupt sequence. The contents of the index register, program counter, accumulators, and condition code register are stored away on the stack automatically. On the first interrupt, the interrupt mask bit is automatically set so no further interrupts may occur until this interrupt is processed. At the end of the cycle a 16-bit address will be placed on the address bus that points to a vectoring address located in memory locations FFF8 and FFF9. An address loaded at these locations causes the MPU to jump to an interrupt routine in memory similar to the way it jumped to the beginning of the user routine during power on. The halt line must be in a high state for interrupts to be serviced. Interrupts will be latched internally if halt is low. The IRQ input has a wired OR capability so that several different interrupt generating inputs may be tied together to cause an IRQ. If IRQ is not being used it would require a 3K minimum external pull-up resistor to +5 volts.

Software   The MC6800 has seventy-two different instructions including binary and decimal arithmetic, logical, shift, rotate, load, store, conditional or unconditional branch, interrupt, and stack manipulation instructions. Figure 5–3 gives a complete microprocessor instruction set. Figure 5–3 also shows the instruction addressing modes and associated execution times. The MPU actually has seven address modes and most of its instructions are usable in all seven modes.

    1. Immediate Addressing.   Immediate addressing is an addressing technique in which the first byte of the instruction contains the operator. The second byte contains the operand. During the first half-cycle of Ø1 the program counter's current address is put on the line. R/W goes high, designating a read operation, and VMA goes high, designating that the current address is valid. During the second half-cycle of Ø1 the operator code is put on the data bus from memory and loaded into the MPU. The MPU program counter is incremented and the operand (which is usually data) is loaded into the MPU on cycle number 2. The operator of the next instruction follows on the next cycle. Immediate addressing is used to allow you to load literals into given registers. The command LDAA 01 would put a 01 into Accumulator A at the end of MPU cycle 2.

    2. Direct Addressing.   In direct addressing, the address of the operand is contained in the second byte of the instruction. Direct addressing allows the user to directly address the lowest 256 bytes in the machine, location 0 through 255 (0 through FF hexidecimal). In this case, the command (LDA) will be followed by a byte which will contain the lower 8 bits of the 16-bit address. The upper 8 bits are forced to all zeros.

This is a sort of "addressing shorthand" that can be used to speed up execution time. It is wise to store data which will be moved around a great deal in lower memory locations to take advantage of shorter direct addressing. In most configurations 0000 through 00FF will be RAM.

The sequence of operation goes something like this—the address in the program counter is put on the address bus and the operator code (LDA) is loaded into the MPU during cycle number 1. Next the program counter is incremented, and during cycle 2, 8 bits of address are loaded into the address bus low (ABL register) which contains the lower 8 bits

FIGURE 5–3. The complete instruction set for the 6800 microprocessor. The figure shows the addressing modes for each command as well as cycle times ($\sim$) and number of program bytes (#) used for each instruction and mode. (Courtesy of Motorola, Inc., Semiconductor Group)

INDEX REGISTER AND STACK MANIPULATION INSTRUCTIONS

		IMMED			DIRECT			INDEX			EXTND			IMPLIED				COND. CODE REG.					
																			5	4	3	2	1	0
POINTER OPERATIONS	MNEMONIC	OP	$\sim$	#	OP	$\sim$	#	OP	$\sim$	#	OP	$\sim$	#	OP	$\sim$	#	BOOLEAN/ARITHMETIC OPERATION	H	I	N	Z	V	C
Compare Index Reg	CPX	8C	3	3	9C	4	2	AC	6	2	BC	5	3				$X_H - M, X_L - (M + 1)$	●	●	⑦	↕	⑧	●
Decrement Index Reg	DEX													09	4	1	$X - 1 \rightarrow X$	●	●	●	↕	●	●
Decrement Stack Pntr	DES													34	4	1	$SP - 1 \rightarrow SP$	●	●	●	●	●	●
Increment Index Reg	INX													08	4	1	$X + 1 \rightarrow X$	●	●	●	↕	●	●
Increment Stack Pntr	INS													31	4	1	$SP + 1 \rightarrow SP$	●	●	●	●	●	●
Load Index Reg	LDX	CE	3	3	DE	4	2	EE	6	2	FE	5	3				$M \rightarrow X_H, (M + 1) \rightarrow X_L$	●	●	⑨	↕	R	●
Load Stack Pntr	LDS	8E	3	3	9E	4	2	AE	6	2	BE	5	3				$M \rightarrow SP_H, (M + 1) \rightarrow SP_L$	●	●	⑨	↕	R	●
Store Index Reg	STX				DF	5	2	EF	7	2	FF	6	3				$X_H \rightarrow M, X_L \rightarrow (M + 1)$	●	●	⑨	↕	R	●
Store Stack Pntr	STS				9F	5	2	AF	7	2	BF	6	3				$SP_H \rightarrow M, SP_L \rightarrow (M + 1)$	●	●	⑨	↕	R	●
Indx Reg → Stack Pntr	TXS													35	4	1	$X - 1 \rightarrow SP$	●	●	●	●	●	●
Stack Pntr → Indx Reg	TSX													30	4	1	$SP + 1 \rightarrow X$	●	●	●	●	●	●

JUMP AND BRANCH INSTRUCTIONS

		RELATIVE			INDEX			EXTND			IMPLIED				COND. CODE REG.					
															5	4	3	2	1	0
OPERATIONS	MNEMONIC	OP	$\sim$	#	OP	$\sim$	#	OP	$\sim$	#	OP	$\sim$	#	BRANCH TEST	H	I	N	Z	V	C
Branch Always	BRA	20	4	2										None	●	●	●	●	●	●
Branch If Carry Clear	BCC	24	4	2										$C = 0$	●	●	●	●	●	●
Branch If Carry Set	BCS	25	4	2										$C = 1$	●	●	●	●	●	●
Branch If = Zero	BEQ	27	4	2										$Z = 1$	●	●	●	●	●	●
Branch If ≥ Zero	BGE	2C	4	2										$N \oplus V = 0$	●	●	●	●	●	●
Branch If > Zero	BGT	2E	4	2										$Z + (N \oplus V) = 0$	●	●	●	●	●	●
Branch If Higher	BHI	22	4	2										$C + Z = 0$	●	●	●	●	●	●
Branch If ≤ Zero	BLE	2F	4	2										$Z + (N \oplus V) = 1$	●	●	●	●	●	●
Branch If Lower Or Same	BLS	23	4	2										$C + Z = 1$	●	●	●	●	●	●
Branch If < Zero	BLT	2D	4	2										$N \oplus V = 1$	●	●	●	●	●	●
Branch If Minus	BMI	2B	4	2										$N = 1$	●	●	●	●	●	●
Branch If Not Equal Zero	BNE	26	4	2										$Z = 0$	●	●	●	●	●	●
Branch If Overflow Clear	BVC	28	4	2										$V = 0$	●	●	●	●	●	●
Branch If Overflow Set	BVS	29	4	2										$V = 1$	●	●	●	●	●	●
Branch If Plus	BPL	2A	4	2										$N = 0$	●	●	●	●	●	●
Branch To Subroutine	BSR	8D	8	2											●	●	●	●	●	●
Jump	JMP				6E	4	2	7E	3	3				See Special Operations	●	●	●	●	●	●
Jump To Subroutine	JSR				AD	8	2	BD	9	3					●	●	●	●	●	●
No Operation	NOP										01	2	1	Advances Prog. Cntr. Only	●	●	●	●	●	●
Return From Interrupt	RTI										3B	10	1		─ ─ ─ ─ ⑩ ─ ─ ─ ─					
Return From Subroutine	RTS										39	5	1		●	●	●	●	●	●
Software Interrupt	SWI										3F	12	1	See Special Operations	●	●	●	●	●	●
Wait for Interrupt *	WAI										3E	9	1		●	⑪	●	●	●	●

*WAI puts Address Bus, R/W, and Data Bus in the three-state mode while VMA is held low.

FIGURE 5-3 (cont.)   **ACCUMULATOR AND MEMORY INSTRUCTIONS**

OPERATIONS	MNEMONIC	IMMED OP	~	=	DIRECT OP	~	=	INDEX OP	~	=	EXTND OP	~	=	IMPLIED OP	~	=	BOOLEAN/ARITHMETIC OPERATION (All register labels refer to contents)	H	I	N	Z	V	C
Add	ADDA	3B	2	2	9B	3	2	AB	5	2	BB	4	3				A + M → A	↕	•	↕	↕	↕	↕
	ADDB	CB	2	2	DB	3	2	EB	5	2	FB	4	3				B + M → B	↕	•	↕	↕	↕	↕
Add Acmltrs	ABA													1B	2	1	A + B → A	↕	•	↕	↕	↕	↕
Add with Carry	ADCA	89	2	2	99	3	2	A9	5	2	B9	4	3				A + M + C → A	↕	•	↕	↕	↕	↕
	ADCB	C9	2	2	D9	3	2	E9	5	2	F9	4	3				B + M + C → B	↕	•	↕	↕	↕	↕
And	ANDA	84	2	2	94	3	2	A4	5	2	B4	4	3				A · M → A	•	•	↕	↕	R	•
	ANDB	C4	2	2	D4	3	2	E4	5	2	F4	4	3				B · M → B	•	•	↕	↕	R	•
Bit Test	BITA	85	2	2	95	3	2	A5	5	2	B5	4	3				A · M	•	•	↕	↕	R	•
	BITB	C5	2	2	D5	3	2	E5	5	2	F5	4	3				B · M	•	•	↕	↕	R	•
Clear	CLR							6F	7	2	7F	6	3				00 → M	•	•	R	S	R	R
	CLRA													4F	2	1	00 → A	•	•	R	S	R	R
	CLRB													5F	2	1	00 → B	•	•	R	S	R	R
Compare	CMPA	81	2	2	91	3	2	A1	5	2	B1	4	3				A − M	•	•	↕	↕	↕	↕
	CMPB	C1	2	2	D1	3	2	E1	5	2	F1	4	3				B − M	•	•	↕	↕	↕	↕
Compare Acmltrs	CBA													11	2	1	A − B	•	•	↕	↕	↕	↕
Complement, 1's	COM							63	7	2	73	6	3				M̄ → M	•	•	↕	↕	R	S
	COMA													43	2	1	Ā → A	•	•	↕	↕	R	S
	COMB													53	2	1	B̄ → B	•	•	↕	↕	R	S
Complement, 2's	NEG							60	7	2	70	6	3				00 − M → M	•	•	↕	↕	①	②
(Negate)	NEGA													40	2	1	00 − A → A	•	•	↕	↕	①	②
	NEGB													50	2	1	00 − B → B	•	•	↕	↕	①	②
Decimal Adjust, A	DAA													19	2	1	Converts Binary Add. of BCD Characters into BCD Format.	•	•	↕	↕	↕	③
Decrement	DEC							6A	7	2	7A	6	3				M − 1 → M	•	•	↕	↕	④	•
	DECA													4A	2	1	A − 1 → A	•	•	↕	↕	④	•
	DECB													5A	2	1	B − 1 → B	•	•	↕	↕	④	•
Exclusive OR	EORA	88	2	2	98	3	2	A8	5	2	B8	4	3				A⊕M → A	•	•	↕	↕	R	•
	EORB	C8	2	2	D8	3	2	E8	5	2	F8	4	3				B⊕M → B	•	•	↕	↕	R	•
Increment	INC							6C	7	2	7C	6	3				M + 1 → M	•	•	↕	↕	⑤	•
	INCA													4C	2	1	A + 1 → A	•	•	↕	↕	⑤	•
	INCB													5C	2	1	B + 1 → B	•	•	↕	↕	⑤	•
Load Acmltr	LDAA	86	2	2	96	3	2	A6	5	2	B6	4	3				M → A	•	•	↕	↕	R	•
	LDAB	C6	2	2	D6	3	2	E6	5	2	F6	4	3				M → B	•	•	↕	↕	R	•
Or, Inclusive	ORAA	8A	2	2	9A	3	2	AA	5	2	BA	4	3				A + M → A	•	•	↕	↕	R	•
	ORAB	CA	2	2	DA	3	2	EA	5	2	FA	4	3				B + M → B	•	•	↕	↕	R	•
Push Data	PSHA													36	4	1	A → MSP, SP − 1 → SP	•	•	•	•	•	•
	PSHB													37	4	1	B → MSP, SP − 1 → SP	•	•	•	•	•	•
Pull Data	PULA													32	4	1	SP + 1 → SP, MSP → A	•	•	•	•	•	•
	PULB													33	4	1	SP + 1 → SP, MSP → B	•	•	•	•	•	•
Rotate Left	ROL							69	7	2	79	6	3				M	•	•	↕	↕	⑥	↕
	ROLA													49	2	1	A	•	•	↕	↕	⑥	↕
	ROLB													59	2	1	B	•	•	↕	↕	⑥	↕
Rotate Right	ROR							66	7	2	76	6	3				M	•	•	↕	↕	⑥	↕
	RORA													46	2	1	A	•	•	↕	↕	⑥	↕
	RORB													56	2	1	B	•	•	↕	↕	⑥	↕
Shift Left, Arithmetic	ASL							68	7	2	78	6	3				M	•	•	↕	↕	⑥	↕
	ASLA													48	2	1	A	•	•	↕	↕	⑥	↕
	ASLB													58	2	1	B	•	•	↕	↕	⑥	↕
Shift Right, Arithmetic	ASR							67	7	2	77	6	3				M	•	•	↕	↕	⑥	↕
	ASRA													47	2	1	A	•	•	↕	↕	⑥	↕
	ASRB													57	2	1	B	•	•	↕	↕	⑥	↕
Shift Right, Logic	LSR							64	7	2	74	6	3				M	•	•	R	↕	⑥	↕
	LSRA													44	2	1	A	•	•	R	↕	⑥	↕
	LSRB													54	2	1	B	•	•	R	↕	⑥	↕
Store Acmltr.	STAA				97	4	2	A7	6	2	B7	5	3				A → M	•	•	↕	↕	R	•
	STAB				D7	4	2	E7	6	2	F7	5	3				B → M	•	•	↕	↕	R	•
Subtract	SUBA	80	2	2	90	3	2	A0	5	2	B0	4	3				A − M → A	•	•	↕	↕	↕	↕
	SUBB	C0	2	2	D0	3	2	E0	5	2	F0	4	3				B − M → B	•	•	↕	↕	↕	↕
Subtract Acmltrs.	SBA													10	2	1	A − B → A	•	•	↕	↕	↕	↕
Subtr. with Carry	SBCA	82	2	2	92	3	2	A2	5	2	B2	4	3				A − M − C → A	•	•	↕	↕	↕	↕
	SBCB	C2	2	2	D2	3	2	E2	5	2	F2	4	3				B − M − C → B	•	•	↕	↕	↕	↕
Transfer Acmltrs	TAB													16	2	1	A → B	•	•	↕	↕	R	•
	TBA													17	2	1	B → A	•	•	↕	↕	R	•
Test, Zero or Minus	TST							6D	7	2	7D	6	3				M − 00	•	•	↕	↕	R	R
	TSTA													4D	2	1	A − 00	•	•	↕	↕	R	R
	TSTB													5D	2	1	B − 00	•	•	↕	↕	R	R
																		H	I	N	Z	V	C

LEGEND:

OP	Operation Code (Hexadecimal);	+	Boolean Inclusive OR;	
~	Number of MPU Cycles;	⊙	Boolean Exclusive OR;	
=	Number of Program Bytes;	M̄	Complement of M;	
+	Arithmetic Plus;	→	Transfer Into;	
−	Arithmetic Minus;	0	Bit = Zero;	
·	Boolean AND;	00	Byte = Zero;	
MSP	Contents of memory location pointed to be Stack Pointer;			

CONDITION CODE SYMBOLS:

H Half-carry from bit 3;
I Interrupt mask
N Negative (sign bit)
Z Zero (byte)
V Overflow, 2's complement
C Carry from bit 7
R Reset Always
S Set Always
↕ Test and set if true, cleared otherwise
• Not Affected

Note − Accumulator addressing mode instructions are included in the column for IMPLIED addressing

of the 16-bit address register of the MPU. The upper 8 bits which are contained in the ABH register are forced to all zeros. In the third cycle the new address is put on the address bus and the operand is loaded into the MPU. It is clear then that the direct addressing mode takes one more cycle to execute than the immediate addressing mode. In the example given, LDAA followed by FO will put whatever data is located in memory position FO into the A accumulator.

An STA instruction is handled in the same manner as LDA instruction, except that there is an additional cycle required. Due to the MPU architecture, this additional cycle is required to move the accumulator internally inside the machine. During this cycle the data bus is in an indeterminate state and VMA goes low. The actual storing of the data occurs on the next cycle.

3. Indexed Addressing.   In indexed addressing, the address contained in the second byte of the instruction is added to the index register's lowest 8 bits. The carry, if there is any, is then added to the higher 8 bits of the index register. These are two byte instructions. Remember that these instructions require the index register to have a memory address loaded in it. This 2-byte instruction becomes useful by loading an address of, say, 0100 in the index register to start. An instruction, such as LDAA FF, is able to address 256 bytes higher than the 0100 located in the index register. Indexed addressing is a shorthand method of addressing, like direct addressing, but by using the index register you are able to access memory in any area in the microcomputer.

In the first two cycles of an indexed address instruction, the LDA operator code would be loaded into the MPU followed by the index offset. In the third cycle the low order byte of the index register is loaded into the adder within the ALU, and it is added to the offset. During the next cycle the carry, if any, is added to the upper 8 bits of the index register in the adder. The VMA goes low during these two cycles while the MPU is preparing the indexed address. The new address then goes on the line during cycle number 5. The STA indexed instruction is handled in the same manner as the LDA instruction, except that an additional cycle is again required due to the MPU architecture. The VMA is held low then for three cycles for the STA instruction, instead of for the previous two cycles.

4. Extended Addressing.   In extended addressing, two bytes follow the instruction. These two bytes carry the address of the operand. The second byte of the instruction is the eight higher-order address bits and the third byte contains the eight lower 8 bits of the address. This is an absolute addressing scheme and a three-byte instruction. Extended addressing is the same as direct addressing except the address field is a full 16 bits allowing access to 2^{16} or 65,000+ address positions. A typical command could be LDAA CF80. Contents of the accumulator would be loaded with the data located at memory position CF80. Cycle by cycle, the extended addressing mode is exactly like the direct addressing mode, except that an additional cycle is required to fetch the higher order 8 bits of the address.

   5. *Implied Address.*   The implied addressing mode comes in two types—those which don't require an address, and those which do require an address. The implied instructions are 1-byte instructions. An example of an instruction which does not require an address is CBA (compare B to A). Here the contents of accumulator A are compared with those in accumulator B and the results stored in the condition code register. The data bus and address bus are valid only on the first cycle of the instruction. Some one-byte instructions do require an address. Even though the address is not determined by the programmer, the address is determined by the microprocessor. One of these instructions is the PSH (push) instruction where the data contained in one of the accumulators is pushed onto the stack. Another example of this type instruction is the PUL (pull) instruction. The data is taken from the stack and put into the accumulator.

   The data and address buses are valid to begin with in order to fetch the "push" operator. Next, the MPU moves data internally and VMA does not go low. During this time the address bus contains the address of the next instruction in ROM, and the MPU is doing an invalid read. During the next cycle the stack pointer is loaded into the address bus buffers and data is written into the stack. On the next cycle VMA goes low and the stack pointer is decremented. The next instruction follows.

   6. *Relative Addressing.*   In relative addressing the address contained in the second byte of the instruction is added to the program counter's lowest 8 bits plus 2. The carry or borrow is then added to the high 8 bits. This allows the user to address data within a range of -126 to +129 bytes of the present instruction. These are two-byte instructions, a form of shorthand which is used to perform branch functions.

   First the operator code is fetched from the memory location stored in the instruction register during cycle number 1. These are the instructions shown in Figure 5-3 beginning with the letter "B" but excluding bit test, BIT. During the MPU's cycle 2, the program counter offset is loaded into the MPU. The offset is added to the low order bits of the program counter during cycle number 3, and during cycle 4 the carry is added to the higher order bits. During these two cycles VMA goes low while the

MPU is operating on the offset data. The next instruction is loaded during cycle number 5.

Here is an example of how this instruction works: Program command CBA, compare accumulator B to accumulator A, is performed. The command BNE then comes into the processor, and the processor takes a look at the condition code register. If the two compared sets of data are not equal, the branch command is valid and the address is formed as mentioned before. A BNE 08 means Branch if the two are Not Equal to an address that is eight positions away from the present program counter address. Remember that the program counter this time is actually sitting at the address of the next instruction during this time. Therefore, the 8 bits plus 2 are added to the program counter address at the time of the BNE command. The two extra bits compensate for the fact that the program counter has already advanced internally in the MPU. Therefore, ten positions away from the BNE instruction there will be a new instruction which is the one that will be processed if the contents of accumulator A and accumulator B are not identical. If the contents of accumulator A and accumulator B are identical according to the conditions shown in the condition code register, the branch instruction offset will be skipped and the processor will continue to execute instructions where the program counter is pointing (which is two bytes away from the branch command). If the BNE had been F8 the relative address would have been 8 bytes in the opposite direction from the branch instruction.

Backstep calculations are a little more complicated, but work the same way. You calculate the number of steps backwards in essentially the same manner as before (again adding 2 to the branch instruction address). To calculate the backstep, take into account the fact that the offset is a signed binary number—meaning that if the Left MSByte is a one, the computer jumps backwards. To jump backwards, write the number of backsteps in binary. Decode each hex digit as four binary digits. Take the 2's complement of the binary number. Finally, add 1. For *example:*

The number of backsteps is 25_{16}—in binary, 0010 0101

Take the complement (invert each digit)—1101 1010

Now add 0000 0001—this gives you 1101 1011

Now change to hex DB

Thus the backstep value following the branch is DB_{16}

Through use and experimentation with your personal computer system you will gain a good feel for how the relative address is really implemented.

7. Accumulator Addressing. Finally, there is accumulator only addressing in which either accumulator A or accumulator B is specified.

These are all one-byte, two-cycle instructions like the CBA instruction that has already been used in previous examples. The address and data bus are active only during the first cycle of the instruction when the operator is being loaded in from memory. During the second cycle the machine performs the operation and holds VMA high.

All the addressing modes will become clearer when you actually start programming the 6800 microprocessor, but a good idea of the function of each is necessary at this time because of the close interrelationship between software and hardware in a microprocessor system of any type.

The microprocessor has six processor control lines which have already been mentioned, RESET, NMI, HALT, VMA, TSC, and DBE. Two of the control lines, RESET and VME, are required for all systems, and the remaining control lines can be utilized depending on the system application. The simplicity of each of these control lines results from the simple way that the 6800 processor is set up. We will discuss each of the important microprocessor controls in more detail.

The RESET input is used to reset and start the MPU from a power-down condition upon initial start-up of the processor or from a power failure. This input can also be used to reinitialize the machine at any time after start-up by connecting a simple push button affair to the RESET line. When a high level is detected in this input, it signals the MPU to begin the reset sequence. In other words, as long as the reset line is low, the machine is held in reset condition. When the reset sequence begins, the contents of FFFE and FFFF will be loaded into the program counter to point to the beginning of the reset routine, as already mentioned. At this time the interrupt mask bit in the condition code register is set and must be cleared on the program control before the MPU can be interrupted by an IRQ. Also the state of the stack pointer may not be known, and the stack pointer must be initialized to that area of memory which has been reserved to act as the stack register. While reset is low the MPU output signals will be in the following state: VMA will be low, BA will be low, the data bus will be in a high impedance state, R/W will be high (in a read state), and the address bus will contain the reset address FFFE. After the power supply reaches 4.75 volts minimum, a minimum of eight clock cycles are required for the processor to stabilize in preparation for restarting. During these eight cycles, VMA will be in an indeterminate state. Any devices that are enabled by VMA which could accept a false write during this time, such as a RAM that is battery backed to keep it from losing data, must be disabled until VMA is forced low after eight cycles. Reset can go high any time after the eighth cycle of clock. Its position relative to system clock does not matter. That is why a simple push button can be used as a reset switch to reinitialize reset at any time during the operation of the system. Although reset will have to be low for the duration of a minimum of at least three complete Ø2 cycles, complex switching circuits are still not needed because the normal switch closure time of at least a few milliseconds will allow enough one microsecond Ø2 cycles to occur.

The nonmaskable interrupt NMI, the IRQ or maskable interrupt, and the "Wait for Interrupt" instruction control the external sources which can interrupt normal operation of the MPU and cause it to go process a different routine located somewhere else in memory. The IRQ signal is maskable, the NMI signal is not. This sets up sort of a priority handling basis within the MPU itself. Under any condition the NMI will be serviced even if the processor is in the middle of servicing an IRQ. The address of the interrupt service routine is fetched from FFFC and FFFD for an NMI interrupt and from FFF8 and FFF9 for an IRQ interrupt. Upon completion of the interrupt service routine, the execution of RTI instruction return from interrupt pulls the program counter, index register, accumulators, and condition code registers off the stack. At this time the stack pointer will be what it was prior to the interrupt. The interrupt mask bit in the condition code register is reset, too. The WAIT instruction can be executed as part of the program and allows you to speed up the MPU's response to the interrupt, because the WAIT instruction actually causes the stacking of the program counter, index register, accumulators, and condition code register before the interrupt occurs. While the MPU is waiting for the interrupt, BA goes high, VMA is low, the address bus, R/W, and data bus are all in the high impedance state. After the interrupt occurs, it is serviced as previously described and the next instruction is executed. After the interrupt service routine will come the instruction that occurs immediately after the WAIT instruction in the user's program.

The HALT line provides an input to the MPU to allow control of program execution by an outside source without interrupting and causing the interrupt routine to be run. If HALT is high the MPU will execute the instruction. If it is low the MPU goes to an idle mode. A response signal, Bus Available (BA), provides an indication of the current status of the MPU.

If BA is high, the MPU has halted and all internal activity has stopped; when bus available is low the MPU is in the process of executing its control program. When BA is high, the address bus, data bus, and R/W line will be in a high impedance state effectively removing the MPU from the system bus. This allows another MPU to share the system bus. The VMA is forced low so the floating system bus will not activate any device on the bus that is enabled by VMA unless the VMA signal is generated from another source.

While the MPU is halted there is no longer any program activity, and if either an NMI or IRQ interrupt occurs, it will be latched into the MPU. As soon as the MPU is taken out of the halted mode, the interrupt service routine will occur. If a reset command occurs while the MPU is halted, the following states occur: BA low, VMA low, data bus high impedance, R/W high, and the address principle contains address FFFE as long as reset is low. As soon as the halt line goes high, the MPU will go to locations FFFE and FFFF for the address of the reset routine.

When HALT goes low, the MPU stops after completing execution of the current instruction. The transition of halt must occur before the trailing edge of Ø1 of the last cycle of an instruction. HALT must not go low any time later than the minimum amount specified in the 6800 specification sheet. For instance, the fetch of the instruction by the MPU is the first cycle of any instruction. If HALT had not been low at least halfway into the clock cycle of the first part of that instruction, but had gone low during Ø2 of that cycle, the MPU would have halted after completion of the next instruction.

Sometimes it is advantageous to step through programs instruction by instruction to debug programs. In order to set up your personal computing system to operate on a step-by-step basis, HALT must be brought high for one MPU cycle and then returned low during the next cycle so that even during processing a single byte instruction, the microprocessor will take only one step at a time. In order to perform single instruction execution for debugging systems, a small amount of external circuitry is needed.

The TSC (three-state control) line can only be stopped for a maximum of four Ø1 clock cycles without destroying data within the MPU because the 6800 is a dynamic device in which some of the logical 1 states are stored in capacitors that must be refreshed or recharged in order to maintain the data within. When the TSC line is a logic 1, the address bus and the R/W line are placed in a high impedance state. VMA and BA are forced low whenever TSC is a 1 to prevent false reads or writes on any devices enabled by VMA. While TSC is held high the Ø1 and Ø2 clocks must be held high and low respectively, in order to delay program execution. TSC can then be used in short direct memory access application. This application is known as "cycle stealing." During the time when the microprocessor is stopped by the TSC line, some peripheral device connected on the address and bus line can actually perform operations in memory just like the microprocessor. In effect the peripheral is "stealing" a few cycles of the microprocessor's operation to perform its function. Keep in mind that this DMA application can be no longer than three Ø1 clock pulses in length. Note: if TSC is in the high state, bus available will be low.

The DBE or data bus enable is a three-state control signal for the MPU data bus. This enables bus drivers, and when in the high state, it's TTL compatible. However, in normal operation, it will be driven by the Ø2 clock. During MPU read cycle the data bus drivers will be disabled internally. When it is desired that another device control the data bus for DMA, DBE should be held low by the controlling device.

SECTION IIA.
6802 MICRO-
PROCESSOR

The 6802 is an 8-bit microprocessor that contains all the registers and accumulators of the MC6800 plus an internal clock oscillator and driver on the same chip. In addition it has 128 bytes of RAM on board located at Hex addresses 0000 to 007F. The first thirty-two bytes of this RAM (to 001F) may be backed up in a low power battery storage mode allowing you to retain this portion of memory during a power-down situation. This is especially helpful in situations where information that was on the stack when power went out must be retained in order to keep the program running properly when power is restored. The 6802 is completely software compatible with the 6800 as well as with the entire 6800 family of parts. Figure 5–4 shows the pin assignment connection for the

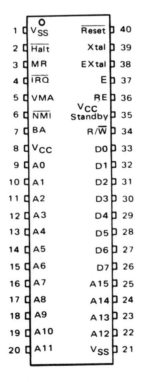

FIGURE 5–4. The 6802 microprocessor, IC pin assignment. (Courtesy of Motorola, Inc., Semiconductor Group)

6802, and we shall only go over the differences between the 6800 and the 6802. The expanded block diagram is shown in Figure 5–5. Several of the signals that were available at pins on the 6800 are no longer available on the 6802 because they are not needed. Some signal and timing lines have been added. For instance, TSC, DBE, Ø1 and Ø2 inputs, and two unused pins have been eliminated. The following signals and timing lines have been added: RAM enable, RE; crystal connections, EX(TAL) and

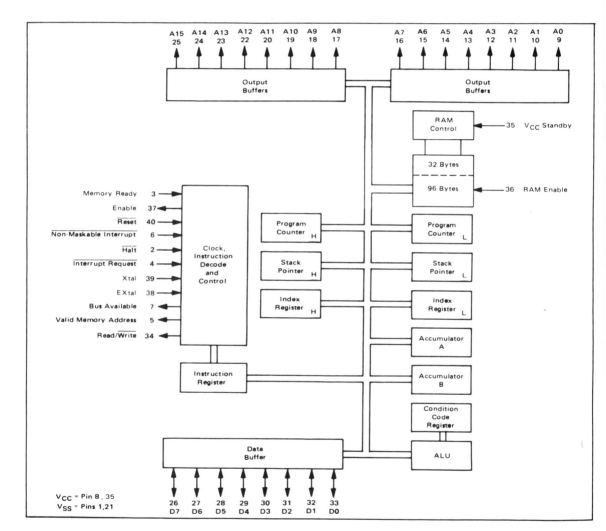

FIGURE 5–5.   Expanded block diagram of the 6802 microprocessor IC. This figure shows the similarity between the 6800 and the 6802 IC's. The only differences (other than pinout) are the on-board clock and the RAM and its respective circuitry. (Courtesy of Motorola, Inc., Semiconductor Group)

X(TAL); memory ready, MR; VCC standby enable; Ø2 output is at E. All other signals are self-explanatory and operate the same way they did in the 6800. The RAM enable signal (RE) is a TTL compatible RAM enable input to control whether or not you use the ON chip RAM of the 6802. When this is a logic 1 the ON chip memory is enabled. In the low state the RAM is disabled and you may use external RAM memory.

Since the 6802 has an internal oscillator that may be crystal controlled, the connections for series resonant fundamental crystal EX and X are provided. A divide-by-four circuit has been added to the 6802 so you can use a cheaper four-megahertz crystal instead of the more expensive 1 MHz. Basic system timing is still operating at 1 MHz just like the 6800. The EX line may be driven externally by a TTL input signal for applications where a separate clock is required. If operating in that mode, pin 38 is just left open.

On the occasion when slower memory might be used or when it would be convenient to stretch out the operating time of the Ø2 clock signal in the 6800 system, the MR memory ready signal is a TTL compatible input control signal allowing this sort of operation. When MR is low, E may be stretched into integral multiples of half-periods. The enable pin E supplies the clock for the MPU and the rest of its system. This is a single phase TTL compatible clock that may be conditioned by the memory ready signal. This is equivalent to Ø2 on the 6800.

Finally the VCC standby pin supplies the DC voltage to the first thirty-two bytes of RAM as well as the RAM enable control logic. Maximum current drain here is eight milliamps at 5.25 volts. Five nicad batteries connected through a diode would supply sufficient voltage to operate the unit in the VCC standby mode for many hours. The basic thirty-two registers in which data is to be stored can be used to retain stack data or they can be used for any other data that one does not wish to lose should power fail.

When Motorola introduced the 6802 it also introduced another member of the M6800 family, the MC6846 ROM, I/O, timer. This device allows a cost-effective microcomputer to be fabricated by merely using the 6802 and the MC6846 which contains 2K bytes of ROM, ten I/O lines, and three timer lines. The ROM in this IC is mask-programmable and up to this point no one has made available a premasked monitor comparable to MIKBUG for the 6802/6846 combination, but the 6846 is a natural choice to make a very low cost two-chip microprocessor for high volume manufacture.

This concludes the basic discussion of the 6800 processor chip. We will now look at each one of the other members of the 6800 processor family to be covered in sufficient detail for you to get an idea of how a

6800 processor system using certain of the family of 6800 processor chips would work. We have also chosen to show some other support chips which are necessary in the operation of our personal computer. Further, to allow you to expand properly the personal computer system that we are including in this book, we are providing data on some chips which will be used in the expansion but which are not used in the personal computer system given in this book.

SECTION III.
MCM6810 A
RAM

The 6810 RAM is a static memory. That means each logic 1 data is stored in an individual flip-flop within the RAM. It is organized in an 8-bit/byte fashion and has been designed to interface directly to the MC6800 microprocessor. (Refer to the MCM6810 spec sheet in Appendix D.) The RAM has six chip select inputs—four are active low, two are active high. These chip selects interface directly to the address bus. Since all the members of the family operate with the same drive capability, the data addressing control lines can be interconnected without using any external buffers. Memory timing specifications have been set to permit simple operation at full speed with the MC6800 microprocessor. Address lines A0 through A6 are used to decode the addresses within the RAM chip. Further addresses can be decoded by judiciously using the CS1 through five chip select signals. Note that VMA is used on the CS3 line to enable the RAM only during a valid memory address. Data is transferred into and out of the RAM by bidirectional data lines D0 through D7. Read or write operations are controlled by the R/W signal. In actual operation the 6810 must have its four-chip select lines at the logic 0 state in order to function. To illustrate the operation, we will assume chip selects 1, 2, 4, and 5 are all grounded. Note that chip select 3 and chip select 0 are active highs. Also note that since we are only decoding six of the fifteen available bits on the address line, we will ignore the upper nine available address lines. The maximum address we will be able to decode is the group of bits A0 through A3 (four bits represented by hexidecimal F) and the bits A4 through A6 (represented by hexidecimal 7).

The easiest way to understand the hexidecimal conversion here is to realize that the four bits A0 through A3 are the least significant bits with which we are working. Bits A4, 5, and 6 are the most significant bits and if we were to turn the RAM array so the *data* bits would be perpendicular to the writing on this page, we would then write the binary number that would influence the RAM as 0 (actually a "don't care" state, or a state that is connected to, say, chip select 1, 2, 4, and 5). As the first bit on the address line that we are concerned with, bits A6, 5, and 4 will all be one, one, one. These first four bits are binary 0111 and represent a hexidecimal 7. The last four bits, A3 through A0, are binary 1111 represented by hexidecimal F. (The binary 1, binary 2, binary 4, and binary 8 bits are present, indicating the decimal equivalent value of the number is 8 + 4 + 2 + 1 or 15. (Hexidecimal equivalent to 15 is F.)

The chip select 0 signal will be driven by 02 clock so that operations occurring within the RAM array will be synchronized with the operations occurring in the MPU. The R/W signal will again be used to indicate whether data is to be written into the RAM array or read out.

When R/W equals a one, a read from RAM array is being called for by the MPU. As soon as the memory address lines stop bouncing around, the MPU will produce a VMA signal. This lets the RAM know that the address located on A0 through A6 and any of the chip select lines is valid. During the next 02 clock cycle on the chip select 0 line to the RAM array, the data bits will represent the data that is present at the address pointed to by the A0 through A6 lines. For instance, if we had previously stored a C5 at address 5F in the RAM array, as soon as the processor addressed location 5F, the next occurrence of 02 clock would cause the data lines D0 through D7 to output a 1100 (C) on bits D7 through D4, and would cause bits D3 to D0 to be a 0101 (5). The MPU could then process this data accordingly.

The access time of any memory used with any MPU is a critical factor. As mentioned before the 6810 has its access time adjusted such that it will interface easily with the 6800 MPU. There are two versions of the MC6810 X, a 350-nanosecond version and a 450 version. With a one-microsecond clock powering the MPU, the memory access time would have to be within half a clock cycle or 500 nanoseconds. The 450-nanosecond 6810 device falls well within this category. Any memory device used with the 6800 microprocessor running at 1 MHz would have to be able to settle into valid data present on the data bus within 500 ns.

SECTION IV.
MCM6830 ROM

The 6830 ROM is a static read only memory member of the "family." All output drivers and timing are compatible with the M6800. This ROM is organized in an 8-bit/byte fashion similar to the 6810 RAM. It has ten address lines and four chip selects. The ROM itself is mask programmable which means you supply a logic table or program listing to the manufacturer, and he then sets up the read only memory to operate according to your specifications. Three of the four chip selects on the 6830 are used to provide address decoding in this system; they are also mask programmable for a logic 1 or logic 0 input. The ROM bus interface is identical to that of the RAM. The R/W input is not necessary on this chip and the VMA signal may or may not be used on one of the chip select lines depending on the application. Obviously, a personal computer system that has a customized program to be stored in a read only memory will not be able to afford to do the volume necessary to justify a mask-programmed ROM. Later we describe an EPROM (erasable programmable read only memory) which can be programmed by the user. The well-known MIKBUG ROM is available from Motorola as part number MCM6830L7, and is widely used in personal systems. The ROM contains a program prepared by Mike Wiles of Motorola which allows the 6800 microprocessor to be configured into a system that can communicate with serial-added devices (such as a teletype) and that allows commands from the teletype to let the user inspect and load data into whatever memory location he uses; or it lets the user choose to punch paper or cassette tapes and to load paper or cassette tapes into the 6800 personal computing system. Since the MIKBUG ROM is used in the Southwest Technical Products personal microcomputer system, its input/output routines are sometimes needed to make available software functions perform. Other computers not using MIKBUG are not necessarily tied to the functions of the MIKBUG debug monitor, but they often design their software so that MIKBUG memory addresses are compatible. By at least taking care of address compatibility you would be able to run such things as Southwest Tech 8K BASIC on your homemade personal computer system, like the one described in this book. Part of Engineering Note 100 from Motorola is included as part of this book to explain the MIKBUG software.

**SECTION V.
MC6820
PERIPHERAL
INTERFACE
ADAPTOR (PIA)**

The PIA provides a universal parallel interface from the outside world to the computer system using 6800 family parts. The PIA makes available two 8-bit bidirectional data buses and four control lines. No external logic is required for interfacing to most peripheral devices. Functionally, the PIA is programmed by the microprocessor via software during system initialization. Each one of the peripheral data lines can be programmed to act as an input or output. Each of the four control/interrupt lines may be programmed for one of several control modes. Thus the interface provides a high degree of flexibility in parallel interface situations.

PIA's may be used to drive such things as parallel printers in handshaking modes. Handshaking modes are modes where the processor places data on the parallel data line, then, by means of a separate signal, tells the printer that there is valid data on the line. The printer then "shakes hands" with the PIA indicating that it has taken data, has finished printing the data, and is ready for new data. These handshaking peripheral interfaces are common in computerized equipment. The PIA system interface lines are made up of data bus lines D0 through D7, R/

W, enable E, register selects RS0 and RS1, reset, chip selects CS0, 1 and 2, and the interrupt request lines IRQA and B.

The reset line initializes a PIA to a sort of cold start position where it is ready to receive its programming from the MPU. Register select lines RS0 and RS1 serve the same purpose in the PIA as address lines do in memory. Indeed the PIA looks like memory to the microprocessor.

There are six locations within the PIA that are accessible to the microprocessor data bus. There are two peripheral registers, two data direction registers, and two control registers. Selection of these locations is controlled by the RS0 and RS1 inputs together with CRA2/CRB2 in the control register which is internal to the PIA. After reset initialization of the PIA the control register may be addressed. When RS1 is a 0 and RS0 is a 1, the computer is talking to control register A. When RS1 is a 1 and RS0 is a 1 the computer can talk to control register B. The chip selects in the PIA are merely used to distinguish one device from another as they were in the RAM and ROM parts already described.

The PIA is one of the most useful devices in the M6800 family and is often used by other families, such as the 650X processor group, to provide parallel outputs from the computer to outside world peripherals. While operation of the PIA itself is straightforward, it is sometimes a little tricky for people to understand. An understanding of the operation of the PIA is important because it is the basis of interface to such things as a simple dot matrix line printer or, perhaps, a floppy disc system that uses a parallel port and handshaking. Figure 5–6 is a detailed drawing of the internal structure of the PIA.

To make the PIA as simple as possible to understand, we will begin by explaining the different sections and data lines out of the PIA, as by now the data lines into the PIA from the MPU should be self-explanatory. We will then concentrate on one side or the other of the PIA to describe the operation and how it is programmed. This should make the operation fairly clear and easy to understand. Also, since the operation of one side can be applied to the other side of the PIA, it will be simple to implement the PIA in a situation where both 8-bit data ports are used.

Section A peripheral data (PA0 to PA7) provides data lines that can be programmed to act as inputs or outputs. This is accomplished by setting a 1 in the corresponding data direction register bit for those lines which are to be outputs. A logic 0 in this bit of the data direction register causes the corresponding peripheral data line to act as an input. During an MPU "read peripheral data" operation, the data on the peripheral lines programmed as inputs appears directly on the MPU data bus. During an MPU "write peripheral data" mode, identical data to that on the data bus will appear at the peripheral interface bus lines programmed to act

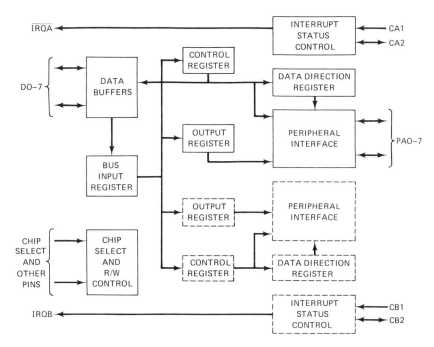

FIGURE 5-6.   Detailed internal view of the PIA. The dotted lines indicate the "B" side of the PIA and are not covered in the detailed operating description in the text.

as outputs. Logical 1's written into the register will cause a high on the data line while 0's result in a low state. In other words, the PIA is noninverting. Data in Output Register A may be read by an MPU "read peripheral data A" operation when the corresponding lines are programmed as outputs. Output register A acts as an extension of the computer's memory. When data is written into the output register, that same data will be read out of the output register unless the peripheral interface is programmed to act as an input, at which time the contents of output register A depends on the parallel data in on lines PA0 through PA7. If the voltage on peripheral data lines PA0 through PA7 is greater than two volts it will be read as a logic 1. Voltages lower than .8 volt produce a logic 0. Voltage levels in between these levels are not considered proper and may cause false reading. Data transferred into the MPU on a read operation may differ from that contained in the respective bit of output register A, depending on how it is programmed.

Section B peripheral data PB0 through PB7, on the other hand, while still being programmed similar to PA0 through PA7, has output buffers which differ from those driving line PA0 through PA7. The section B peripheral drivers have tristate capability allowing them to enter a high impedance state when a peripheral data line is used as an input. In addition, data on the B side will be read properly from lines programmed as outputs even if the voltages are below two volts for a logic 1. Outputs on the B side are TTL compatible and may be used as a source of up to 1 milliamp at 1.5 volts to directly drive the base of a transistor switch.

Interrupt input lines are CA1 and CB1 while peripheral control lines are CA2 and CB2. CA1 and CB1 are input only lines that set the interrupt flags of the control registers via the MPU, IRQ, or NMI lines. The active transition of these signals is programmed by the two control registers. The CA2 and CB2 lines, however, can be used as either inputs or outputs. The CA2 and CB2 lines are both TTL compatible. The CB2 line is high impedance input and provides a high current source output of 1 milliamp at 1.5 volts.

This is a detailed description of only the A side of the PIA. Keep in mind that the B side operationally is the same although it has different output drive levels and input drive requirements. A low reset line has the effect of zeroing all the registers in the PIA, setting the PA0 through PA7 and CA2 as inputs, and disabling all interrupts. The PIA must be configured by the user's software program immediately following reset or immediately before PIA use if not used immediately after reset. Otherwise all PIA registers are zero and all interface lines are inputs. When the two register select lines are 0 and the control register bit is a 0, as will be shown in more detail later, it is the data direction register that is enabled.

The data direction register allows the MPU to control the direction of data through each corresponding data line. A data direction register bit set at 0 configures the data line as an input, while a 1 results in an output. The peripheral control lines CA1 and 2 are controlled by the control register.

The control register is addressed by having RS1 at a 0 and RS0 at a 1. This means the data direction register and the control register have their own separate addresses. If there were no other addresses in the system, an address of 0000 would address the data direction register, while an address of 0001 would address the control register. The control register has another use, too. It allows the MPU to enable the interrupt lines and to monitor the status of the interrupt flags. If the IRQ output on the PIA is not hooked directly to the IRQ on the MPU, an interrupt on the CA1 line will still register within the PIA but will not cause an interrupt in the MPU. So the processor could come over and occasionally look at the control register by addressing it and reading the data in it to determine whether or not an input had come in on the CA1 line in the

PIA. If the IRQ line is hooked up, not only would an input on CA1 cause the control register to indicate that an interrupt had occurred, but the IRQ output from the PIA would also initiate an interrupt routine in the MPU. This way the MPU can be set up to determine which of many peripherals that may be connected to it generated a given interrupt.

In other words, if you had five parallel data terminals connected by means of PIA's and each one was to be processed on a time-sharing basis, the MPU could be doing whatever processes it normally does in the course of carrying out its program. When one of the buttons on the keyboard on one of the terminals was depressed, it would generate the IRQ through the PIA. This IRQ would send the MPU into an IRQ service routine. That routine could consist merely of scanning the various PIA's to determine which one generated the interrupt. Information can be stored as to which terminal generated the interrupt, and the MPU could return from the interrupt routine to the main routine. In the course of running its main routine, the MPU could service the proper peripheral.

The control word format shown in Figure 5-7 is one that allows the control register to program the CA1 and CA2 line. The first six bits are those of main concern. The last two bits are merely to show whether or not an interrupt came in on CA1 or CA2 (depending on how the control register had programmed the PIA). Bit number 0 on the logic 0 disables the MPU interrupt request. As can be seen in the figure, the first two bits of the control word control whether or not CA1 performs an interrupt operation and determine whether or not a CA1 input is an active high or active low. Bit number 2 in each control register allows selection of either the peripheral interface register or the data direction register, when the proper register select signals are applied to RS0 and RS1. Because of this, the control register must be addressed first whenever you are initializing your PIA or setting it up for proper operation. Bits 3, 4, and 5 of the control register determine control of CA2 as interrupt input, again covering whether interrupt CA2 is to be high or low. They also control whether or not CA2 will be used as an output, determining whether or not the active output is to be high or low.

Assume peripheral lines PA0 through PA7 are going to read from our external peripheral so it must be established as an input. Let CA1 provide the interrupt input so it must be conditioned to recognize incoming positive transitions. Now CA2 will be used to signal that data has been read. For handshaking purposes CA2 will be established as an output. The following sequence can be used. Select output register A; set the mode control for A side by using a 2F.

The constant 2F in binary is equal to a 00101111 loaded into the control register. It has the following effect: Bit 0 equals 1 enables a CA1 interrupt; Bit 1 equals 1 selects positive transition for interrupt recognition; Bit 2 equals 1 selects output register A (the initial zeros caused by

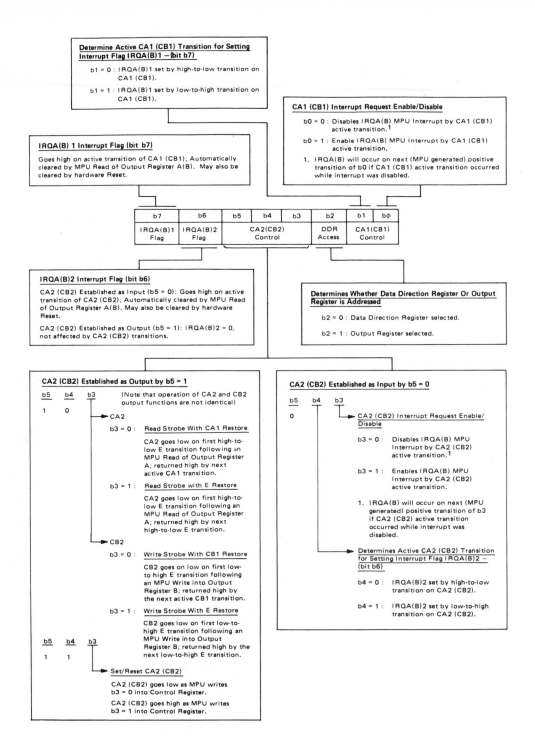

FIGURE 5–7. PIA control word functional breakout. (Courtesy of Motorola, Inc., Semiconductor Group)

the hardware system reset establishes PA0 through PA7 as inputs); Bit 3 equals 1, B4 equals 0 selects read strobe, with an E restore; B5 equals 1 establishes CA2 as an output; B6 and B7 are "don't cares" since the MPU can't write into those two positions. If there was no assurance that the PIA internal registers were initially zero, and system reset had occurred, you would have to use the following sequence prior to loading the 2F into the control register: You would have to load logic 0's into control register A, then load logic 0's again at address 00 which would be establishing PA0 through PA7 as inputs via the data direction register. Then the 2F would be loaded into the control register or memory location 01 to control the A side.

To establish the A side for transmitting data, the A side PA0 through PA7 would have to be established as outputs. We could use CA2 again as an output for signalling that there is data ready and use CA1 to accept a negative transition acknowledgment signal from the peripheral. Again recreating a handshaking type mode of operation, we could load an instruction 24 into the control register. This would have the following effect: B0 equals 0 disables IRQ A interrupt by CA1 transition (it is assumed that the MPU will read flag bit B7 to check for acknowledgment rather than allowing an interrupt); B1 equals 0 selects recognition of negative transition on CA1 for setting flag bit 7; B2 equals 1 selects output register A; B3 equals 0, B4 equals 1 selects write strobe with CA1 restore; B5 equals 1 establishes CA2 as an output; and again B6 and B7 are "don't cares."

If there is no assurance this time that the PIA internal register bit positions are zeroed by a system reset, the following sequence can be used. Load a 00 into control register B. Now load an FF into position 00 or select the PA0 through PA7 lines as outputs. Insert a 24 into control register A to select output register A and set mode control for the side as was already covered. Notice in both cases that if the initialization sequence is started from a known reset condition, only half as many instructions are required.

**SECTION VI.
MC6850
ASYNCHRONOUS
COMMUNICA-
TIONS
INTERFACE
ADAPTOR (ACIA)**

The parallel data of the bus system is transmitted serially and receives full duplex (meaning it can transmit and receive simultaneously) by the ACIA (see Figure 5–8) with proper formatting and error checking. Like the PIA, the ACIA is programmed via the data bus during system initialization. A programmable control register provides variable word lengths, clock division ratios, transmit control, receive control, and interrupt control. Three control lines are also provided for controlling external peripherals, MODEMs, or whatever. A status register is available to the MPU and is updated constantly with current status of the

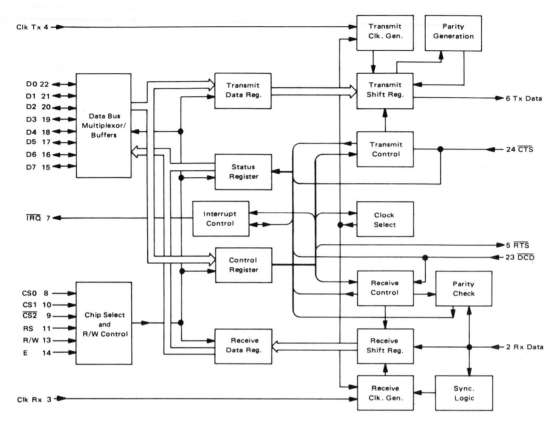

FIGURE 5-8. ACIA synchronous communications adapter, detailed block diagram. (Courtesy of Motorola, Inc., Semiconductor Group)

transmitter and receiver. At the bus interface, the ACIA, like one half of the PIA, appears as two addressable memory locations. Inside the ACIA there are four registers—two read only and two write only. The read only registers are status and receive data; the write only registers are control and transmit data. The two serial input and output lines have independent clocks so that you could actually transmit at one rate and receive at another.

After the MPU performs a status read operation to find out whether or not the transmit data register is empty, characters may be written into the transmit data register. The complete character is transferred to a shift register where it is serialized and transmitted from the transmit data output line. It is preceded by a start bit and followed by one or two stop bits. Internal odd or even parity can be optionally added to the character and will occur between the last data bit and the first stop bit. After the first character is written in the data register, the status register can be read again to check for a transmit data register empty condition. If the register is empty, another character can be loaded for transmission even though the first character is in the process of being transmitted. This is because the ACIA uses double buffering. If two characters are in the ACIA at the same time, the second character will automatically be transferred into the shift register when the first character transmission is completed. This is the sequence that will be used until all desired characters have been transmitted.

In receiving, the status register is read to determine if a character has been received. If the receiver data register is full, the character is then placed on the 8-bit ACIA bus. Whenever a read command is received from the MPU, the receiver strips the parity bit automatically so data alone is transferred to the MPU. The receiver is double buffered so a character can be read from the data register as another character is being received into the shift register. A divide-by-one clock ratio is provided for externally synchronized clock while divide-by-16 and -64 ratios are provided for internal synchronization. Faster clock ratios allow the ACIA to sample smaller intervals of the received data to insure precisely when a transition from one to zero comes and to make for more error-free operation. The receiver section of the ACIA causes an interrupt when the receiver interrupt enable is set and the receive data register is full. To clear the interrupt, you merely read data or reset the ACIA.

The ACIA control register is an 8-bit write-only buffer that controls a function of the reciever/transmitter interrupt enables and the request to send control output. Bit 0 and 1 are used in combination to control the divide ratio of transmit and receive sections of the ACIA. These bits can also provide a Master Reset for the ACIA which clears the status register and initializes both the receiver and transmitter, but it does not affect the other control register bits. Clock divide ratios are: divided by 1 and divided by 16 and subdivided by 64. Bits 2, 3, and 4 are used to select word length, parity, and number of stop bits. Bits 5 and 6 provide control of the interrupt from the transmit data register empty condition, or the request to sent output, and the transmission of a break level. The receive interrupt enable is controlled by bit number 7.

The MPU can read the status register in the ACIA at any time. It's a read only register and information stored indicates the status of the transmit data register, the receive data register, error logic, and the peripheral or modem inputs to the ACIA. Bit 0 is the receive data register full bit indicating that receive data has been transferred to the receive data register. This indicates whether or not a complete data word has been transmitted. The data carrier detect bit, 2, will be high when the

BCD input to the ACIA goes high to indicate in case of a MODEM that no carrier is present. Bit 3 is a clear-to-send bit indicating the state of the clear-to-send input to the ACIA. Bit 4 is a framing error indicating that the received character is improperly framed by a start and stop bit. This is detected by the absence of the first stop bit. It indicates a synchronization error caused by faulty transmission or a break condition. The framing error flag is set or reset during the receive data transfer time so it is present throughout the time the associated character is available. Bit 5 is a receive overrun error flag indicating that one or more characters in the data stream were lost. In other words characters were received but not read from the receive data register before more characters came in. Bit 6 is the parity error flag indicating that the number of ones in the character does not agree with the preselected odd or even parity. Odd parity is said to occur when the total number of ones is odd; even parity, when the total number of ones is even. Finally, bit 7 of the status register in the ACIA is the interrupt request bit indicating the state of the IRQ output. Any interrupt condition with its applicable enable will be indicated in this status bit. This bit is cleared by a read operation to the receive data register or write operation to the transmit data register.

SECTION VII. 6843 FLOPPY DISC CONTROLLER (FDC) AND 6845 CRT CONTROLLER (CRTC)

Although there are other members of the 6800 family, such as MODEM chips, etc., we have chosen to cover two chips which may be of interest to the reader who is considering expanding the personal computer system found in this book for his own use. These are the MC6843, FDC, floppy disc controller, and the MC6845 CRTC, CRT controller.

The floppy disc controller performs a complex MPU/floppy interface function and was designed to eliminate much software normally involved in integrating floppy disc functions. The controller has a macro command set. These macro commands are treated like microprocessor commands but actually are used to direct the internal microcontrol unit inside the FDC to allow control of the floppy disc. The FDC contains twelve directly accessible internal registers together with a microcontroller ROM network. There are parallel-to-serial and serial-to-parallel conversion registers which are not accessible to the programmer, as well as things such as data clock pattern generation and detection. The data in/out registers in CRC control communicate between the disc drive and MPU. Disc operation is monitored by the MPU with three status registers inside the FDC. There are also separate registers provided for track and sector address information. A set-up register allows generation of a programmable delay corresponding to the seek time of the particular drive in use. The other section provides a programmable settling time delay. Thus the FDC can interface a wide range of different drives with an absolute minimum of external hardware. The format is compatible with the IBM3740 or is user programmable. It operates both cycle stealing and direct memory access, data transfer mode. One bit in the command register is reserved to select either program control I/O or direct memory access. When the macro command is being executed inside the floppy disc controller, an interrupt at macro end allows the FDC to be processing at the same time the MPU is processing. This is called "parallel processing." The 6843 requires a minimum of external hardware and is the easiest way to hook up a 6800 microprocessor to a floppy disc.

The macro command set that the 6843 is capable of performing is STZ seek track 0, SEK seek, SSW single sector write, SWD single sector write with delated address mark, SSR single sector read, RCR read the CRC, MSW multiple sector write, MSR multiple sector read, FFW free format write, FFR free format read. Figure 5-9 shows the various input and output lines along with a programming model of the registers that are available.

The MC6845 CRT controller provides a programmable interface between the microprocessor and raster scan CRT. It contains eighteen registers and allows programmable screen and character formats with two different types of scanning, limited or full graphics display, hardware scrolling, and hardware paging. It also has fourteen address lines to allow it to access up to 16K of refresh memory and provide line bufferless refreshing. A multiplexer is used to switch the memory

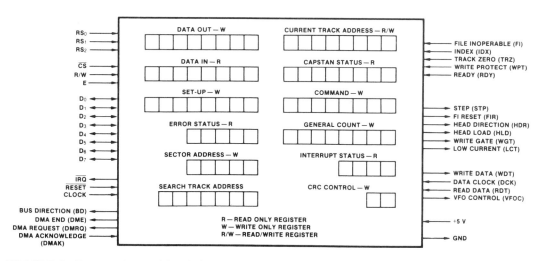

FIGURE 5-9. Programming model and signal lines for the 6843 floppy disc controller IC. (Courtesy of Fairchild Camera and Instrument Corporation)

address lines from the CRTC to the MPU. This means the memory that the CRTC is using to create a display is accessible as memory to the MPU. As data is written into the registers, characters appear on the screen almost instantly. A light pen strobe is available too, so the CRT display can be used with a light pen. Complete cursor control is possible with control of the rate the cursor blinks, making the cursor solid or no cursor at all under software control. The height as well as the position of the cursor within the character block can also be programmed. Complete details are given in the spec sheet located in Appendix D.

On the horizontal axis you can have character displays and formats in excess of 132 characters per line. Sync width, sync position, how much of the horizontal raster is used to display, etc., are all under software command as well as are vertical parameters. The vertical sync pulse width is not programmable; it is fixed at sixteen rasters. Interfacing the CRTC to the MPU is done over data bus lines, a read/write line, chip select line, enable line, and a register select line. An address register routes the signals through to the desired register within the CRTC, leaving the 6845 CRTC to be programmed during initialization just like the PIA and ACIA.

SECTION VIII.
1702 EPROM

Now we leave the family of 6800 microprocessor parts and enter into the world of nonfamily support chips. The 1702 EPROM was selected because of its availability to the experimenter on the surplus market. It is inexpensive, and once understood it allows the reader to understand the other various types of EPROM's that are available on the market. The 1702 is organized 256 words by 8 bits. It is electrically programmable and it is erasable through the application of ultraviolet light through a quartz window which is built right into the integrated circuit. After erasure through exposure to ultraviolet light, a new pattern can be written into the device. It is packaged in a twenty-four pin dual in line package. The circuitry of the 1702 is entirely static; no clocks are required. The inputs and outputs are TTL-compatible. The appropriate lines have tristate outputs so memory expansion is quite simple. There is a chip select input lead. Programming the PROM itself is rather a complicated ordeal—unless you have a PROM programmer, it is not the kind of thing you would want to do. Figure 5–10 shows both a block diagram and a connection diagram of the 1702 PROM. After the chip has been programmed and you are using it in the read mode, the program pin (pin 13) is connected to +5 volts. One less desirable feature of the 1702 is that it requires a -9 volt power supply. A logic 0 or ground on pin 14 is what does the enabling. In operation, the microprocessor would select an address which would be decoded by the A0 through A7 bits in

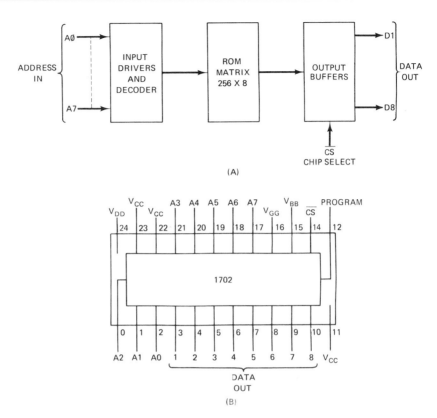

FIGURE 5–10. 1702 erasable programmable read-only memory. Functional diagram is shown at (A) with the pinouts for the IC shown at (B).

the 1702. The chip select would be driven by the combination of two signals R/W and VMA. As soon as a valid memory address is available on A0 through A7, confirmed by the MPU, and read, command is given by the MPU and the chip select goes low. This enables the tristate drivers on the data line, and whatever data is located in the ROM matrix is output on the data lines to the MPU.

**SECTION IX.
74154 OF 16
DECODER**

Figure 5–11 shows a simple decoder circuit that is taking any of four different inputs and creating up to sixteen different outputs. The decoding scheme is very simple and in effect gives us one of sixteen outputs for the four inputs on the A, B, C, and D lines. If lines A, B, C, and D are all 0's, the output of the 74154 will be a low or a 0 on pin 1. If pin A is a 1, pins B, C, and D are 0's; we will move our logic 0 from pin 1 to pin 2.

logic

FUNCTION TABLE

G1	G2	D	C	B	A	0	1	2	3	4	5	6	7	8	9	10	11	12	13	14	15
	INPUTS											OUTPUTS									
L	L	L	L	L	L	L	H	H	H	H	H	H	H	H	H	H	H	H	H	H	H
L	L	L	L	L	H	H	L	H	H	H	H	H	H	H	H	H	H	H	H	H	H
L	L	L	L	H	L	H	H	L	H	H	H	H	H	H	H	H	H	H	H	H	H
L	L	L	L	H	H	H	H	H	L	H	H	H	H	H	H	H	H	H	H	H	H
L	L	L	H	L	L	H	H	H	H	L	H	H	H	H	H	H	H	H	H	H	H
L	L	L	H	L	H	H	H	H	H	H	L	H	H	H	H	H	H	H	H	H	H
L	L	L	H	H	L	H	H	H	H	H	H	L	H	H	H	H	H	H	H	H	H
L	L	L	H	H	H	H	H	H	H	H	H	H	L	H	H	H	H	H	H	H	H
L	L	H	L	L	L	H	H	H	H	H	H	H	H	L	H	H	H	H	H	H	H
L	L	H	L	L	H	H	H	H	H	H	H	H	H	H	L	H	H	H	H	H	H
L	L	H	L	H	L	H	H	H	H	H	H	H	H	H	H	L	H	H	H	H	H
L	L	H	L	H	H	H	H	H	H	H	H	H	H	H	H	H	L	H	H	H	H
L	L	H	H	L	L	H	H	H	H	H	H	H	H	H	H	H	H	L	H	H	H
L	L	H	H	L	H	H	H	H	H	H	H	H	H	H	H	H	H	H	L	H	H
L	L	H	H	H	L	H	H	H	H	H	H	H	H	H	H	H	H	H	H	L	H
L	L	H	H	H	H	H	H	H	H	H	H	H	H	H	H	H	H	H	H	H	·L
L	H	X	X	X	X	H	H	H	H	H	H	H	H	H	H	H	H	H	H	H	H
H	L	X	X	X	X	H	H	H	H	H	H	H	H	H	H	H	H	H	H	H	H
H	H	X	X	X	X	H	H	H	H	H	H	H	H	H	H	H	H	'H	H	H

H = high level, L = low level, X = irrelevant

functional block diagram and schematics of inputs and outputs

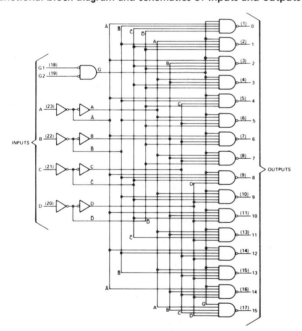

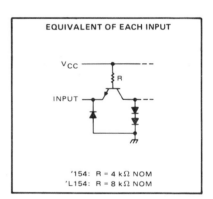

EQUIVALENT OF EACH INPUT

'154: R = 4 kΩ NOM
'L154: R = 8 kΩ NOM

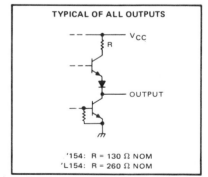

TYPICAL OF ALL OUTPUTS

'154: R = 130 Ω NOM
'L154: R = 260 Ω NOM

FIGURE 5–11. Block diagram, pinout, and truth table for the 74154 decoder that is used in the PC-68 personal computer system described in the text. (Courtesy of Texas Instruments, Inc.)

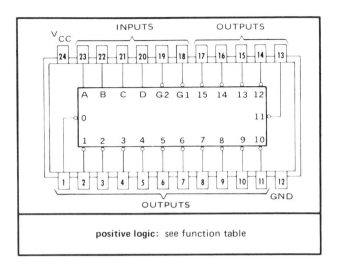

INPUTS   OUTPUTS

positive logic: see function table

FIGURE 5-11 (cont.)

When A, B, C, and D are all logic 1's, equivalent to hexidecimal F (decimal 15), pin 17 will be the output. All this assumes, of course, that G1 and G2 are logic 0 to enable the chip to operate. G1 and G2 come in very handy, for we can use these to bring in our VMA signal from the MPU and mix in Ø2 clock to make sure the system is synchronized. Thus in a situation where we may be reading or writing from memory, we will have to enable that memory with one of the sixteen outputs of 74154. All the necessary timing will have already been performed in the decoding process.

**SECTION X.
8833, 8835
QUAD THREE-
STATE
PARTY LINE
TRANSCEIVERS**

This is a very interesting chip set. The 8833 is a noninverting quad transceiver. The 8835 is its identical partner except that it inverts data on a bidirectional bus. Figure 5-12 shows the two. The drivers are the AND gate-shaped devices. All the receivers are the inverter-shaped devices. Each driver and receiver has its own enable/disable line. By connecting the disable lines together through an inverter we can control the transceiver via a three-state control line such as R/W. Since there are four transceivers per package, it takes two packages to handle all eight data lines associated with the 6800 microprocessor. A logic 1 on either the driver or receiver disable lines disables the appropriate driver or receiver set. The output driver is a high current device while the receiver is an extremely sensitive noise-immune device which allows many common TTL loads to be connected along the bidirectional bus. A

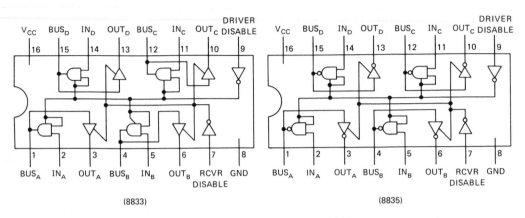

FIGURE 5–12.   Pinout and functional representation of the 8833 and 8835 three-state transceivers.

device like this is necessary when one starts driving nonfamily peripheral chips to create a microprocessor system using a device like the 6800 MPU.

SECTION XI. THE 8097, 8098 HEX THREE-STATE BUFFERS

Figure 5–13 shows the inverting and noninverting versions of high speed hex (meaning six units) buffers with three-state outputs. They are organized so they can be connected as a single 6-bit or a 2-bit/4-bit device. By choosing either the 97 or 98 version you get inverting or noninverting outputs. The output enable is high. The outputs are forced to high impedance "off" state no matter what the inputs to each individual buffer are. If the E enable signal lines go to logic 0, the inverter stages are enabled, and whatever data is present at the input of the inverter will appear either normally or inverted at the output

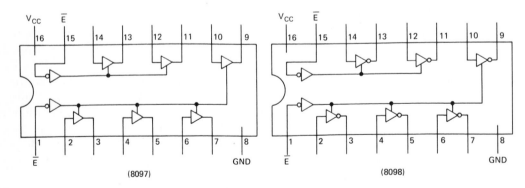

FIGURE 5–13.   Pinout and functional representation of the 8097 and the 8098 three-state bus drivers.

depending on which version you use. These devices are handy when expanding the address bus of the 6800 MPU in that they are high current devices which can drive multiple TTL loads.

SECTION XII. 2102 STATIC AND 4044 RAMS

If there is a standard in the personal computer memory marketplace it is the 2102 RAM which is a very versatile static RAM similar to the 6810 already discussed under the M6800 logic family of devices. The organization of a 2102 is 1,024 bits by 1. Eight of the units must be connected in parallel and decoded as one in order to get eight parallel data bits. Eight of the devices give you a 1,000-byte RAM storage which is adequate for many small programs in a personal computer system. By sequentially enabling groups of eight 2102 RAM's connected as described, you are able to build multiple thousand byte memory systems. A typical block memory system using 2102's is a 4K RAM board. This requires thirty-two packages.

The 2102 shown in Figure 5–14 is extremely popular because it's readily available and inexpensive. It is being displaced somewhat in home computer systems by such chips as the 4044 4K-by-1 static RAM chip. By using the 4K RAM's, one can build an 8K memory board using

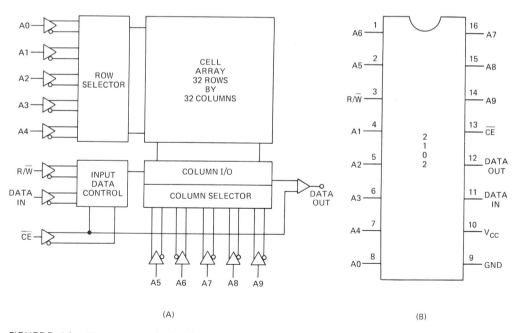

(A)

(B)

FIGURE 5–14.   The super-popular 2102 1K X 1-bit RAM. Shown in both functional and pinout form.

only sixteen chips. Figure 5–15 shows the hookup interconnections for the 4044. The 4044 is still moderately expensive, but in situations where space is at a premium and power requirements are to be minimized, the 4K-by-1 bit part is an excellent choice.

There are other memory systems available. There are dynamic RAM's in which memory storage takes place in a capacitor which must be refreshed and recharged as in the dynamic section of the 6800 microprocessor. The dynamic memory has some problems. It is not as easy to hook up as a static RAM because it takes special onboard chips to take care of refreshing the memory. There are also RAM's organized as 1K-by-4 which are four bits wide and 1K deep in storage (these are still 4K RAM's), and 16K dynamic RAM's are gaining popularity at this point. A complete 16,000-byte memory may be built using only eight chips.

All in all, the review of the 6800 family and support chips that we have gone over in this chapter should have been in sufficient detail to allow you to understand the construction and to begin programming here on the personal computer system which we will cover in the next chapter.

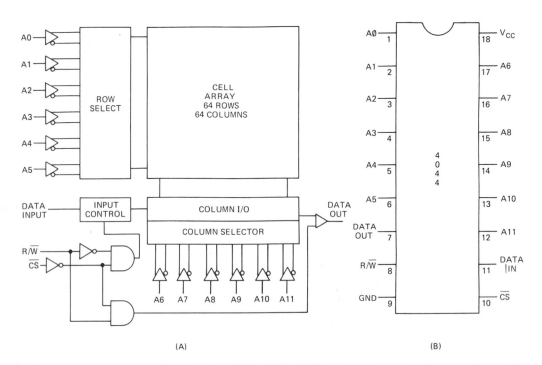

(A)   (B)

FIGURE 5–15. The simple-to-use-and-interface 4044 4K X 1 RAM uses the latest technology to produce a 4K static RAM. Note the similarity between this and the 2102 RAM.

A Personal Computer System You Can Construct

While experts in any field can be expected to disagree on varying points, one point that microprocessor experts all agree on is that the best training and experience in microprocessors comes from getting your "hands on" and trying out a system. Learning the interrelationship between the hardware and the software and mastering software design to the point where you know what you can demand from a given system can only be learned by using a micro to run your own software.

Software generation is the one largest cost in microcomputers, but it is the lowest cost in personal computers. If that sounds slightly contradictory, it is not. In the commercial application of a microprocessor some estimates say you will have to pay between $20 and $50 per byte of program in order to generate the software. In the personal computer system you are buying the hardware with the idea that you will generate the software as a hobby for the pleasure of making the machine work in your given application. Thus, in the personal computing system, the software you generate is free. Here is an example. The so-called "8K Basic" (meaning an 8,000- byte Basic Interpreter) for your personal computer may have cost $40,000 to generate in its first version. You will take advantage of the fact that the manufacturer expects to sell many, many copies of 8K Basic so he is willing to sell one to you at, for instance, $40.

Now you write a program in BASIC using the interpreter to run it (and write it, too). Say it's one you have designed to balance your checkbook. Unless you get the program listing from some book, you will generate the code. You might spend five nights in a row with a total of twenty hours in writing the program. If you were figuring your pay for the time spent, even at $5 per hour you have invested $100 worth of time in the project. You don't get a $100 payment, however; what you get is the satisfaction of knowing that you were able to produce a useful program for the personal computer. Since your time was free, you have actually generated the program for a much lower cost than a manufacturer could have done it.

To optimize your investment in personal computers you would do well to look carefully at the hardware investment you make. It is wise to bring the cost of hardware as closely in line with the cost of your software (free) as possible. In the beginning, you will be satisfied with simple software programs that merely perform some singular function, play a game, etc. But somewhere down the road you will want to build some software that performs more complex functions, multiple functions, or whatever. You will have to consider the expansion capabilities of your hardware with an eye to the future. You will also want to carefully optimize your investment so that expanding the system is possible within the limits of your pocketbook.

Sometime in the discussion of the personal computer system comes the build or buy point. This is where you must decide for yourself whether or not you wish to scratch build your system or build from a kit or plans (plan building is close to "scratch" building except that plans are supposedly proven to work) or whether you wish to buy the unit preassembled. There is a great deal to be said for all of those approaches. If you buy the system ready-made, you are ready to sit right down and get on with the writing of software to make the system perform. If you build from a kit, you will probably save money and learn something about the makeup of the personal computer system. Although most personal computer kits are not going to teach you much about the hardware per se, having put the kit together gives you the feeling that you are capable of at least jumping in and trying to service the computer when it goes down. Although you may not know a great deal about electronics, the scratch building approach has the advantage that you will learn a great deal about the local sources of certain electronic parts. Scratch building is the lowest cost approach of all, but you're on your own if the system doesn't work at power-up time and later when the unit needs service. Nevertheless, there is hardly a better way to get familiar with the internal parts of the personal computer.

From the standpoint of speed, the fastest way to get your system up is to buy one that is already running and tested by a reputable manufacturer or computer dealer. The next fastest method is the kit, where someone else has done all the parts shopping for you and has brought everything together in one place. The slowest method by far is scratch building, where it may take weeks to order and receive one part from one outfit located many miles away. But scratch building breeds familiarity with the internal circuits making up your personal computing system and further provides the self-confidence needed not only to work on, but also to expand your system. The scratch builder's perspective changes; he looks for analog to digital converter chips rather than for A-D converter boards for his system. You are able to put one of these chips into action usually long before some manufacturer actually uses one as an add-on board to its particular system. Keep in mind, however, unless you design your own system or are present for the design of the system you are going to use, you may know less about it than about a well-designed kit when you are finished. Then the only advantage to scratch building may be the cost.

Consider, too, the looks. If you plan on keeping your computer locked away in the basement, then you have no problem. But if your plans include writing special software that will allow your kids to use the computer to learn math or allow your wife to keep the menus, you had better consider the looks of the computer as a major factor— especially if you are trying to win others (laymen) over to personal computers. This is not to say, however, that a homemade system cannot look as nice as a kit or prebuilt unit, it is only to say that sometimes a scratch-built computer is nothing more than a printed circuit board full of parts. While this is generally the lowest cost approach to the personal computer, it leaves much to be desired in the field of man/machine esthetics.

With all these considerations, it is hard to make a recommendation; in fact we will leave it up to the manufacturers to sway you with the beautiful cabinets and the claims of performance while we give you an example of a personal computing system you can build that tries to fill all the above requirements. It is nice enough looking (at least in most eyes), cost is minimal for the initial system, expansion is possible, and finally, it is simple enough so that we shall go through the design step by step. We shall call the computer the "PC–68," for Personal Computer 6800.

The PC–68 computer provides a simple, low cost exposure to personal computers. As is, the unit is capable of running simple programs that allow you to learn the functions of, and demonstrate to others, the personal computer. Because of its simplicity, the PC–68 computer makes an excellent controller. Since you are in on the early design stage, you are better qualified to expand the system using either your own scratch-built boards, or by modifying readily available boards for various computer systems. You will be familiar with the basic signals and power requirements of your system, and you will know what must be done to expand the system to accept other boards. It is the PC-68 system that will be used in the remainder of this book to write the software that will be used to illustrate the art of programming. (Note: This does not preclude the use of the software on other 6800 systems or the possibility of rewriting for 6502, 8080, or Z-80.)

From this point on we are going to consider that the reader has made the decision to fabricate a PC-68 personal computer. Even if you haven't, read on anyway. The insight gained into the makeup and design of a personal computer system of any type is invaluable to you. In other words, whether you build this unit or not, this "guided tour" is likely to teach you more about microprocessors than you may already know. If you are already a microprocessor hardware expert, you may take exception to some of the design methods employed, but keep in mind this is being written with an eye to the "how it works" more than the "how to."

To begin the task of designing a personal computing system, we must begin at a top level. We must write the design specifications. The things we bring out in the "specs" will be our guidelines or road map. These are the goals which we hope to be able to reach by the time the design is finished. During the course of implementing the spec into our design, we may find that some of the things we want our system to do are impractical. For instance, we may write that we want the system to directly interface 20 MB (20 mega, or million, bytes). Well, if we then write that we want to use an 8-bit microcomputer chip in the personal computer, something is going to have to give. It could be that one of the points in the spec says that it will have to be low priced. This precludes use of some special computer chip that will directly address 20 M bytes and we either change our spec or wait until our knowledge of computer systems allows us to build a virtual memory system interface to the 8-bit microcomputer. Because it is still in a state of flux at this time, we call the first "brain dump" of proposed computer capabilities, the preliminary specifications.

Our design specification goals will be:

To provide a low cost system (probably 8-bit).

To use a common, easy-to-program chip.

To make a unit that can use available software (such as SWTPC 8K Basic).

To make it expandable with both scratch-built and available boards.

To make the unit small and attractive.

To make the initial unit powerful enough to program without expanding.

To keep it simple.

Now we merely refine the spec sheet and make sure everything we have written as a preliminary spec is an achievable goal. It is. We next move on to breaking down each goal for design into its component parts and providing a solution based on our knowledge.

It is at this point in the spec-writing process that we may have to do some research. Here we must find prices of each chip as part of the first design goal:

LOW COST

We must know if any one chip takes more support chips than another. Then we must compare the chip and support chips against what may appear to be a more expensive chip until we consider the system price. We can zero in on the lowest cost—6800, 6502, 8080, and Z–80—as well as other chips that were not covered in the first part of this book. Of course, assuming your only knowledge to this point is of the chips covered in the text, it would take additional research to look at the ones not covered. Within these limitations we can reduce support chips by picking a unit with internal clock. This limits us to consider the 6802, 8085, and 6502.

Since a further look shows that 6802 also has built-in 128- $\times$ -8-bit scratch pad memory (meaning we further reduce chip count), we shall lean toward 6802 in this category with 6502 and 8085 holding equal status in second place.

PROGRAMMA-BILITY

Here we are talking machine language level, and we are only working with the chips provided by our own specification to be those in the first step. Through research, we find that two of the three have "minicomputer-like" instruction sets, the 6502 and the 6802. So far so good.

AVAILABILITY OF SOFTWARE

How readily available is 6502 software, such as interpreters, compilers, etc.? Not nearly as available as many programs for the 6800. If we were to design our system so that it thinks it is running some popular system monitor, like the MIKBUG monitor, we also help insure software compatibility. Nearly all monitors for 6800 systems are at least MIKBUG compatible. This step narrows the choices to 6802.

ABILITY TO EXPAND

This step almost takes care of itself. There are many available boards for 8-bit microcomputers and they can at least be modified to operate with nearly any computer system. Scratch boards are no problem because you are customizing them for your system anyway. By the way this step further reinforces the decision to go with 6802 because it is very simple to interface, and it is possible to connect nearly any board for almost any bus to a 6802.

APPEARANCE   By doing a little scratching and using plastic sheets glued together we can come up with a pretty decent looking enclosure for the PC-68.

POWER   By using a minimum of chips in line with the first requirement (low cost), the 6802 gives us 128 bytes of scratch pad memory to work with. This means we have the capability within the small system of running some nifty software. We can also provide serial ports, etc., in order to have the system perform some rather sophisticated functions (for a little guy).

KEEP IT SIMPLE   Because of the structure of the 6802 and because of the possibility of using a minimum of hardware support chips, this requirement can easily be met.

With all these design parameters in mind, we can write the engineering spec for the system at this time. It will now go something like this: The system will use the 6802 8-bit microprocessor chip. System clock will run at 1 MHz and the unit will provide 128 bytes of RAM memory, expandable to several K bytes. The program memory shall use EPROM for maximum flexibility. The EPROM memory shall be designed for expandability. The PC-68 shall have a serial port under software control for the purpose of connecting a full alphanumeric terminal. Capabilities shall exist for expanding the unit for parallel output. (Here is where we use a PIA.) The entire design shall be done to provide maximum system efficiency with a minimum of overall cost in the basic unit. Now all good engineering specs end with the following: "This specification subject to change without notice."

So far, the design plan is beginning to unfold into a personal computer system that is being honed to a fine edge. We shall use the requirements listed in the engineering spec as we begin the generation of the block diagram and then as we refine the block diagram into a schematic diagram from which we build the unit.

Basically, the block diagram as shown in Figure 6-1 is generated by using the specifications to come up with the blocks. The serial data output requirement is filled by the serial I/O block in the diagram. The

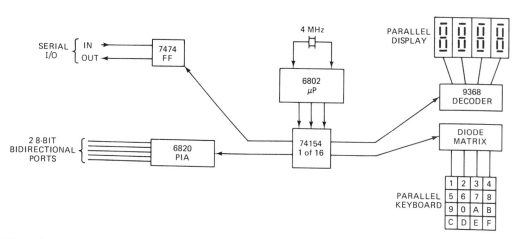

FIGURE 6-1. Block diagram of the PC-68 personal computer system described in the text. Cost of parts for the computer system is quite low. The 6802 microprocessor is extremely powerful and is quite easy to program. This unit makes an excellent starter computer and is upward expandable like the other systems on the market at this time.

computer block will be filled in the final (schematic diagram) by the 6802 processor. Internal computer I/O lines or data and address buses are driven by bus drivers. To get the system clock to run at 1 MHz as in the spec, we must use a 4 MHz crystal. To give the unit programmability, we have the ROM block in the block diagram. The system expandability of RAM will happen on the address and data buses. All buses shall be available to the user for expansion. The parallel I/O block is reserved for a PIA, so some addresses and the data bus are required for its operation. To do the address decoding, we have the decoding block shown in the block diagram. With the completion of the block diagram, we are ready to create the preliminary schematic diagram.

The schematic diagram must remain flexible and changeable through the "design troubleshooting" step. To eliminate unrealistic design stages in this book, we shall go to the actual, final schematic diagram of the unit we shall build (Figure 6-2). It should be obvious now how the schematic would step through its stages of development. A rough schematic would be used to give us the preliminary drawings from which we would normally fabricate the breadboard. We start at some central area in the block diagram and work our way through the block diagram, making a schematic of each section and testing each section as we go. By using only ROM area and microprocessor chip, a short program can be written. Of course, to make sure the ROM area works, you will need the address decoding section, too. With those three

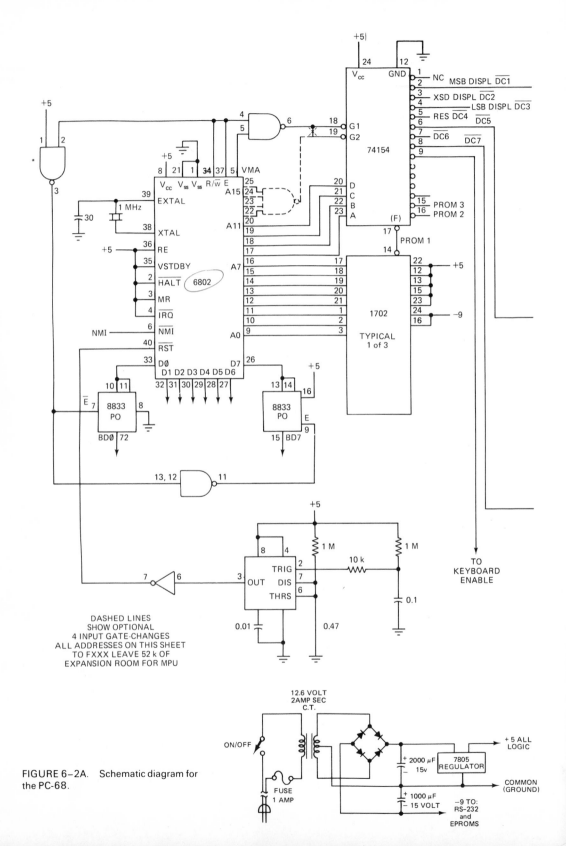

FIGURE 6-2A. Schematic diagram for the PC-68.

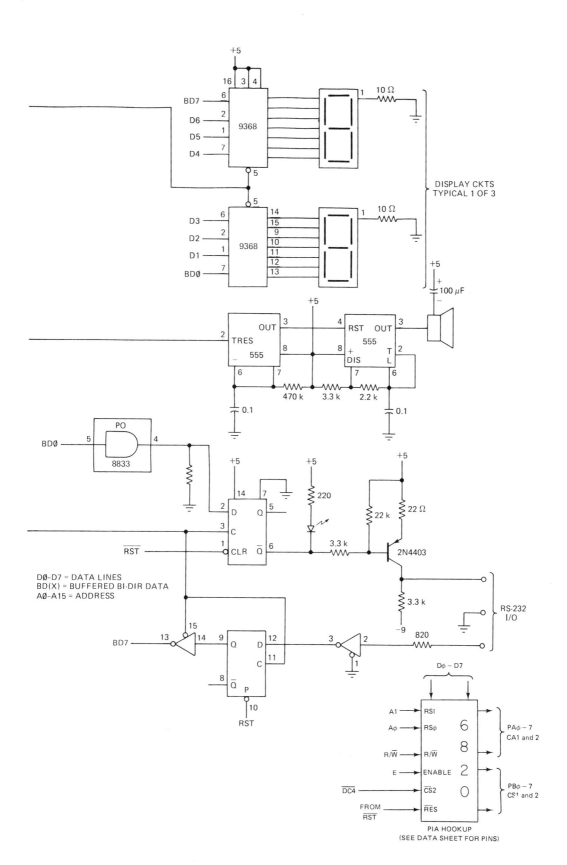

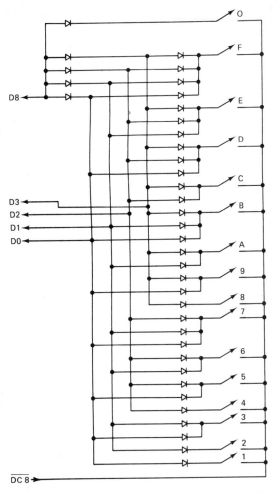

FIGURE 6-2B.   Part of the schematic diagram for the PC-68. This is the keyboard encoder circuit.

areas and an oscilloscope, you can write a program for the personal computer that will show its operation on the face of the scope.

Here we shall be doing two things. First, we shall be learning what to expect in reading programs. Second, we shall be seeing how the actual hardware may be troubleshot through the use of a software routine. We shall display this simple program as the computer would step through it for ease of understanding and to show the computer's method of operation.

This is the program for checking out the microprocessor basic

PC-68 TEST PROGRAM

Address	Contents	Explanation
FFFE	FF00	Sends the UP to the first step of program located at address FF00 (chosen for no special reason).
FF00	4F	CLRA. Clears the A accumulator.
FF01	C6	LDAB. Loads accumulator B with the following byte:
FF02	0A	10_{10} (base 10). Literal byte that goes in accumulator B. This will be used to count ten operations in a loop of program that comes back and repeats itself (ten times).
FF03	97	STAA. Store the contents of accumulator A at the address that follows.
FF04	20	32_{10}. Here we use direct addressing to store the 00 in accumulator A (see FF00) in hex memory position 20 (decimal 32).
FF05	5A	DECB. Decrement accumulator B. This will be used to mark the steps. The first time through the loop the contents of B will be a 4, the second a 3, etc., until B becomes a 00. At that time the next step will allow the program to escape from the loop.
FF06	26	BNE. Branch, not equal to zero. If B is not counted to zero branch to the address indicated in the next step.
FF07	FB	This is the hex number representing the jump backward to address step FF03, thus completing the loop operation. (More on computing this number in the programming section.)
FF08	B7	STAA. Store the 00 in accumulator A at the memory location contained in the next two bytes.
FF09&0A	F357	Where we store the byte in accumulator A. The address was chosen to key the decoder to an output on its F3 decoding line, but the 57 was a random choice, it could well have been F300, anything to trip the decoder.

| FFOB | 7E | Jump to the address contained in the next two bytes. The program is finished, but to get a good look on the scope, we are going back to the start and repeat the program so it will loop itself till we turn off the power to the unit. |
| FFO6&OD | FFOO | Address where the program will proceed from. This is the beginning of the original program, so the program itself is in a never ending loop and will continue to operate like this till power is removed. |

function, power supply, and address decoder, as well as the condition of the EPROM used. In operation, the scope shows five outputs on pins of the 74154 address decoder, except that at time six there will be a hole. Moving the scope across the output decoder, output pins will show no outputs except at address F3XX. If the scope is dual trace you can see that the pulse output at pin 1 occurs during the "hole" in the output at pin 3. If this series of wave forms is what you are getting, you have checked out the circuits.

In the development of the microprocessor design, this success would not mean that we finalize this portion of the schematic diagram yet because we are not sure that something will not have to change in the final diagram. We can finalize the drawing after all the microcomputer circuits are fully functional.

Although we could do some other circuit, a logical circuit to fabricate at this stage of the design checkout or breadboarding would be the display decoder circuits. Again, a simple program could be written that would allow the display of characters or something on the display of the computer system. After the display circuits, we could fabricate the keyboard circuits and talk to the display via the microprocessor. It is doubtful that any of your friends would share your thrill as you pushed the number 5 on the keyboard and the display lit up with the number 5. But you would have the satisfaction of knowing that you had built a complete computer that was functioning properly and that you had written a real computer program that was actually operating the display and keyboard circuits.

Some of the things found in the display circuits are worth noting. One is the way the decoder drives the latch enables to the display circuits. Each decoder output drives two latches and then the eight data lines are split into four lines, each feeding each of the same two decoders. Thus a read of data on the data lines from an accumulator or memory position actually causes two of the display decoders to operate, displaying the entire contents of the byte being addressed by the computer. Thus, to display the contents of a byte in, for instance, the A accumulator, you simply store the A accumulator (STAA) in memory position F100. This causes the 01 decoder output to pulse low and drives the latch, displaying the A accumulator in eight bits (two hex numbers) such as C6, or F4, or 33, whatever the contents of the accumulator is. This is a very simple interface as far as software goes. The ease of software interfacing was weighed against some other schemes such as having the processor drive the display and do the decoding. Since a hex decoder is available and since the ease of programming this personal computer was a factor to be considered, we opted to use decoders in the design of the PC-68.

The keyboard circuits on the other hand could be simplified by the addition of an IC decoder rather than by the diodes shown here, but the diodes are cheap, readily available, and they illustrate the method of decoding that goes on inside the IC should you decide to go with a decoder in place of the diodes. Note in the diode circuits, the presence of some hardware/software trickery. See how the keypressed decoding circuitry (actually diodes hooked up as an OR gate) actually feeds its output on data line 8. When the decoder addresses the keyboard, the software need only test bit 8. If bit 8 is a logic 1, the software knows that a key is down and it can read the other bits. If no key is down, the processor can go do some other chore, coming back periodically (another loop) to check on the status of the keyboard. If a given key is down, the data bits are going to show up as the lower four bits of data. Thus you can read the keyboard easily.

After a test of bit 8 shows that a key is down, you merely LDAA with the contents of the memory position designated by the decoder. That is F8XX in the PC-68. Once the keyboard word is loaded into the accumulator, it must be stripped of the keypressed bit at bit 8 or this will confuse things by always displaying an 8 as the higher order bit. If you then displayed the contents of accumulator A, you would show an 86 and not the desired 06. The 6800 has some simple commands that can be used to mask bits out and one of these is the AND command.

The logical AND command in the 6800 may be performed in any of the traditional addressing modes available with the other commands. In our example, that of masking out bit 8 we would use the immediate mode of addressing. This is the command mode that will cause the contents of the register to be ANDed with the contents of the following byte (the literal). To AND accumulator A, we would use ANDA or hex 84. Written for an assembler, the source code for the command that would mask bit 8 would be:

ANDA #$0F assembled to become: ANDA 84 0F.

This has the effect of blocking off the higher order bits in the accumulator because of the AND function (when both A and B are logical 1's, the output is logical 1). Since for the most significant nybble of the command the A functions are 0000, the output will be 0000 no matter what the B side has on it (and it has a 1000). For the least significant nybble the A side is 1111, so the output will be whatever is in the B side. Where the B bits are 1, the AND function provides for an A and B of 1 equals 1 out. Where the B bits are 0 the AND function is A of 1, B of 0 equals 0 out.

The serial data interface is provided in the PC–68 by a very simple one flip-flop interface. The interface is driven by both the data and address decoder circuits. Bidirectional bus transceivers were used in the circuit so data direction could be controlled, and the MPU could use the I/O port just like a memory position. To output data on the serial line, the computer simply stores data at the memory position provided by the output of the address decoder. This is any address in the F7XX series. Notice, however, that only one data bit (bit 8) is used for outputting data and only one other bit is used to input data. The bit word to be output is stored in the A accumulator, and Accumulator Shift Commands are used to output the bits to the proper data lines. By using data line D7 (bit 8) the most significant data bit is output first. This is in keeping with the standard serial data transfers from a teletype. By using bit 0, data input D0, you merely shift the data around in the accumulator and the incoming MSB moves across the accumulator to become the MSB of the accumulator contents. Note the use of the R/W signal to provide the data direction. When the R/W signal is a logic 1, input register is selected; when R/W is a logic 0 (indicating a write signal from the MPU), the output register is addressed and D7 is output. The output signal from the FF goes through a simple one transistor inverter and level changer circuit. The output of the level changer is an RS–232 compatible data signal that can handle serial output to and from peripherals such as CRT Terminals and TTY Terminals as well as some printers. By properly timing the output of the MPU, you can actually control the baud rate of the serial port so that you can interface peripherals running at various speeds. The software is also the controller of such things as start bits, number of stop bits, and whether or not data out is inverted.

The programming necessary to operate the serial data output port is fairly simple and follows. This listing will bring the computer program more into conformity with a standard listing. Here, we list the command proper and any other associated bytes on the same line similar to the way an assembler would list the computer's machine language.

PC-68 SERIAL OUTPUT PORT TEST

Address	Contents	Explanation
FFFE	FF00	Start jump vector to beginning of the program.
FF00	86 80	LDAA #$80 (# means immediately). Load the A accumulator with binary 10000000.
FF02	B7 F700	STAA I/O Address. Store the accumulator contents at address 0700. This causes the output of the flip-flop to go to a logic 1.
FF05	C6 FF	LDAB #$FF ($ means hex). Puts an FF_{16} or a 256 count in the B accumulator. This is preparatory to a loop that will count down the B accumulator to keep the serial output high for a time.
FF07 LOOP	5A	DECB. Counts down the 256 in B accumulator.
FF08	26 FD	BNE "LOOP." Branch if not counted to zero, back to the loop (FF07) beginning and stall a while longer.
FF0A	4F	CLRA. Loop is done, so clear the contents of A accumulator.
FF0B	B7 F700	STAA I/O Address. Store the A accumulator at the serial I/O address. This makes the data line go to logic 0.
FF0E	7E FF00	JMP Beginning. Jump to FF00 and do the whole thing again.

The serial data output port need not only be used for outputting and inputting data from terminals, but can be used for anything that requires a control voltage output such as a relay driver. In some of the experiments you will perform with the PC-68 system you can use the serial port for driving Light Emitting Diodes, etc. Also it is possible to use the output line for driving an amplifier/speaker so that we can program the PC-68 to play musical tones. Another application is to use the output line to drive a relay driver that will interrupt the telephone line, simulating the action of a dial telephone. In this manner the PC-68 can be used to recall and dial your most used phone numbers. Truly, this serial data port is going to offer our unit a lot of flexibility to the outside world.

With the expandability criteria in mind, we can see how it is possible to expand our computer to operate with parallel output devices by adding the parallel output PIA port. The PIA port simply interfaces the processor via the address decoder and the two lowest order address bits. The lower order address lines allow us to address all the internal registers in the PIA and thus bring it under complete software control. There are actually four different register addresses to be selected in the PIA itself. Tradition has it that you use the lower order address bits. This way the registers in the PIA are addressed sequentially. Although it would be perfectly permissible to use more of the address decoder outputs to provide addresses for the PIA (such as F800, F900, FA00, FB00), it is more frugal in terms of memory to give the PIA an address, such as FB00. With the register, select lines tied to the lower address bits so that the PIA is addressed at FB00, FB01, FB02, and FB03.

With the PIA connected to the computer it is possible to make a music player that uses several of the parallel port terminals to feed a resistor network. This forms an ADDER circuit. When all the ports outputs are logical 1's, all the voltages add and the output is highest. When the ports are partly at logic 1 and partly at logic 0 (or ground), the resistors work as voltage dividers and the total output voltage goes lower. By controlling how many networks are at logic 0 and logic 1, you can actually make the output wave form from the adder simulate an analog signal. The analog signal can be a moderately complex wave form so you can reproduce a musical note by switching various port terminations at different rates of speed. By writing a short program for the PC-68, we will be able to play a musical tune on the parallel I/O port. The internal operation of the PIA port is explained in another chapter so we shall assume at this point that you have a basic understanding of the PIA ports' internal registers and their functions. We shall write a program that will put a logic 1 out of the PIA ports and then move the logic 1 along the port terminals. It would take an eight-trace scope to see the thing in operation, so we shall make the computer do each step and stop waiting for a keyboard command before it proceeds to the next step in walking up the PIA. Each port can then be observed with a scope to insure that the thing is operational and the programs fully work. Again, we shall display each step, but this time we shall set the op code in mnemonic form (like the LDAA and STX) at the first of the line after the address.

The software that was given in the preceding paragraphs was being used to check out the working of the hardware. Software that is

PC-68 PARALLEL PORT TEST

Address	Mnemonic	Machine Code	Explanation
FFFE	none	FFOO	Jump start address.
FFOO	LDX#$0800	8E F800	Initialize the index register.
FFO3	CLRA	4F	Set accumulator A to zero.
FFO4	STAA 1,X	A7 01	Store the A accumulator one space forward of the index register's address. This puts a O in the control register.
FFO6	STAA 3,X	A7 03	Store the contents of the A accumulator three places forward of the address in ''X.'' This addresses the control register. This tells it that we want to talk to the data direction register.
FFO8	NEGA	40	Complements the contents of A accumulator. Makes it FF.
FFO9	STAA O,X	A7 00	Makes DDR set up for output.
FFOB	STAA 2,X	A7 02	Makes DDR (B) set up for output.
FFOD	STAA 1,X	A7 01	Completes setup of PIA.

FF0F	STAA 3,X	A7 03	Completes setup of PIA(B).
FF11	LDAA #1	86 01	Puts 00000001 in A accumulator.
FF13 LOOP	TST KEYIO	7D F200	Check for any key down
FF16	BEQ LOOP	27 FB	If no key is down go back.
FF18	STAA $0700	B7 F700	Put out the rotating bit and scan for key down.
FF1B	ASLA	49	Shift A left one bit.
FF1C	JMP LOOP	7E FF13	Jump back and do it again.

used in this manner is called "diagnostics." It is possible to have the computer go through its own diagnostic routine on command and check itself for correct operation. This is another of the many advantages to using the microprocessor in a dedicated control system. Self-diagnostics is not as useful a feature when using a personal computing system such as the PC–68, because the diagnostics are only needed when something goes wrong with the processor. A knowledge of the use of diagnostics and how to use them in your system will be invaluable, since any system can be expected to develop some kind of problem at some point in its lifetime.

Once the system is checked out and found to be functional in all ways, the next step in this creation of a personal computer is to put the final version of the unit together. In the case of the PC–68, the so-called "breadboard" is also the final version. Since you already have the advantage of this unit having been fully checked out, you can skip the troubleshooting you could expect to have had in the diagnostics phase.

This system could be constructed on perfboard, but there are two much better alternatives to that type of construction—wirewrap and the solderboard. The original PC–68 was put together on solderboard. Solderboard construction simply means that individual sockets are soldered on the board and then wires are soldered to the solder pads. Wirewraps are basically similar except that the terminals on the sockets are longer than the solder tail types. The connections between circuits are performed by wrapping wires around the terminal posts. The actual wirewrapping can be performed by twisting a hand wirewrap tool, or by an electric inverted drill-like device. With a powered wirewrap, you can make an amazing number of connections in a short period of time.

Figure 6–3 shows the general layout used in the PC–68. While the layout is not absolutely critical, it would probably be best to use a layout similar to the one shown to ensure operation of the computer under all possible conditions. The power supply is not critical although one should use general good engineering layout practices in putting the thing together.

Since power required to operate the unit is not too heavy, a simple power supply such as the one shown in the schematic is more than adequate. Location of the mechanical things such as the switches, etc., is

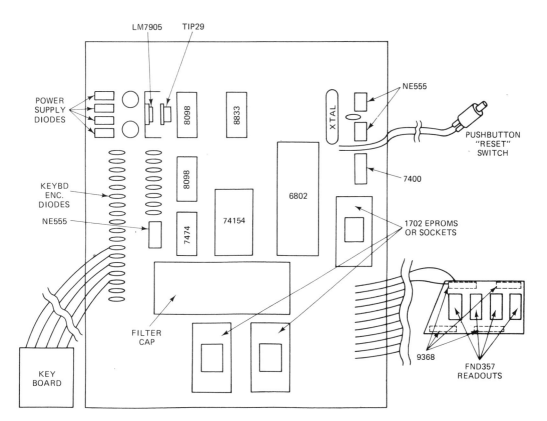

FIGURE 6–3.   Pictorial layout of the PC-68 personal computer used in the text.

not critical. The power transformer runs hot and should be located as far as possible from the IC's in the unit. Definitely do not put the transformer underneath the circuit board to heat the board itself. To keep demand on the regulator low, the power supply is actually split into two sections. One section is the UA7805 regulator IC and the other is a high current pass transistor that is hooked up as an emitter follower and has a fairly constant voltage output slightly lower than the five volts out of the regulator. This higher current five-volt supply is used to drive the higher current displays and display drivers. The critical levels are at the TTL and the MPU chip. These run off the main five-volt regulator. The power supply section actually has a positive and negative supply. The negative supply serves two purposes. One is supplying the negative voltage to the 1702 EPROM's, and the other is supplying the negative voltage to the transistor making up the RS–232 converter circuit (the transistor on the output of the flip-flop). Since the demands on the negative supply are extremely small and both the EPROM's and the RS–232 converter are tolerant, the negative supply is unregulated.

The cabinet is fabricated according to the drawings in Figure 6–4. The material used in the cabinet is simple polypropylene plastic. Cutting is accomplished by scribing the flat plastic sheets with an X-acto plastic scoring tool. After the sheet is scored, you merely lay the sheet on the edge of the table scored side up and close to the table edge. Push the outer edge of the sheet until the sheet breaks clean along the scored area. Light sanding of the outer edges brings them to a finish. Since each sheet is relatively small and easy to handle, it is easier to put the sandpaper rough side up on a flat surface such as a workbench or table top and then move the edge of the plastic back and forth across the edge to be finished.

The plastic is glued with a liquid acetone-type glue. A small container with a nozzle is available at plastic supply houses for the purpose. The outside edges of the box should be glued together first. The outsides of the box thus formed can be held with masking tape till the glue dries. Then secure the top of the unit to the four sides already glued. This should bring the cover assembly into square. The inside corner braces are next. Finally, glue the plexiglass window into place on the front panel. This is where the display will show through to the operator. All the seams should be glued by running a bead of acetone along the inside joints of the plastic and the entire unit set aside for drying. After at least six hours, the plastic will be hardened and the front sloping panel can be drilled for the keyboard. Also the holes for AC power cord and transformer mounting can be drilled in the rear cross piece.

In actual use, the PC board fits up inside the cabinet and is held in place by corner braces. For working on the PC–68, the board can be left

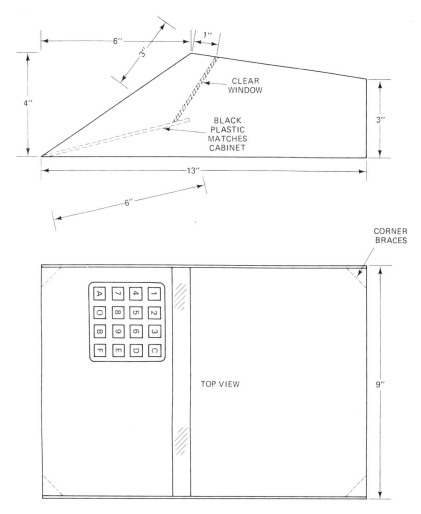

FIGURE 6–4.   Outline drawings of a PC-68 cabinet.

unsecured. If you are finished with the construction of the unit, then you are ready to fasten the PC board to the corner pieces with self-tapping screws through enlarged holes in the plastic corners and smaller gripping holes in the PC material itself. Now the cabinet not only provides more conventional looks for the unit, but it also protects the electronic components that would otherwise be exposed.

Using the PC-68 system will be quite like using any other personal computing system, except that without any add-ons, the PC-68 will be best suited for controller applications, as mentioned before. As a versatile personal computer system, you will need to add on more RAM memory. With the proper amount of RAM, however, you can program the PC–68 computer system like any other 6800 system now available to personal computer users. By adding PIA ports or other necessary hardware, you will be able to do such things as run a floppy disc-based system. By having a deep understanding of the hardware involved in the personal computer system, you will not only be able to get more out of the PC–68, but will be able to understand any personal computer system that you encounter.

7

Putting It All Together with Programming

If by now you have actually put together the PC-68 or have in your possession a microcomputer system, you are probably itching to get down to the writing of programs. Making the machine do what you want it to do is most of the fun of personal computer ownership. Programming is one of the finer parts of enjoying your own creativity with a personal computer system. By programming your computer properly you not only are able to make it perform functions for you, but are also able to trade programs and ideas with others so they can reproduce and duplicate your efforts.

Some conventions need to be assumed in the writing of your programs, that is, you need to use some accepted methods for writing programs that will enable someone else to read the program you have written and understand what you have done. Further, if need be, you or someone else would ideally be able to take the program you have written for one machine or language and convert it for use on another personal system which may or may not even use identical software commands. Even if the other system uses the same basic parts, it may not use the same addresses as the one you used to write things on.

Another advantage of using some standards and conventions in writing your own programs is that of being able to read and understand what you did even after weeks or months have passed. Say you write a program for adding and subtracting decimal numbers early in the game. Later, you want to lift the program and use it in a more complex math routine that includes multiplication and division. If you have forgotten much of the thought process that went into the first simpler program, you will likely have trouble reorienting yourself on how it all originally worked. That will make it tough for you to put the programs together into the master program.

If you always use the same guidelines in writing your programs, you will not have to figure out your program from scratch in order to be able to use it again. If you do it right the first time you will not have to do it over again. This chapter will try to introduce you to some accepted programming techniques so that you can use them from the start in writing programs. This should help you write effective programs and additionally will allow you to interpret other programs long after this book has become nothing but a reference work on the shelf somewhere. As was mentioned earlier in this book, programming conventions were originally adapted to allow others working on the same large project to be able to work together and put their work into a main unit. It is like the chapters in a book. Each chapter will follow the other in logical thought and in actual physical preparation. While the format of different books will change, the various chapters in the book will conform in layout and style and content. Books from a given publisher sometimes are controlled as to format so that even though each comes from a different author, they all go together to form a series providing a wide range of information on a given subject.

The first part of this chapter will provide some rules and definitions which will help you generate good, operating code for your personal computer. Once a solid background into general programming has been given, we will apply the principles to the actual generation of operational code for the PC–68. Throughout the entire text, we shall use the mnemonic and machine codes for the 6800 microprocessor, except where a general reference to another chip is in order. We shall also cover the nybbles and bytes of programming rather than try to tackle the major tasks of programming right off the top. With the programming rules we are offering, you would theoretically be able to tackle a large programming job with little difficulty, but it is better to eat bread before the meat. We will stick with operating systems, etc., before tackling the software design of a Fortran compiler for the 6800. Actually, the approach of breaking things down into smaller tasks serves you best even when working with some phenomenally huge program. Also, for the home computerist, the task of writing a compiler, for instance, would be phenomenal because of the time needed. The task of writing subroutines for the compiler will look much more achievable and will allow you to accomplish some goals on the way to the major overall production.

Breaking down the programming task and working on the individual parts also helps you overcome the discouragement you're bound to feel when you are working on a large task. You can feel the sense of accomplishment with the completion of each of the smaller tasks. There are, of course, pitfalls to avoid, such as the so-called "bottom-up" programming where you work on the smaller tasks first without regard to the overall task, then toil with the process of trying to interconnect the whole mess into one big array. Suppose you write the simple add/subtract routine mentioned before, complete with I/O routines, that allows you to enter a number followed by a plus or minus then followed by another number. The computer executes the program with speed and precision and prints the answer on the CRT screen. Now, let us say you used some place in memory as a scratch pad memory or a spot that is used to store some part or parts of the problem or solution temporarily while you perform some manipulations. Later, you write a multiply/divide routine from the bottom up. Say you accidentally use the same set of registers for parts of the scratch pad memory in the multiply/divide routine. At some future time when you try to combine the two programs, you have trouble getting the program to run because you are making the computer write over its own data in the course of operation. These address conflicts can be very difficult to find and require a great deal of debugging.

On the other hand, suppose you had written the add/subtract part of the program from the top down. That is, you realized that the program was to be a part of a larger program in the future and so, by using proper structure in your program writing, you took care of the address conflicts at the outset. In fact, because you knew of the total program picture, you might even have related the addresses in the scratch pad to each other in such a manner as to have saved programming steps. By using structured approaches to your task and using some other simple hints while keeping the overall objective in mind, you would have made immensely more useful programs.

Structured programming is a method name. It actually means that you construct your software in small, independent sections within the already small sections we have discussed. These sections are written in such a manner as to minimize the interaction within the parts. By eliminating or at least minimizing the criss-cross interconnections within the program, you eliminate confusion when you (or someone else) try to read the program at a later time. Of course, too much of anything can be bad, so even a great system like structured programming has its problems when carried to the extreme. If one was to eliminate all interaction within a program entirely, one would have to rewrite the routines that could more effectively be shared in a given program. For example, suppose the I/O routine contains 45 bytes in a given program. Further, suppose you were to call upon the services of the CRT terminal ten times in a given routine, you would have to supply the code for the I/O routine each time. The program would be 450 bytes long before you even had started. This kind of wasted space in a personal computer is unthinkable because of the extra memory requirements that would cost more than the original computer and certainly much more than our ideal target system of $500. Therefore, it would be permissible to breach the absolute requirements of the definition of structured programming to get efficiency. So to maintain order, we could write a clearly named I/O routine and cause our program to jump to that subroutine and perform the function called for. Even though the literal interpretation of the rules of the game of structured programming would not allow the interaction necessary to call on the services of a subroutine, it will be better at times to worry about getting the job done.

When possible, of course, it is better to waste some bytes of programming in order to make the program appear clearer to the user. For this reason, somewhere along the line the Macroinstruction came into being. A macroinstruction, or just plain "macro," is a series of instructions that are written to perform some task in a computer. While the macro is like a miniroutine, it is not like a subroutine. It is complete and is meant to be a part of a main program. In fact, the macro comes into play in the process of assembly. For instance, if you have a macro called "MOVNYB" (for Move Nybble) or move the contents of a designated accumulator over ½ byte or a nybble, you merely use the mnemonic MOVNYB like a command word for the microprocessor. The assembler then inserts the several bytes of code that make up the macro right in the middle of the other instructions in the place where you called it. This procedure can only be done by a macro assembler program, and it is very effective in saving writing out the programming steps when you are programming with the assembler.

The difference between the macro and the subroutine is that when the code is listed by the assembler the subroutine stands alone and is only written once. When the program needs to use the function provided by the subroutine, the program jumps to the subroutine, performs the function, then jumps back to where it was in the original program. The macro, once coded by the assembler, merely blends in with the other code and there is no interaction between the program parts as the program jumps around to the subroutine and back again. Keep in mind though, if the subroutine and the macro both use up 15 bytes, the macro will eat up 15 bytes of code every time it is called upon, where the subroutine will only use the original 15 bytes plus a byte or two to call the subroutine when it is used.

Both the macro and the subroutine use a series of instructions which are the basic instructions that are recognized by the microprocessor chip and are a part of the micro's repertoire. The commands are actually binary digital command words, such as 00111001 in hexidecimal, 39. Since these command words perform a function such as Return from Subroutine and since words are a little easier to remember than numbers, we generate a short name or mnemonic for the function. Thus the Return from Subroutine command mnemonic is RTS. We can simply remember the function to be performed RTS and then if we are hand coding our program we can look up the hex command for that mnemonic, 39. Thus we consider the computers command codes to be the equivalent words for such functions as ADDA (ADD accumulator A) and CBA (Compare accumulator B with A), etc.

In some computers such as the LSI–11 system, we have a further breakdown of the basic instruction into actual steps that cause it to perform the basic command step. These are called "microinstructions" and are actually part of any microcomputer although in most microcomputers you do not have access to the microcode or microinstructions as the programmer. The microinstructions are the steps the computer may make to perform the instruction that is basic, such as ADDA or LDX. Microinstructions are the atoms of programming, the smallest element possible in the computer's instruction sets, which compare to the molecule. Then the macroinstruction is comparable to the element made up of atoms. Your program consists of the elements you put together to perform a function and to become the final piece or object.

The better built the object, the more useful it is. You can use the tools of programming to create objects from the elements. Your objects will be most effective as you apply some of the principles of programming, such as structured programming, and still use enough sense to know when a compromise in the absolute rules is necessary. It is necessary to understand the basic rules of the structured program in order to use it more effectively. Again, the structured program is put together in such a way that there are no loops back to some obscure place in the program or within the program steps. All the moves in pure structured programming are in the same direction and there are three basic building blocks that are used.

The first building block is the sequence. This is a segment of program wherein the steps are operations that follow in order. If the program flow chart is written horizontally, the sequences follow each other from left to right. It is possible to write an entire program made up only of sequences. A more complex program will require the program to make conditional moves or to perform other operations based on conditions of the data.

The second program sequence is the IF THEN ELSE module. The triangular block represents the IF test in Figure 7–1. The THEN is the sequence of events or path that is occurring on the upper line (also called the "True Line"). The ELSE portion or the false portion occurs when the test is negative; it may have more or less sequences than the upper line. An IF THEN ELSE sequence of events could go like this: IF data is greater than 25 THEN make accumulator A a zero and go on to the next step, ELSE just go on to the next step. Often, in some higher level languages, the ELSE part is done by letting program flow instead of branching off to some other step.

The DO WHILE block is also shown in the figure. In this module, system conditions are tested by the triangular block again, and either some function is performed and the instruction is executed again, or the DO WHILE condition is met and the computer stops DOing. So WHILE a certain condition exists (as proven by the triangular test block) the computer will DO something. The DO WHILE part can be used for timing a certain thing in the computer. Say you start with the B accumulator at a 5 count and you enter the DO WHILE. Each time you test to see if B is a zero; if it is not, you perform the function or DO a decrement of B. You will decrement accumulator B five times then move on to the next part of the program. If you know the exact number of

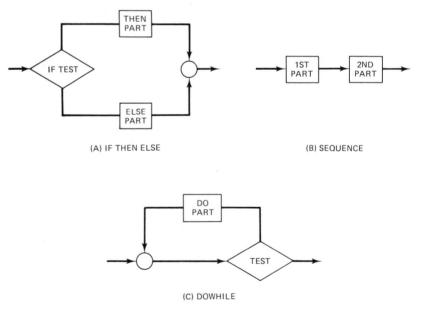

(A) IF THEN ELSE   (B) SEQUENCE

(C) DOWHILE

FIGURE 7–1.   Structured programming parts.

steps of the computer's timing it takes to perform the test and the decrement, you can achieve a desired time delay by choosing the proper constant to put in accumulator B before entering the DO WHILE block.

To begin the sequence of programming steps to properly use the three types of modules, you first develop the solution algorithm. An algorithm is a mathematical or logical solution to a given problem. You will merely develop the series of program steps that will solve the problem you have. You structure the algorithm, usually a block diagram, so it can be read sequentially in small, visible segments using the three parts already discussed. Your machine needs to have equivalent instructions that will allow you to put together the IF THEN ELSE and DO WHILE statements properly before you go on to the next step.

Next, you will perform a check for the following conditions. First, see that there is only one input and one output line. For every node in the program, or every point where a function is performed, make sure the program has a path from the input through the node to the output. This is a preliminary program check to make sure you have covered all the other steps in a structured manner. Finally check each step in the IF THEN ELSE and the DO WHILE parts to make sure they meet the criteria already covered in the definitions of each. If your program passes or is modified to pass the tests outlined, you are ready to convert to code. While programming in this manner will make for clear, clean, concise, uncluttered, and easy-to-read programs, it will be memory costly; since that is a factor in the micro, you can use another step.

While the top down approach is good for micros, as well as memory rich systems, the micro demands that you conserve program and memory space somewhat. The final step with a system that is short on memory would be to go through the structured program and look for duplicate code. When the duplicate functions are found they can often be turned into subroutines that will be called by our programs. Be careful to make sure you are memory conservative. Remember that if a subroutine is very far away you will eat up three bytes handling it. Consider the confusion it adds to your program flow, and if you have only a short four-or-five-byte routine, you would best handle it as a macro.

Now let's use the top down, structured approach for generating some useful programs for our PC–68 micro. Begin by writing down what we want the system to do. Remember that our computer must be told everything to do, so we will need a program for getting the data from the keyboard and for displaying data on the digits on the front of the unit. We will also want to be able to program our unit by giving it commands. We will want to be able to read the data located at a given address and also to load in new data at a certain address. Then we will want some kind of "execute" command that will cause the program we put in to run. Armed with this little operating system, we should be able to program the PC–68 to do whatever we want and need within the limits of the memory and add-ons we have available. Because of the structure of the PC–68 system, we have only four displayable digits. To make the operating system function within these constraints, we will use two different key inserting modes. One of the two modes will be the five key mode, so that from reset or power on, the PC–68 will accept the next five keys input. Four of the first five keys the PC–68 will interpret as address data, the fifth will be the command key. The command key can void the first four entries (erase the keys already input), make the program begin running at the given address, or enter the byte-level entry programs, or the ones that take only three inputs.

The second mode of operation is the byte level mode, in which a two-key byte is entered and is followed by a command key. The display will keep track of the byte entry and at the same time display the least significant bits of the address where it is working. In the memory examine mode, the byte display will be the data that is located at the displayed memory position. In this mode one of the command keys that is normally used for erase will be used as the command to exit this mode of operation.

Now that we have kind of a design goal for the system, we can make the key assignments that will be used in the system for the programming of the unit. Keys 0–F will be used for data entry when they are pushed as the first four keys in the power on mode, or the first two keys in the data mode. Keys 0–F may be used as control keys with keys A–F preferred. These are the keys that are pressed as the fifth key in the power on mode and the third key in the data mode. Since the function of the data entry or address entry keys is self-explanatory, we shall now specify how each of the control keys is to be set up.

Command key F will be the command key that causes the unit to return to the power on, or idling condition. After the F key is depressed at any time as a command key, the unit will beep twice in succession and return to the power on mode. The display will show 0000. This function shall be valid both for the address mode and the data mode.

In the power on mode, the E key will work as the memory examine key. Depressing this key in the power on mode as the command key will make the unit jump from the address entry program in the power on mode to the data entry program in the data mode. The display shall show the least significant byte of the address spelled out in the first four keys. The other two digits will provide the data that is resident at the location shown. While operating in the memory examine program, you need only operate on key to use the program to look at the various data in the machine. The A key causes the address to advance and display the new data. The B key causes the address to go backward and display the new data at the previous location. Depressing the D key causes the operating system to jump into a new program, and that is the memory change function.

In the memory change function, the address will not advance from where it was in the examine function. Instead the program will display the current contents of the current address and then you can enter two digits which will be the new contents. The unit then jumps out of the change mode and goes back to the examine mode at the same address. At the same time, the unit beeps twice to indicate that it has performed its function properly.

With the unit back in the memory examine mode, the functions described before are active. To get out of the memory examine mode you must reenter the power on mode by depressing the F key.

Back in the power on mode, the only other active control key is the C key. After entering the starting address and seeing it is correct, you depress the C key to get the computer to begin executing the program you have written for it. There is no way back to the power on program unless you either push the reset pushbutton or build something into your program that will allow you to make a jump if certain conditions are met.

The following table shows the command keys that are valid for the various modes and shows the function of some proposed keys that can be used later to expand the function of the operating system by offering a way to dump and store programs on punched paper tape. It is suggested if you use the expansion to paper tape that you use a MIKBUG compatible format for your paper tape. This format is clearly spelled out in detail in the Motorola Engineering Note 100 given in Appendix D. By using the MIKBUG format, you make the PC-68 capable of swapping programs with other computers that are already on the market.

By working from the top down we have now defined the complete operating system in sufficient detail to begin the actual programming task. The first step after defining the system parameters is to create the flow chart. Since we are really involved with several separate programs in our operating system, we shall have to have several different flow charts describing each program. First we will have the executive program or the power on routine. We shall draw it out as the first phase of our software design.

Our flow chart is a sort of symbolic outline of the program. Some people compare the software flow chart to a sort of hardware schematic diagram. However, the first software flow chart should be used more as

PC-68 PERSONAL COMPUTER COMMANDS

Mode	Recognizes	Function
Power On	F	Clears the entry and reenters Power On.
Power On	E	Memory examine function.
Power On	C	Jumps to user program and begins execution.
*Power On	D	Dumps data to Mikbug compatible paper tape.
*Power On	B	Takes in Mikbug compatible tape.
Examine	F	Rejoins Power On mode
Examine	A	Advances memory and displays new data.
Examine	B	Decrements memory position and displays.
Examine	D	Enters a data Entry mode.
Entry	XX	Puts two digits in mem position in display.

*Reserved for future expansion.

a block diagram with each block of the flow chart describing some function. There are several levels of software generation and, other than the listing of functions, the flow chart is the most primitive level. It is possible to refine the flow chart to one lower level, sort of a detailed block diagram. The most specific level is the specific written program instructions and this listing is probably the most comparable to a schematic diagram.

In our software block diagram, we shall use certain accepted symbols to represent the given major functions such as a pure, old, functional operation. The operation is shown in the flow chart as a rectangular box. A question or, more properly, a decision is represented by a diamond-shaped box. The decision will branch out in one of two possible directions from the diamond box depending on whether or not the decision is True (yes answer) or False (no answer), just as was formerly described in the functional modules of structured programming. Figure 7–2 shows the accepted flow-charting symbols that are used in this series of programs and that you will encounter throughout your working with the personal computer.

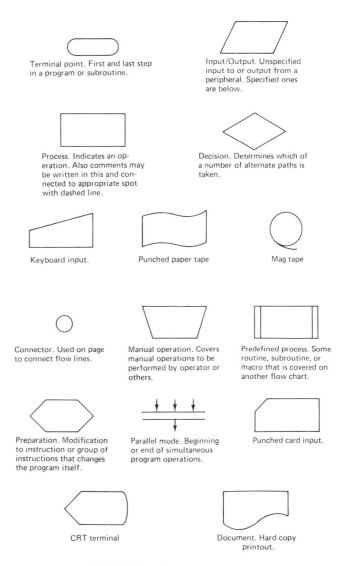

Terminal point. First and last step in a program or subroutine.

Input/Output. Unspecified input to or output from a peripheral. Specified ones are below.

Process. Indicates an op-eration. Also comments may be written in this and con-nected to appropriate spot with dashed line.

Decision. Determines which of a number of alternate paths is taken.

Keyboard input.

Punched paper tape

Mag tape

Connector. Used on page to connect flow lines.

Manual operation. Covers manual operations to be performed by operator or others.

Predefined process. Some routine, subroutine, or macro that is covered on another flow chart.

Preparation. Modification to instruction or group of instructions that changes the program itself.

Parallel mode. Beginning or end of simultaneous program operations.

Punched card input.

CRT terminal

Document. Hard copy printout.

FIGURE 7–2.   Flow-chart symbols.

Figure 7-3 shows the flow chart depicting the power on mode of operation for the PC-68. Before we actually fill in the code for each block or set of blocks to create the actual program, we will see that there is a gap in the program. That is, we have assumed in the block diagram flow chart of the software that there is a way to get data in and out of the

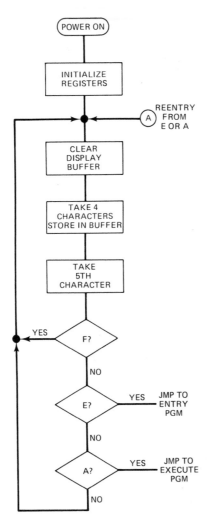

FIGURE 7-3.   Power on. Routine flow chart.

computer. This is one place that we shall grossly deviate from the procedure of writing complete programs without using any subroutines. We are about to write two different routines for data entry on the keyboard and data display on the digital display, and treat these as subroutines throughout the rest of our programming. While these are complete routines, we shall use them as subroutines so that the use of them anywhere in our programming is greatly simplified from the standpoint of writing actual code to perform the function. Naming the routines from the beginning will help make their use clearer when we encounter them in our programming even long after this program has been written. The name of the keyboard entry program will be shortened to the mnemonic KEYIN, and the digital display program will be shortened to DISP.

The software flow charts for the I/O routines are going to be a little complex, but are relatively easy to follow. The output routine DISP is given in Figure 7-4. This is an example of a program that is merely a series of sequences. Here we put the contents of the data buffer in the two accumulators and then store the two accumulators' contents in the display latches. This is an example in which the simplicity of the hardware design causes the software to be very simple.

While it would be very simple to code this routine at this time, we shall move on to the KEYIN routine and look at its flow chart before moving into the coding. Figure 7-5 gives the flow chart for the KEYIN

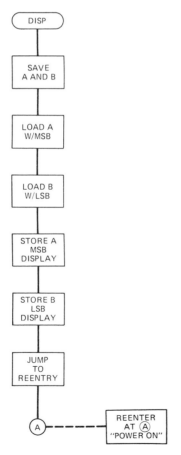

FIGURE 7-4.   Parallel display. Routine flow chart.

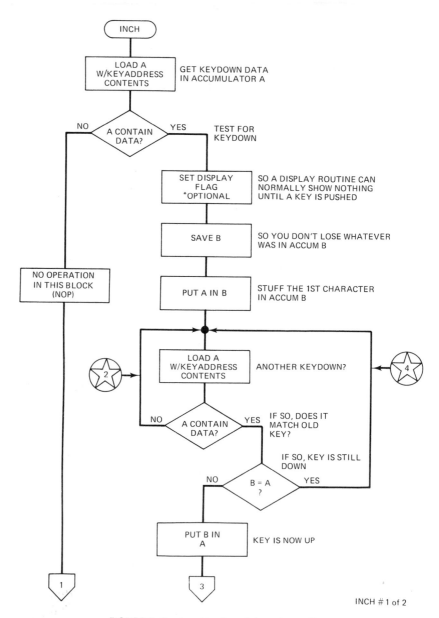

FIGURE 7–5. Input keyboard character routine.

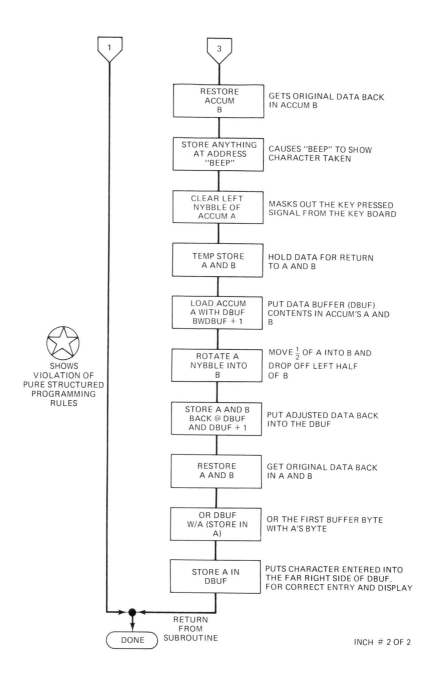

```
                                    ┌───┐                    ┌───┐
                                    │ 1 │                    │ 3 │
                                    └───┘                    └───┘
                                                              │
                                              ┌──────────────────────────────┐
                                              │          RESTORE             │  GETS ORIGINAL DATA BACK
                                              │          ACCUM               │  IN ACCUM B
                                              │            B                 │
                                              └──────────────────────────────┘

                                              ┌──────────────────────────────┐
                                              │      STORE ANYTHING          │  CAUSES "BEEP" TO SHOW
                                              │      AT ADDRESS               │  CHARACTER TAKEN
                                              │        "BEEP"                 │
                                              └──────────────────────────────┘

                                              ┌──────────────────────────────┐
                                              │       CLEAR LEFT             │  MASKS OUT THE KEY PRESSED
                                              │       NYBBLE OF              │  SIGNAL FROM THE KEY BOARD
                                              │       ACCUM A               │
                                              └──────────────────────────────┘

                                              ┌──────────────────────────────┐
                                              │      TEMP STORE              │  HOLD DATA FOR RETURN
                                              │      A AND B                 │  TO A AND B
                                              └──────────────────────────────┘

                                              ┌──────────────────────────────┐
                                              │      LOAD ACCUM              │  PUT DATA BUFFER (DBUF)
                                              │   A WITH DBUF                │  CONTENTS IN ACCUM'S A AND
                                              │   BWDBUF + 1                 │  B
                                              └──────────────────────────────┘

                                              ┌──────────────────────────────┐
                                              │       ROTATE A               │  MOVE ½ OF A INTO B AND
                                              │    NYBBLE INTO               │  DROP OFF LEFT HALF
                                              │         B                    │  OF B
                                              └──────────────────────────────┘
```

SHOWS
VIOLATION OF
PURE STRUCTURED
PROGRAMMING
RULES

STORE A AND B
BACK @ DBUF
AND DBUF + 1 — PUT ADJUSTED DATA BACK INTO THE DBUF

RESTORE
A AND B — GET ORIGINAL DATA BACK IN A AND B

OR DBUF
W/A (STORE IN
A) — OR THE FIRST BUFFER BYTE WITH A'S BYTE

STORE A IN
DBUF — PUTS CHARACTER ENTERED INTO THE FAR RIGHT SIDE OF DBUF. FOR CORRECT ENTRY AND DISPLAY

RETURN
FROM
SUBROUTINE

(DONE)

INCH # 2 OF 2

routine. Getting the actual keyboard data into the computer is again simple because of the hardware design. The rest of the program is a little more complex though, because the program has to be able to put the information from the keyboard into the buffer which is merely a designated area of memory. In this routine, as in the DISP routine, we first save the contents of registers so we don't spoil any important data. (Remember, this is a subroutine and everything must be returned intact at the end of the routine.) Next we merely get data in the A accumulator for the proper address for the keys, and then we test the A accumulator to see if any keys are down. If no keys are down we are finished; if one is down we must go through the steps of the program and get the proper data.

At this point we have enough flow-charting done in three separate routines to "go to code." Before we jump right in and start coding, however, it would be good to learn a little about the proper format for presenting our code. Here we must keep in mind the things we have covered with structured programming so that we present the facts as clearly and concisely as possible. Remember that the only compromises we shall make in the structured approach to programming are those that more effectively accommodate our personal computer system. Rather than stilt our programming by saying such things as the first 100 lines of our program are reserved for comments, we shall say that we will use as many lines of our listing as are needed to clearly comment on the program. We can then be more efficient in even the presentation of the microcomputer software.

This is the logical place to cover assemblers. If we don't have a fancy computer program for assembling our code for us, we can act as if we do and provide hand coding that is at least as systematic and effective as the machine-coded material should be. It will also be nice to learn to write programs in the style that can be accepted by an assembler, so that when the time comes that an assembler is available, you will not have to relearn programming techniques all over again.

Assembler programs actually take the source code which is supplied by the programmer and then convert it to object code which is the machine language. Assemblers allow the naming of routines such as DISP and KEYIN; from then on the routine only need be referenced by name, an easier task than trying to remember a vague address location. For example, program step 36 might be memory location 0678 and this could be a routine called "OUTPUT." We could load a given character into the A accumulator and then jump to step 36 or to memory location 0678 every time we wanted to output data. Or, we could simply tell the assembler to JMP OUTPUT. Now the assembler takes care of all the work for us by figuring out the address for OUTPUT and by converting the JMP command to the proper machine code. This is especially handy when you are going into the program and inserting steps so that the actual address of step 36 is changing all the time. It would be a lot of work trying to keep track of the new address of the OUTPUT routine as you added and took away program steps.

Each line that is entered in the assembler is numbered, sometimes by the assembler and sometimes by another software aid that works hand in hand with the assembler and that is called the "editor."

The editor is a software program that allows you to change commands around and work with the program you are designing. The data that goes into the assembler goes in via the editor and some software packages are called "CORES" for COResident Editor and aSsembler. (There is a package named CORES for the 6800.) With an editor and assembler that are working coresident in the same computer you can jump back and forth from the editor and assembler while preparing your program. This way you can write the program, assemble it, check it out, and then come back to the editor to make needed adjustments. With the Motorola CORES you can use the assembler to put object code right into memory, too. This means you can write code in the editor, assemble it directly into the machine code, put it in the machine and run it to test it, come back to the editor to make needed changes, then repeat the procedure. This gives you versatile programming capabilities.

In writing the source code for an assembler, more rules come into play. This is because there are certain ways the data must be entered into the assembler. There are also assembler commands which tell the assembler what to do with the object code and and what to print out, etc. These assembler commands are called "assembler directives." The programmer must keep all this in mind as he writes the source code. Most assemblers have fairly flexible input requirements, but they must be followed within reason in order to get workable results out.

The characters must be entered into the assembler in zones. First comes the line number followed by at least one space (denoting a new zone) which tells the assembler that the line number is completed. Next comes the zone containing the label or the function name. The command zone is next where either the assembler directive or the assembly language mnemonic is contained. This zone is followed by another space (or more) and a new zone which tells where in memory something is to happen. This may be numerical or name information, depending on how you wish to specify the address. If the address has been defined (or will be later) and given a name, you can use the name. If you are using numeric address information, you can specify whether the numeric information is binary, hex, or base ten. You can also command the assembler to convert to the ASCII equivalent of a letter or symbol. For instance, the 6800 resident assembler uses the following conventions. Where there is no preface, the numerical data is assumed to be decimal. A dollar sign ($) prefacing the numeric information specifies that the data that follows is hex. The octal data prefix is "@," and the "%" indicates that the data is binary. An ASCII literal is preceded by an apostrophe (') so that to LDAA or load the A accumulator with 'A would put in a $41 (hex, 41). This same zone is also used to specify the addressing mode when necessary.

While the data itself is preceded by a preface symbol or prefix, so the prefix symbol is preceded by a symbol that specifies the addressing mode. Of course, inherent mode, or one-byte commands do not even require this field when source code is being written, but the others may be specified. If there is no symbol preceding the data information symbol, then the direct or extended mode of addressing will be used with the assembler using the direct mode when it is possible. Using the pound-weight sign (#) as the preface causes the assembler to use the immediate mode. Therefore, our previous example would more accurately be written in source code:

LDAA #'A which would generate code that would be 86 41.

The last mode is the indexed mode which is written "(distance) ,X." The ",X" is the mode and the "(distance)" is the offset. For instance, if you wished to write source code that would have the A accumulator load up with whatever data was in a memory location that was located two memory positions away from the address in the index register, the source code would be:

LDAA 2 ,X   This would translate to machine code: A6 02.

Once the so-called operand data from this field is all filled in in the source code, you merely enter another space if desired to write in comments. The comment field is very important although the assembler performs no operation on the data therein. The only place the comment field will show is in the listing called the "assembly listing," but this is where it is needed. The comments are not essential to a working program, but they do help guide others and yourself, at a later date, through the program and thus understand the logic that generated it.

It is the comment field that can save you the most grief later. Most firms want programmers capable of presenting a clear and concise picture of what the program is doing all along the way. You will want to annotate your program so that you can reference what is going on, too. It is not necessary to comment on every single step within a program so the use of the comment field in the assembler is optional.

In addition to these zone requirements, some assemblers have rules that must be followed in order to make them operate properly. For instance, the 6800 resident assembler requires that the first directive or statement in the program must be the assembler directive that names the program, the NAM directive. Any other directive or statement in the first line of the program generates an error.

Armed with the facts about how assemblers operate, we shall write our first source code for the PC-68 computer. We will use the conventions that are required of the 6800 resident assembler/editor, since if you end up expanding the PC-68 this will be the setup you will most likely use. For the first program we still assume that we do not have an operational assembler for the 6800 and that we must assemble the program "by hand." This is not as difficult as one might think if one uses the same rules for generating the source code that the assembler requires. Also, by using the kind of coding techniques that the actual assembler will use, we can convert the source code to machine code. Since we are using these techniques, as a side benefit we will get an assembler listing as a byproduct of the whole process.

For the sake of clarity, we shall start the process with the easier, parallel display routine showing the source code:

```
 10  NAM DISP ASSBLY LISTG FOR PARA DISPL SUBROUT
 20 DFLAG EQU $0032 REGISTER CALLED DFLAG
 30 PADR1 EQU $F100 ADDRESS OF LSDIGITS TO DISPLAY
 40 PADR2 EQU $F200 ADDRESS OF MSDIGITS TO DISPLAY
 50 *
 60 * THIS IS A PGM TO DISPLAY THE CONTENTS
 70 * OF THE BUFFER (DBUF) ON THE HEX DISPLAYS
 80 *
 90  ORG $F000 PGM TO ORIGINATE BEGINNING AT $F000
100 START PSHA
110  PSHB SAVE ACCU A AND ACCU B
120  LDAA DBUF GET MSBYTE IN A
130  LDAB DBUF+1 GET LSBYTE IN B
140  STAA PADR2 DISPLAY MSB
150  STAB PADR1 DISPLAY LSB
160  PULB
170  PULA GET ORIG A AND B BACK FROM STACK
180 DONE RTS RETURN FROM SUBROUTINE
190  END
```

Now if we run this source code through an assembler, we will get an error. The assembly process itself takes place in two passes in the 6800 CORES. The first pass looks for labels and makes up a table of them to be used to reference the second pass which actually fills in the code. Our second pass would show reference to address DBUF and there would be no such address provided in the first pass; therefore, we would get an error. The problem is easy to fix. We simply go back into the editor, and add a step between existing steps; for instance, to fix our program so it will assemble, we would add the following:

25 DBUF EQU DFLAG + 1 DATA BUFFER ADDRESS

Note that we keyed the address definition off the already defined DFLAG address. That is perfectly legitimate because we have already defined the other address and the assembler can do math. Line by line we can look at each statement to provide an explanation for clarity.

As you look at each line be sure to note that there are extra spaces on the lines in various select places. As already covered, these are the spaces that actually provide the zone information for the assembler. Line 10 contains a double space to put the assembler directive NAM for Name in the proper zone. Then the comment zone makes this directive perfectly clear; this is where the program name DISP is given. This must be the first directive given for the assembler.

In line 20 we use the EQU statement which is the EQUals statement that tells the assembler that we wish to make the memory address called DFLAG EQUal to Hex 32. Line 25 is our newly inserted line which defines the address for the data buffer memory. Line 50 and the following lines have an asterisk (*) where the label would be. This shows the assembler that a comment is coming and inhibits the assembler from producing code (which would certainly cause an error in this case) and will merely print the comments when the source code is assembled.

The ORG statement in line 90 is another assembler directive that tells the assembler that the actual program code is to begin at address ORiGinating at memory position F000 Hex. Line 190 contains the END directive. Until the assembler gets the END statement, it will charge along trying to come up with line numbers and put together a program. If there is no END statement the assembler will lock up in a constant error printing mode.

Now if we run the source code generated through an assembler and command the assembler to provide a printout, we will get the assembly listing that will contain both a source code and the object code listing in a form that will be easily readable:

0010			NAM	DISP	assbly LISTG FOR PARA DIS SUBR
0020	0032	DFLAG	EQU	$0032	REGISTER CALLED DFLAG
0025	0033	DBUF	EQU	DFLAG+1	DATA BUFFER ADDRESS
0030	0100	PADR1	EQU	$0100	ADDR OF LSDIGITS TO DISPLAY
0040	0200	PADR2	EQU	$0200	ADDR OF MSDIGITS TO DISPLAY
0050		*			
0060		*	THIS IS PGM TO DISPLAY THE CONTENTS		
0070		*	OF THE BUFFER (DBUF) ON THE HEX DISPLAYS		
0080		*			
0090	F000		ORG	$F000	PGM TO ORIGINATE AT F000
0100	F000 36	START	PSHA		SAVE ACCU A
0110	F001 37		PSHB		AND ACCU B
0120	F002 96 32		LDAA	DBUF	GET MSB IN A
0130	F004 D6 33		LDAB	DBUF+1	GET LSB IN B
0140	F006 B7 F200		STAA	PADR2	DISPLAY MSB
0150	F009 F7 F100		STAB	PADR2	DISPLAY LSB
0160	F00C 33		PULB		
0170	F00D 32		PULA		GET ORIG A AND B BACK FM STK
0180	F00E 39	DONE	RTS		RETURN FROM SUBROUTINE
0190			END		

Note that the actual source code appears on the right-hand side of the page all neatly spaced out according to the various zones. Also note that the object code is on the left. Also observe that some of the comments were changed slightly to shorten them so they would fit on the page. An actual assembler would not be able to shorten the comments and you would have to do that via the editor.

In the beginning, you may not have the convenience of having an assembler program at your command, so you will have to hand code your programs. You should follow the same basic procedure, but as you write the source code you should leave space on the right to go back and fill in the addresses and code for the machine. Also, you will not really need the assembler directives, although if you take the time to insert them now, you will find it easier to assemble the program on an assembler when one becomes available. The only problem is that you may not know all the assembler directives that are available if you do not already have the assembler program. The hand assembly process for the same program would go as follows:

```
10                  START   PSHA
20                          PSHB            SAVE ACCU A
                                            AND ACCU B
30                          LDAA    DBUF     GET MSB IN A
40                          LDAB    DBUF+1   GET LSB IN B
50                          STAA    PADR2    DISLAY MSB
60                          STAB    PADR1    DISPLAY LSB
70                          PULB
80                          PULA             GET A AND B
                                             FROM STACK
90                  DONE    RTS              RETURN FROM
                                             SUBROUTINE
```

Now in hand coding, you will go back to the original listing of source code and plug in the addresses just like in the assembler listing:

```
10   F000 36     START   PSHA
20   F001 37             PSHB            SAVE ACCU A
                                         AND ACCU B
30   F002 96 32           LDAA   DBUF     GET MSB IN A
40   F004 D6 33           LDAB   DBUF+1   GET LSB IN B
50   F006 B7 F200         STAA   PADR2    DISPLAY MSB
60   F009 F7 F100         STAB   PADR1    DISPLAY LSB
70   F00C 33              PULB
80   F00D 32              PULA            A AND B BACK
                                          FM STK
90   F00E 39      DONE    RTS             RETURN FROM
                                          SUBROUTINE
```

These are the principles that will allow us to write all manner of good software programs for the personal computer. By using these techniques your programs will be readable by anyone working in the personal computer field. You will also be able to submit programs for publication in the personal computer magazines. All people who are familiar with personal computers will be able to read your programs with relative ease, and, depending on how well you have annotated the code, will be able to understand the programs. At this point you are referred to the program listing for the MIKBUG debug program provided in the back of this book. As a good exercise, you will do well to go through several of the routines contained there to see how the code is written and see how they approached the programming chore.

You are also referred to Figure 7-6 which is the program listing for a debug program written for the PC-68 personal computer. This program will allow you to enter programs on your own PC-68 and is merely there to help you get started. It should be burned on PROM and should reside in the PC-68 from power on so you can get your own programs going. Notice that you will find the code for the routine DISP in the beginning of the program listing. This listing was done on a 6800 personal computer system using CORES for the assembler/editor chores.

It would be nice if this text could cover all the aspects of programming the personal computer in sufficient detail so that no part of the whole would go uncovered, but the fact remains that personal computer programming is not just a one-shot process. You will learn programming from following articles and programs written by others and from the most important factor of all: practicing on your own personal computer system. The biggest roadblock you will encounter in learning to program well is just plain sitting down and doing it. It is really easy for one to sit down and run programs that someone else has written to play games with the personal computer or even to provide some useful function such as checkbook balancing, etc. It is quite another thing to generate your own programs for your very own personal system. Let's hope you do the latter rather than fall into the trap of the former.

Who knows? Perhaps you will be the one who builds the machine and writes the applications software for the microcomputer that will change the world.

Good luck!

FIGURE 7-6. Program listing for the PC-68.

PAGE 001

```
00010                        NAM      PC-68     DEBUG PGM
00020               *
00030               *
00040               * REGISTERS
00050               *
00060  0020                   ORG      $20
00070  0020 0001   DFLAG      RMB      1
00080  0021 0002   DBUF       RMB      2
00090  0023 0002   TEMPX      RMB      2
00100  0025 0001   DCNT       RMB      1         DIGIT COUNT
00110               *
00120               *
00130               * CONSTANTS
00140               *
00150       0800    KEYADR     EQU      $0800
00160       0500    BEEP       EQU      $0500
00170       0100    DISAD1     EQU      $0100
00180       0200    DISAD2     EQU      $0200
00190               *
00200               *
00210               *
00220               * PAR KEYBD INPUT-INKEY
00230               *
00240  FF00                    ORG      $FF00
00250       FF00    INKEY      EQU      *
00260  FF00 36                 PSH  A
00270  FF01 B6 0800 IN         LDA  A   KEYADR
00280  FF04 4D                 TST  A
00290  FF05 27 FA              BEQ      IN
00300  FF07 7D 0800 WAIT       TST      KEYADR    LOOK FOR KEYDOWN
00310  FF0A 26 FB              BNE      WAIT
00320  FF0C B7 0500            STA  A   BEEP
00330  FF0F 84 0F              AND  A   #$0F
00340  FF11 36                 PSH  A
00350  FF12 37                 PSH  B             PUT THESE AWAY FOR A SEC
00360  FF13 96 22              LDA  A   DBUF+1    GET LEAST SIG BYTE
00370  FF15 D6 21              LDA  B   DBUF      GET MSB
00380  FF17 48                 ASL  A
00390  FF18 59                 ROL  B
00400  FF19 48                 ASL  A
00410  FF1A 59                 ROL  B
00420  FF1B 48                 ASL  A
00430  FF1C 59                 ROL  B
00440  FF1D 48                 ASL  A             MOVING OVER A NYBBLE
00450  FF1E 59                 ROL  B
00460  FF1F 97 22              STA  A   DBUF+1
00470  FF21 D7 21              STA  B   DBUF      PUT ADJUSTED BUFFER IN BUF
00480  FF23 33                 PUL  B
00490  FF24 32                 PUL  A             GET B&A BACK
00500  FF25 9A 22              ORA  A   DBUF+1    PUT IN NEW CHARA
00510  FF27 97 22              STA  A   DBUF+1    STORE IN BUFFER
00520  FF29 32      FINISH     PUL  A
00530  FF2A 39                 RTS
```

FIGURE 7-6 (cont.)

```
00550                    *
00560                    * THIS IS MEMORY EXAMINE PGM
00570                    * ENTER HERE BY PRESSING
00580                    * "E"
00590                    *
00600        FF2B        EXAM   EQU    *
00610 FF2B DF 23                STX    TEMPX
00620 FF2D D6 24                LDA B  TEMPX+1 .
00630 FF2F D7 24         MODIFY STA B  TEMPX+1
00640 FF31 DE 23                LDX    TEMPX
00650 FF33 F7 0200              STA B  DISAD2
00660 FF36 A6 00                LDA A  0,X
00670 FF38 B7 0100              STA A  DISAD1
00680 FF3B 8D C3         LOOP1  BSR    INKEY
00690 FF3D 4D                   TST A
00700 FF3E 27 FB                BEQ    LOOP1
00710 FF40 81 0A                CMP A  #$A
00720 FF42 26 03                BNE    DECR
00730 FF44 5C           INCR    INC B
00740 FF45 20 E8                BRA    MODIFY
00750 FF47 81 0D        DECR    CMP A  #$D
00760 FF49 26 03                BNE    RETURN
00770 FF4B 5A                   DEC B
00780 FF4C 20 E1                BRA    MODIFY
00790 FF4E 81 0F        RETURN  CMP A  #$F
00800 FF50 26 F2                BNE    INCR
00810 FF52 7E FFA9              JMP    RENTRY
00820                    *
00830                    *
00840                    * MEMORY CHANGE PGM ENTER
00850                    * THIS BY PRESSING  THE
00860                    * "C"
00870                    *
00880        FF55        CHANGE EQU    *
00890 FF55 DF 23                STX    TEMPX
00900 FF57 D6 24                LDA B  TEMPX+1
00910 FF59 D7 24         MODIF  STA B  TEMPX+1
00920 FF5B DE 23                LDX    TEMPX
00930 FF5D F7 0200              STA B  DISAD2
00940 FF60 A6 00                LDA A  0,X
00950 FF62 B7 0100              STA A  DISAD1
00960 FF65 8D 99         LOOP2  BSR    INKEY
00970 FF67 4D                   TST A
00980 FF68 27 FB                BEQ    LOOP2
00990 FF6A 8D 94         LOOP3  BSR    INKEY
01000 FF6C 4D                   TST A
01010 FF6D 27 FB                BEQ    LOOP3
01020 FF6F 96 22                LDA A  DBUF+1
01030 FF71 97 25                STA A  DCNT
01040 FF73 8D 8B         LOOP4  BSR    INKEY    COMMAND KEY
01050 FF75 4D                   TST A
01060 FF76 27 FB                BEQ    LOOP4
01070 FF78 81 0E                CMP A  #$E
```

FIGURE 7-6 (cont.)

```
01090 FF7C 81 0A           CMP A  #$A
01100 FF7E 27 0F           BEQ    ENTRY1
01110 FF80 81 0D           CMP A  #$D
01120 FF82 27 0E           BEQ    ENTRY2
01130 FF84 81 0F           CMP A  #$F
01140 FF86 26 DD           BNE    LOOP2
01150 FF88 7E FFA9         JMP    RENTRY
01160 FF8B 96 25   ENTRY   LDA A  DCNT
01170 FF8D A7 00           STA A  0,X
01180 FF8F 5C     ENTRY1   INC B
01190 FF90 20 C7           BRA    MODIF
01200 FF92 5A     ENTRY2   DEC B
01210 FF93 20 C4           BRA    MODIF
01220                 *
01230                 *
01240                 * EXECUTE COMMAND ROUTINE
01250                 * ENTER THE USER PGM WITH
01260                 * AN "A"
01270                 *
01280       FF95     EXECU   EQU    *
01290 FF95 6E 00           JMP    0,X      PGM JMPS INX'D & RUNS
01300                 *
01310                 *
01320                 * DISPLAY ROUTINE DISP
01330                 *
01340 FF97 36       DISP    PSH A           PUTS DISPLAY UP
01350 FF98 37               PSH B
01360 FF99 96 21           LDA A  DBUF
01370 FF9B D6 22           LDA B  DBUF+1
01380 FF9D B7 0100         STA A  DISAD1
01390 FFA0 F7 0200         STA B  DISAD2
01400 FFA3 33              PUL B
01410 FFA4 32              PUL A
01420 FFA5 39       DONE    RTS
01430                 *
01440                 *
01450                 *
01460                 * MAIN ROUTINE PC-68
01470                 *
01480                 * THIS IS THE MAIN ROUTINE
01490                 * WHICH CALLS UP ALL THE
01500                 * OTHER ROUTINES FROM KEY
01510                 * ENTRIES.
01520                 *
01530                 *
01540 FFA6 8E 001F   START   LDS    #DFLAG-1
01550 FFA9 7F 0021   RENTRY  CLR    DBUF
01560 FFAC 8D E9             BSR    DISP
01570 FFAE C6 04             LDA B  #4
01580 FFB0 D7 25     INCH1   STA B  DCNT
01590 FFB2 D6 25     INCH    LDA B  DCNT
01600 FFB4 BD FF00           JSR    INKEY
01610 FFB7 8D DE             BSR    DISP
```

FIGURE 7-6 (cont,)

```
01630 FFBB 5A                DEC B
01640 FFBC 26 F2             BNE      INCH1
01650 FFBE DE 21             LDX      DBUF      PUTS ADDR IN X
01660 FFC0 BD FF00 CMND      JSR      INKEY
01670 FFC3 81 0F             CMP A    #$F
01680 FFC5 27 E2             BEQ      RENTRY
01690 FFC7 81 0E             CMP A    #$E
01700 FFC9 27 0A             BEQ      EXAM1
01710 FFCB 81 0C             CMP A    #$C
01720 FFCD 27 09             BEQ      CHNG1
01730 FFCF 81 0A             CMP A    #$A
01740 FFD1 27 C2             BEQ      EXECU
01750 FFD3 20 D4             BRA      RENTRY
01760 FFD5 7E FF2B EXAM1     JMP      EXAM
01770 FFD8 7E FF55 CHNG1     JMP      CHANGE
01780                        END
```

TOTAL ERRORS 00000

ENTER PASS : 1P,2P,2L,2T

Bibliography

ARNOLD, HALL, and NICHOLS. *Modern Data Processing,* 3rd ed. New York, N.Y.: Wiley, 1978.

BARNA and PORAT. *Introduction to Microcomputers and Microprocessors.* New York, N.Y.: Wiley, 1976.

BASILI and BAKER. *Structured Programming Tutorials.* Compcon '75, Washington, D.C., 1975.

BATES and DOUGLASS. *Programming Language One.* Englewood Cliffs, N.J.: Prentice-Hall, 1975.

BRADY. *The Theory of Computer Science.* London: Chapman and Hall, 1977.

HARMS and ZABINSKI. *Introduction to APL and Computer Programming.* New York, N.Y.: Wiley, 1977.

HUGHES and MICHTON. *A Structured Approach to Programming.* New York, N.Y.: Prentice-Hall, 1977.

LYNCH and RICE. *Computers, Their Impact and Use.* New York, N.Y.: Holt, Rinehart, and Winston, 1977.

POIROT and GROVES. *Computer Science for the Teacher.* Manhaca, Texas: Swift, 1976.

RAMDEN. *JCL and Advanced Fortran Programming.* New York, N.Y.: Elsevier Scientific Publications Company, 1976.

RAYWARD-SMITH, ed. *Proceedings of the Conference on Applications of Algol 68.* Norwich, England: British Computer Society, 1976.

STONE and SIEWIOREK. *Introduction to Computer Organization and Data Structures: PDP-11 Edition.* New York, N.Y.: McGraw-Hill, 1975.

Appendixes

Personal Computer Manufacturers

This is a partial listing of the manufacturers of personal computing systems and peripherals:

Apple Computer Inc.
10260 Bandley Drive
Cupertino, CA 95014
(408) 996-1010

Canada Systems, Inc.
1353 Foothill Blvd.
La Cañada, CA 91011
(213) 790-7957

Central Data Co.
P.O. Box 2484, Station A
Champaign, IL 61820
(217) 359-8010

Compal (Computer Power & Light)
12321 Ventura Blvd.
Studio City, CA 91604
(213) 760-3345

Compucolor Corp.
5965 Peachtree Corners East
Norcross, GA 30071
(404) 449-5961

Computalker Consultants
P.O. Box 1951

Santa Monica, CA 90406
(213) 392-5230

E & L Instruments
61 First Street
Derby, CT 06418
(203) 735-8774

Electronic Control Technology
763 Ramsey Avenue
Hillside, NJ 07205
(P.O.B. 6, Union, NJ 07083)
(201) 686-8080

Electronic Systems
P.O. Box 212
Burlingame, CA 94010
(408) 374-5984

General Micro-Systems
12369 W. Alabama Place
Lakewood, CO 80228
(303) 985-3423

Bill Godbout Electronics
Box 2355
Oakland Airport, CA 94614

The Heath Company
Benton Harbor, MI 49022
(616) 982-3417

IMSAI Mfg. Corp.
14860 Wicks Blvd.
San Leandro, CA
(415) 483-2093

Jade Computer Products
5351 West 144th
Lawndale, CA 90260
(213) 679-3313

Midwest Scientific Instruments, Inc.
220 W. Cedar St.
Olathe, KS 66061
(913) 764-3273

North Star Computers, Inc.
2547 Ninth Street
Berkeley, CA 94710
(415) 549-0858

Noval, Inc.
8401 Aero Drive
San Diego, CA 92123
(714) 277-8700

OAE (Oliver Advanced Engineering)
676 West Wilson Avenue
Glendale, CA 91203
(213) 240-0080

Ohio Scientific
Box 36
Hiram, OH 44234
(216) 562-3101

PCS (Processor Control Systems)
Box 544
Celoron, NY 14720
(716) 664-2871

Percom Data Co., Inc.
318 Barnes
Garland, TX 75042
(214) 276-1968

Quay Corp.
P.O. Box 386
Freehold, NJ 97728
(201) 681-8700

Radio Shack
One Tandy Center
Fort Worth, TX 76102

SD Computer Products
Div. SD Sales
P.O. Box 28810
Dallas, TX 75228
(214) 271-4667
(800) 527-3460

Seals Electronics, Inc.
10728 Dutchtown Rd.
Concord, TN 37922
(615) 966-8771

Shugart Assoc.
435 Oakmead Pkwy.
Sunnyvale, CA 94086
(408) 733-0100

Smoke Signal Broadcasting
6304 Yucca
Hollywood, CA 90028
(213) 462-5652

Solid State Sales
P.O. Box 74
Somerville, MA 02143
(617) 547-4005

Southwest Technical Products Corp.
219 W. Rhapsody
San Antonio, TX 78216
(512) 344-9778

TEI Inc.
c/o CMC Marketing Corp.
5601 Bintliff #515
Houston, TX 77036
(713) 783-8880

Thinker Toys
1201 10th Street.
Berkeley, CA 94710
(415) 527-7548

Vector Electronics Co., Inc.
12460 Gladstone Avenue
Sylmar, CA 91342
(213) 365-9661

Vector Graphic, Inc.
790 Hampshire Road A&B
Westlake Village, CA 91361
(805) 497-6853

Wave Mate
1015 W. 190th Street
Gardena, CA 90248
(213) 329-8941

Numbering Systems

Because a personal computer does not have ten fingers to count with, we have developed other numbering systems more appropriate for it to work with. Basically, computers like the microprocessor work in binary. The binary number system is one of the easiest to understand since it only has two digits to be concerned with. A binary progression compares with the decimal progression like this: First comes 0, then 1, just like their decimal equivalents. The binary equivalent to the decimal 2 is 10, however. No, that's not ten, it is 1–0, or one–zero. When one is talking binary, one must remember that there is a rather significant difference between reading the number one–zero as ten and its equivalent two.

So far we have tried only to limit the number of discrete steps we are using to represent given numbers. We cannot try to limit the number of places necessary for our numbering system. For instance in decimal the number 33 takes up only two places while in binary the same number equivalent is 100001. In binary, we must use up six places to represent the two places in the decimal equivalent. Although binary is simple in one respect, there will have to be a price paid in writing out the binary numbers. Basically, the larger the number base, the fewer places it takes to represent a given number.

In decimal arithmetic, each place to the left or right of the decimal point represents some power of the base number 10 (ten this time). In binary, on the other hand, we are using a power of the base 2 and every place to the right or left of the decimal point represents a power of the base 2. To clear up confusing differences in number base understanding when many bases are being used interchangeably within the same text, we show the base with a subscript; thus in binary, a 2 is written 10_2 while the decimal 10 is written 10_{10}.

Here is where we have come so far: To analyze the number 33_{10} we start with the least significant digit (the 3 on the right) and we know that this represents three of the number that is equivalent to ten to some power. In this position the power of ten is zero, or 10^0. Since any number to the zero power is equal to 1, we say we have three 1's in our number 33_{10}. The next position to the left of the decimal in 33_{10} is another 3; this time it stands for the power of ten that comes next, and that's 10^1. Any number to the first power is that number itself, or this time we are looking at the tens digit. Now our number 33_{10} is made up of three 10's (30) and three is (3) and 30 + 3 = 33!

You analyze the binary number equivalent to the 33 in the same way. This time the number is 100001_2 and the rightmost digit will again be the ones digit ($2^0 = 1$). The next digit to the left will be 2^1 or the twos digit. We progress on and on to the sixth position. Coming up with the number is easy if you keep in mind that you are doubling your number each time you move to the left. You start with the ones place then move left doubling to 2, 4, 8, 16, 32, and so on. To break down the 100001_2 to its equivalent, you start on the left; we have one 1, no 2's, no 4's, no 8's, no 16's, one 32, and that adds up to $32_{10} + 1_{10} = 33_{10}$, and the conversion from binary to decimal is complete.

Of course, there are more numbering systems. We could just as easily have used the number base 3 and have come up with a number base system. It would be a little strange though because not only don't people have three digits on the hand (three fingers), but computers work only on high and low or on and off states. You could count power off as a third state, but you find it hard to operate the computer in the power off condition anyway. The most practical systems for computers are multiples of the binary base 2. One of these multiples of 2 that is particularly handy for computers is the third power of 2, the base 8.

The base 8 is practical in computers because it eliminates some of the places needed with binary in writing out large numbers and because a typical computer byte is 8-bits long. The number 256_{10} is 11111111 in binary and is 377 in octal, or base 8. Note that we still haven't saved any places over the decimal system, but we certainly saved a lot of places over the binary system. Although the octal counting system is thrifty on digits, it doesn't compare to its near brother, the hexadecimal system.

Although octal numbering is popular in some computers, the most popular computer numbering system is the hexadecimal system that uses a base higher than 10 so it is even a shorthand system when compared to decimal. Hex numbers are the base 6 (hex) and the base 10 (decimal) combined for the base 16. Hex 256_{10} simply becomes FF so you save lots of room. You think FF doesn't look like a number? It is—in hex. Look at what happens to a normal number count in hex compared with a decimal count. The digits, 0, 1, 2, 3, 4, 5, 6, 7, 8, and 9 are the same in both hex and in decimal. The difference occurs after 9_{10}. You have just run out of digits in the decimal system, and you still have five numbers to go in the base 16. The hex numbering system fills in the next five places with the letters A through F (always capitals). Now as we continue to count the decimal numbers up to 15 we get (starting at 10_{10}): A, B, C, D, E, and F. Thus, it is not unusual to see hex numbers like CAD and DAD, although commonly hex numbers will appear in groups of two (8 bits) and four (16 bits) when being used with 8-bit personal computer systems. To change from hex to decimal, just make the change keeping in mind that A–F have their respective decimal equivalents. Going from binary to hex and hex to binary is really very simple. That is part of what makes hex so easy to use when working with computers.

From our previous example of binary:100001_2 to hex is easily executed. You have 2^4 (16) different possibilities for each hex digit 0–F. So you just divide the binary number into groups of four. In the example, you will get one four-place number and one two-place number that can be made into a four placer by adding zeros on the left. Starting from the right and moving left we get 0001. That is simply equivalent to a hex 1. Now the left set of four are only 10. By adding zeros we get 0010. This is a hex and decimal 2. So in hex our $100001_2,33_{10}$, is 21. With practice you should be able to look at a number like 21_{16} and see that you have two 16's and one 1 for 33_{10}.

With practice, you can develop strong skills in working with hexadecimal numbers. Use hex numbers and learn to convert them without tables, although tables make larger numbers easier for you to work with. By remembering your powers of 2 and that hex numbers are four binary places long, the conversions are quick and simple in most cases.

CONVERSION TABLE FOR HEX TO DECIMAL AND BINARY NUMBERING SYSTEM

How to Convert to Decimal.   Find the decimal weights for corresponding hexadecimal characters, beginning with the least significant character. The sum of the decimal weights is the decimal value of the hexadecimal number.

How to Convert to Hexadecimal.   Find the highest decimal value in the table which is lower than or equal to the decimal number to be converted. The corresponding hexadecimal character is the most significant character. Subtract the decimal value found from the decimal number to be converted. With the difference, repeat the process to find subsequent hexadecimal characters.

POWERS OF TWO

2^n	n
1	0
2	1
4	2
8	3
16	4
32	5
64	6
128	7
256	8
512	9
1,024	10
2,048	11
4,096	12
8,192	13
16,384	14
32,768	15
65,536	16
131,072	17
262,144	18
524,288	19
1,048,576	20

HEXADECIMAL AND DECIMAL CONVERSION TABLE

15	BYTE		8	7	BYTE		0
15	CHAR	12	11 CHAR 8	7	CHAR	4	3 CHAR 0
HEX		DEC	HEX	DEC	HEX	DEC	HEX	DEC

HEX	DEC	HEX	DEC	HEX	DEC	HEX	DEC
0	0	0	0	0	0	0	0
1	4 096	1	256	1	16	1	1
2	8 192	2	512	2	32	2	2
3	12 288	3	768	3	48	3	3
4	16 384	4	1 024	4	64	4	4
5	20 480	5	1 280	5	80	5	5
6	24 576	6	1 536	6	96	6	6
7	28 672	7	1 792	7	112	7	7
8	32 768	8	2 048	8	128	8	8
9	36 864	9	2 304	9	144	9	9
A	40 960	A	2 560	A	160	A	10
B	45 066	B	2 816	B	176	B	11
C	49 152	C	3 072	C	182	C	12
D	53 248	D	3 328	D	208	D	13
E	57 344	E	3 584	E	224	E	14
F	61 440	F	3 840	F	240	F	15

ASCII Conversion Table

ASC II CONVERSION TABLE

LSB \ MSB	0	1	2	3	4	5	6	7
0	NUL	DLE	SP	0	@	P	`	p
1	SOH	DC1	!	1	A	Q	a	q
2	STX	DC2	''	2	B	R	b	r
3	ETX	DC3	#	3	C	S	c	s
4	EOT	DC4	$	4	D	T	d	t
5	END	NAK	%	5	E	U	e	u
6	ACK	SYN	&	6	F	V	f	v
7	BEL	ETB	'	7	G	W	g	w
8	BS	CAN	(	8	H	X	h	x
9	HT	EM	)	9	I	Y	i	y
A	LF	SUB	*	:	J	Z	j	z
B	VT	ESC	+	;	K	[	k	{
C	FF	FS	,	<	L	\	l	/
D	CR	GS	–	=	M	]	m	}
E	SO	RS	.	>	N	^	n	~
F	SI	US	/	?	O	_	o	DEL

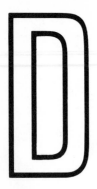

6800 Family
Specification Sheets

Here are abbreviated specification sheets for the members of the M6800 microprocessor family used extensively in the text of this book. They are reprinted here with the permission of Motorola, Inc., Semiconductor Group.

   Also included in this Appendix is the listing of the MIKBUG ROM, which has become a personal computer industry standard operating system for the 6800 microprocessor.

MC6800
(1.0 MHz)

MC68A00
(1.5 MHz)

MC68B00
(2.0 MHz)

8-BIT MICROPROCESSING UNIT (MPU)

The MC6800 is a monolithic 8-bit microprocessor forming the central control function for Motorola's M6800 family. Compatible with TTL, the MC6800, as with all M6800 system parts, requires only one +5.0-volt power supply, and no external TTL devices for bus interface.

The MC6800 is capable of addressing 65K bytes of memory with its 16-bit address lines. The 8-bit data bus is bidirectional as well as 3-state, making direct memory addressing and multiprocessing applications realizable.

- Eight-Bit Parallel Processing
- Bidirectional Data Bus
- Sixteen-Bit Address Bus — 65K Bytes of Addressing
- 72 Instructions — Variable Length
- Seven Addressing Modes — Direct, Relative, Immediate, Indexed, Extended, Implied and Accumulator
- Variable Length Stack
- Vectored Restart
- Maskable Interrupt Vector
- Separate Non-Maskable Interrupt — Internal Registers Saved in Stack
- Six Internal Registers — Two Accumulators, Index Register, Program Counter, Stack Pointer and Condition Code Register
- Direct Memory Addressing (DMA) and Multiple Processor Capability
- Simplified Clocking Characteristics
- Clock Rates as High as 2.0 MHz
- Simple Bus Interface Without TTL
- Halt and Single Instruction Execution Capability

MOS
(N-CHANNEL, SILICON-GATE, DEPLETION LOAD)

MICROPROCESSOR

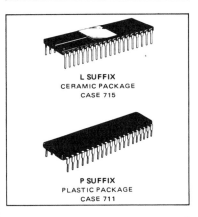

L SUFFIX
CERAMIC PACKAGE
CASE 715

P SUFFIX
PLASTIC PACKAGE
CASE 711

PIN ASSIGNMENT

1	V_{SS}	Reset 40
2	$\overline{Halt}$	TSC 39
3	$\phi1$	N.C. 38
4	$\overline{IRQ}$	$\phi2$ 37
5	VMA	DBE 36
6	$\overline{NMI}$	N.C. 35
7	BA	R/W 34
8	V_{CC}	D0 33
9	A0	D1 32
10	A1	D2 31
11	A2	D3 30
12	A3	D4 29
13	A4	D5 28
14	A5	D6 27
15	A6	D7 26
16	A7	A15 25
17	A8	A14 24
18	A9	A13 23
19	A10	A12 22
20	A11	V_{SS} 21

ORDERING INFORMATION

Speed	Device	Temperature Range
1.0 MHz	MC6800P,L	0 to 70°C
	MC6800CP,CL	−40 to +85°C
MIL-STD-883B	MC6800BQCS	−55 to +125°C
MIL-STD-883C	MC6800CQCS	
1.5 MHz	MC68A00P,L	0 to +70°C
	MC68A00CP,CL	−40 to +85°C
2.0 MHz	MC68B00P,L	0 to +70°C

TABLE 1 — MAXIMUM RATINGS

Rating	Symbol	Value	Unit
Supply Voltage	V_{CC}	−0.3 to +7.0	Vdc
Input Voltage	V_{in}	−0.3 to +7.0	Vdc
Operating Temperature Range—T_L to T_H MC6800, MC68A00, MC68B00 MC6800C, MC68A00C MC6800BQCS, MC6800CQCS	T_A	 0 to +70 −40 to +85 −55 to +125	°C
Storage Temperature Range	T_{stg}	−55 to +150	°C
Thermal Resistance Plastic Package Ceramic Package	θ_{JA}	 70 50	°C/W

This device contains circuitry to protect the inputs against damage due to high static voltages or electric fields; however, it is advised that normal precautions be taken to avoid application of any voltage higher than maximum rated voltages to this high impedance circuit.

TABLE 2 — ELECTRICAL CHARACTERISTICS (V_{CC} = 5.0 V, ± 5%, V_{SS} = 0, T_A = T_L to T_H unless otherwise noted)

Characteristic		Symbol	Min	Typ	Max	Unit
Input High Voltage	Logic	V_{IH}	V_{SS} + 2.0	—	V_{CC}	Vdc
	$\phi1,\phi2$	V_{IHC}	V_{CC} − 0.6	—	V_{CC} + 0.3	
Input Low Voltage	Logic	V_{IL}	V_{SS} − 0.3	—	V_{SS} + 0.8	Vdc
	$\phi1,\phi2$	V_{ILC}	V_{SS} − 0.3	—	V_{SS} + 0.4	
Input Leakage Current		I_{in}				µAdc
(V_{in} = 0 to 5.25 V, V_{CC} = max)	Logic*		—	1.0	2.5	
(V_{in} = 0 to 5.25 V, V_{CC} = 0.0 V)	$\phi1,\phi2$		—	—	100	
Three-State (Off State) Input Current	D0–D7	I_{TSI}	—	2.0	10	µAdc
(V_{in} = 0.4 to 2.4 V, V_{CC} = max)	A0–A15, R/$\overline{W}$		—	—	100	
Output High Voltage		V_{OH}				Vdc
(I_{Load} = −205 µAdc, V_{CC} = min)	D0–D7		V_{SS} + 2.4	—	—	
(I_{Load} = −145 µAdc, V_{CC} = min)	A0–A15, R/$\overline{W}$, VMA		V_{SS} + 2.4	—	—	
(I_{Load} = −100 µAdc, V_{CC} = min)	BA		V_{SS} + 2.4	—	—	
Output Low Voltage (I_{Load} = 1.6 mAdc, V_{CC} = min)		V_{OL}	—	—	V_{SS} + 0.4	Vdc
Power Dissipation		P_D	—	0.5	1.0	W
Capacitance		C_{in}				pF
(V_{in} = 0, T_A = 25°C, f = 1.0 MHz)	$\phi1$		—	25	35	
	$\phi2$		—	45	70	
	D0–D7		—	10	12.5	
	Logic Inputs		—	6.5	10	
	A0–A15, R/$\overline{W}$, VMA	C_{out}	—	—	12	pF

TABLE 3 — CLOCK TIMING (V_{CC} = 5.0 V, ±5%, V_{SS} = 0, T_A = T_L to T_H unless otherwise noted)

Characteristics		Symbol	Min	Typ	Max	Unit
Frequency of Operation	MC6800	f	0.1	—	1.0	MHz
	MC68A00		0.1	—	1.5	
	MC68B00		0.1	—	2.0	
Cycle Time (Figure 1)	MC6800	t_{cyc}	1.000	—	10	µs
	MC68A00		0.666	—	10	
	MC68B00		0.500	—	10	
Clock Pulse Width	$\phi1,\phi2$ — MC6800	$PW_{\phi H}$	400	—	9500	ns
(Measured at V_{CC} − 0.6 V)	$\phi1,\phi2$ — MC68A00		230	—	9500	
	$\phi1,\phi2$ — MC68B00		180	—	9500	
Total $\phi1$ and $\phi2$ Up Time	MC6800	t_{ut}	900	—	—	ns
	MC68A00		600	—	—	
	MC68B00		440	—	—	
Rise and Fall Times		$t_{\phi r}, t_{\phi f}$	—	—	100	ns
(Measured between V_{SS} + 0.4 and V_{CC} − 0.6)						
Delay Time or Clock Separation (Figure 1)		t_d				ns
(Measured at V_{OV} = V_{SS} + 0.6 V @ t_r = t_f ≤ 100 ns)			0	—	9100	
(Measured at V_{OV} = V_{SS} + 1.0 V @ t_r = t_f ≤ 35 ns)			0	—	9100	

TABLE 4 – READ/WRITE TIMING (Reference Figures 2 through 6)

Characteristic	Symbol	MC6800			MC68A00			MC68B00			Unit
		Min	Typ	Max	Min	Typ	Max	Min	Typ	Max	
Address Delay	t_{AD}										ns
C = 90 pF		–	–	270	–	–	180	–	–	150	
C = 30 pF		–	–	250	–	–	165	–	–	135	
Peripheral Read Access Time	t_{acc}	–	–	530	–	–	360	–	–	250	ns
$t_{ac} = t_{ut} - (t_{AD} + t_{DSR})$											
Data Setup Time (Read)	t_{DSR}	100	–	–	60	–	–	40	–	–	ns
Input Data Hold Time	t_H	10	–	–	10	–	–	10	–	–	ns
Output Data Hold Time	t_H	10	25	–	10	25	–	10	25	–	ns
Address Hold Time	t_{AH}	30	50	–	30	50	–	30	50	–	ns
(Address, R/W̄, VMA)											
Enable High Time for DBE Input	t_{EH}	450	–	–	280	–	–	220	–	–	ns
Data Delay Time (Write)	t_{DDW}	–	–	225	–	–	200	–	–	160	ns
Processor Controls											
Processor Control Setup Time	t_{PCS}	200	–	–	140	–	–	110	–	–	ns
Processor Control Rise and	t_{PCr}, t_{PCf}	–	–	100	–	–	100	–	–	100	ns
Fall Time											
Bus Available Delay	t_{BA}	–	–	250	–	–	165	–	–	135	ns
Three-State Delay	t_{TSD}	–	–	270	–	–	270	–	–	220	ns
Data Bus Enable Down Time	$t_{\overline{DBE}}$	150	–	–	120	–	–	75	–	–	ns
During φ1 Up Time											
Data Bus Enable Rise and	t_{DBEr}, t_{DBEf}	–	–	25	–	–	25	–	–	25	ns
Fall Times											

FIGURE 1 – CLOCK TIMING WAVEFORM

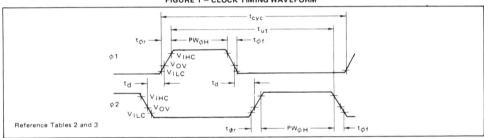

Reference Tables 2 and 3

FIGURE 2 – READ DATA FROM MEMORY OR PERIPHERALS

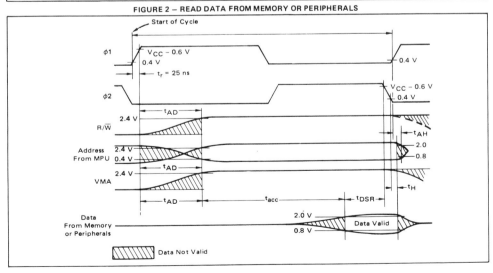

FIGURE 3 — WRITE IN MEMORY OR PERIPHERALS

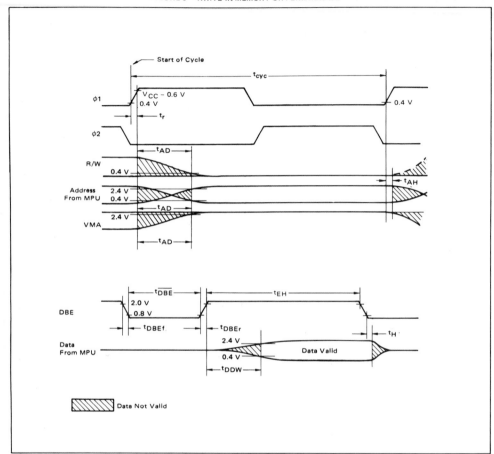

FIGURE 4 — TYPICAL DATA BUS OUTPUT DELAY
versus CAPACITIVE LOADING (T_{DDW})

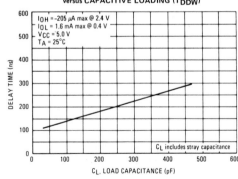

FIGURE 5 — TYPICAL READ/WRITE, VMA, AND ADDRESS
OUTPUT DELAY versus CAPACITIVE LOADING (T_{AD})

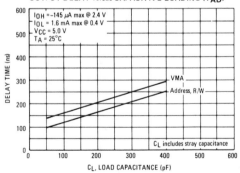

FIGURE 6 – BUS TIMING TEST LOADS

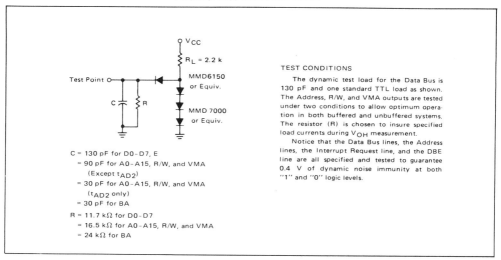

TEST CONDITIONS

The dynamic test load for the Data Bus is 130 pF and one standard TTL load as shown. The Address, R/W, and VMA outputs are tested under two conditions to allow optimum operation in both buffered and unbuffered systems. The resistor (R) is chosen to insure specified load currents during V_{OH} measurement.

Notice that the Data Bus lines, the Address lines, the Interrupt Request line, and the DBE line are all specified and tested to guarantee 0.4 V of dynamic noise immunity at both "1" and "0" logic levels.

FIGURE 7 – EXPANDED BLOCK DIAGRAM

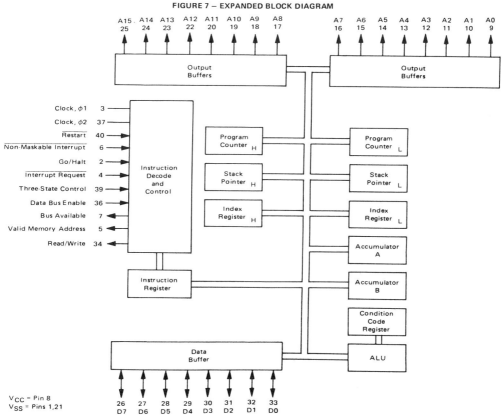

MPU SIGNAL DESCRIPTION

Proper operation of the MPU requires that certain control and timing signals be provided to accomplish specific functions and that other signal lines be monitored to determine the state of the processor.

Clocks Phase One and Phase Two ($\phi1,\phi2$) — Two pins are used for a two-phase non-overlapping clock that runs at the V_{CC} voltage level.

Figure 1 shows the microprocessor clocks, and Table 3 shows the static and dynamic clock specifications. The high level is specified at V_{IHC} and the low level is specified at V_{ILC}. The allowable clock frequency is specified by f (frequency). The minimum $\phi1$ and $\phi2$ high level pulse widths are specified by $PW_{\phi H}$ (pulse width high time). To guarantee the required access time for the peripherals, the clock up time, t_{ut}, is specified. Clock separation, t_d, is measured at a maximum voltage of V_{OV} (overlap voltage). This allows for a multitude of clock variations at the system frequency rate.

Address Bus (A0–A15) — Sixteen pins are used for the address bus. The outputs are three-state bus drivers capable of driving one standard TTL load and 90 pF. When the output is turned off, it is essentially an open circuit. This permits the MPU to be used in DMA applications. Putting TSC in its high state forces the Address bus to go into the three-state mode.

Data Bus (D0–D7) — Eight pins are used for the data bus. It is bidirectional, transferring data to and from the memory and peripheral devices. It also has three-state output buffers capable of driving one standard TTL load and 130 pF. Data Bus is placed in the three-state mode when DBE is low.

Data Bus Enable (DBE) — This input is the three-state control signal for the MPU data bus and will enable the bus drivers when in the high state. This input is TTL compatible; however in normal operation, it would be driven by the phase two clock. During an MPU read cycle, the data bus drivers will be disabled internally. When it is desired that another device control the data bus such as in Direct Memory Access (DMA) applications, DBE should be held low.

If additional data setup or hold time is required on an MPU write, the DBE down time can be decreased as shown in Figure 3 (DBE $\neq \phi2$). The minimum down time for DBE is $t_{\overline{DBE}}$ as shown and must occur within $\phi1$ up time. The minimum delay from the trailing edge of DBE to the trailing edge of $\phi1$ is t_{DBED}. By skewing DBE with respect to E in this manner, data setup or hold time can be increased.

Bus Available (BA) — The Bus Available signal will normally be in the low state; when activated, it will go to the high state indicating that the microprocessor has stopped and that the address bus is available. This will occur if the Halt line is in the low state or the processor is in the WAIT state as a result of the execution of a WAIT instruction. At such time, all three-state output drivers will go to their off state and other outputs to their normally inactive level. The processor is removed from the WAIT state by the occurrence of a maskable (mask bit I = 0) or nonmaskable interrupt. This output is capable of driving one standard TTL load and 30 pF. If TSC is in the high state, Bus Available will be low.

Read/Write (R/W̄) — This TTL compatible output signals the peripherals and memory devices whether the MPU is in a Read (high) or Write (low) state. The normal standby state of this signal is Read (high). Three-State Control going high will turn Read/Write to the off (high impedance) state. Also, when the processor is halted, it will be in the off state. This output is capable of driving one standard TTL load and 90 pF.

Reset — The Reset input is used to reset and start the MPU from a power down condition resulting from a power failure or initial start-up of the processor. This input can also be used to reinitialize the machine at any time after start-up.

If a high level is detected in this input, this will signal the MPU to begin the reset sequence. During the reset sequence, the contents of the last two locations (FFFE, FFFF) in memory will be loaded into the Program Counter to point to the beginning of the reset routine. During the reset routine, the interrupt mask bit is set and must be cleared under program control before the MPU can be interrupted by IRQ. While Reset is low (assuming a minimum of 8 clock cycles have occurred) the MPU output signals will be in the following states: VMA = low, BA = low, Data Bus = high impedance, R/W̄ = high (read state), and the Address Bus will contain the reset address FFFE. Figure 8 illustrates a power up sequence using the Reset control line. After the power supply reaches 4.75 V a minimum of eight clock cycles are required for the processor to stabilize in preparation for restarting. During these eight cycles, VMA will be in an indeterminate state so any devices that are enabled by VMA which could accept a false write during this time (such as a battery-backed RAM) must be disabled until VMA is forced low after eight cycles. Reset can go high asynchronously with the system clock any time after the eighth cycle.

Reset timing is shown in Figure 8 and Table 4. The maximum rise and fall transition times are specified by t_{PCr} and t_{PCf}. If Reset is high at t_{PCS} (processor control setup time) as shown in Figure 8 in any given cycle, then the restart sequence will begin on the next cycle as shown. The Reset control line may also be used to reinitialize the MPU system at any time during its operation. This is accomplished by pulsing Reset low for the duration of a minimum of three complete $\phi2$ cycles. The Reset pulse can be completely asynchronous with the MPU system clock and will be recognized during $\phi2$ if setup time t_{PCS} is met.

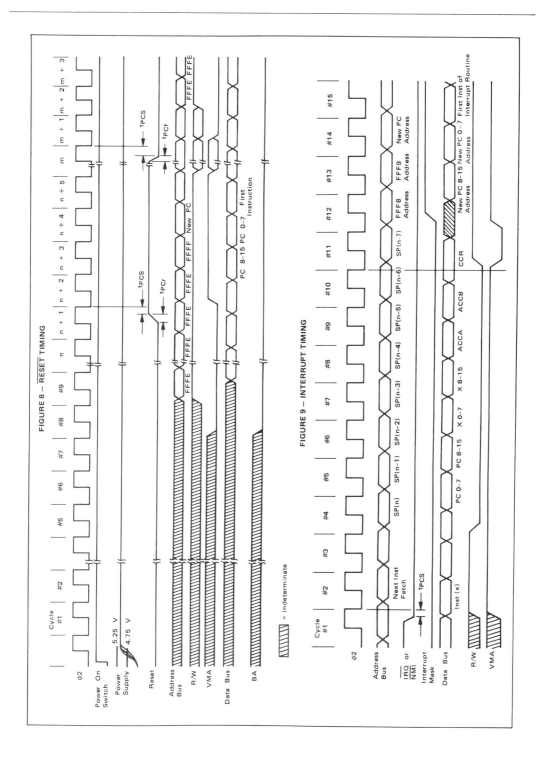

FIGURE 8 – RESET TIMING

FIGURE 9 – INTERRUPT TIMING

Interrupt Request (IRQ) — This level sensitive input requests that an interrupt sequence be generated within the machine. The processor will wait until it completes the current instruction that is being executed before it recognizes the request. At that time, if the interrupt mask bit in the Condition Code Register is not set, the machine will begin an interrupt sequence. The Index Register, Program Counter, Accumulators, and Condition Code Register are stored away on the stack. Next the MPU will respond to the interrupt request by setting the interrupt mask bit high so that no further interrupts may occur. At the end of the cycle, a 16-bit address will be loaded that points to a vectoring address which is located in memory locations FFF8 and FFF9. An address loaded at these locations causes the MPU to branch to an interrupt routine in memory. Interrupt timing is shown in Figure 9.

The Halt line must be in the high state for interrupts to be serviced. Interrupts will be latched internally while Halt is low.

The IRQ has a high impedance pullup device internal to the chip; however a 3 kΩ external resistor to V_{CC} should be used for wire-OR and optimum control of interrupts.

Non-Maskable Interrupt (NMI) and Wait for Interrupt (WAI) — The MC6800 is capable of handling two types of interrupts: maskable (IRQ) as described earlier, and non-maskable (NMI). IRQ is maskable by the interrupt mask in the condition code register while NMI is not maskable. The handling of these interrupts by the MPU is the same except that each has its own vector address. The behavior of the MPU when interrupted is shown in Figure 9 which details the MPU response to an interrupt while the MPU is executing the control program. The interrupt shown could be either IRQ or NMI and can be asynchronous with respect to $\phi2$. The interrupt is shown going low at time t_{PCS} in cycle #1 which precedes the first cycle of an instruction (OP code fetch). This instruction is not executed but instead the Program Counter (PC), Index Register (IX), Accumulators (ACCX), and the Condition Code Register (CCR) are pushed onto the stack.

The Interrupt Mask bit is set to prevent further interrupts. The address of the interrupt service routine is then fetched from FFFC, FFFD for an NMI interrupt and from FFF8, FFF9 for an IRQ interrupt. Upon completion of the interrupt service routine, the execution of RTI will pull the PC, IX, ACCX, and CCR off of the stack; the Interrupt Mask bit is restored to its condition prior to Interrupts.

Figure 11 is a similar interrupt sequence, except in this case, a WAIT instruction has been executed in preparation for the interrupt. This technique speeds up the MPU's response to the interrupt because the stacking of the PC, IX, ACCX, and the CCR is already done. While the MPU is waiting for the interrupt, Bus Available will go high indicating the following states of the control lines: VMA is low, and the Address Bus, R/W and Data Bus are all in the high impedance state. After the interrupt occurs, it is serviced as previously described.

TABLE 1 — MEMORY MAP FOR INTERRUPT VECTORS

Vector		Description
MS	**LS**	
FFFE	FFFF	Restart
FFFC	FFFD	Non-maskable Interrupt
FFFA	FFFB	Software Interrupt
FFF8	FFF9	Interrupt Request

Refer to Figure 11 for program flow for Interrupts.

Three State Control (TSC) — When the Three-State Control (TSC) line is a logic "1", the Address Bus and the R/W line are placed in a high impedance state. VMA and BA are forced low when TSC = "1" to prevent false reads or writes on any device enabled by VMA. It is necessary to delay program execution while TSC is held high. This is done by insuring that no transitions of $\phi1$ (or $\phi2$) occur during this period. (Logic levels of the clocks are irrelevant so long as they do not change.) Since the MPU is a dynamic device, the $\phi1$ clock can be stopped for a maximum time $PW_{\phi H}$ without destroying data within the MPU. TSC then can be used in a short Direct Memory Access (DMA) application.

Figure 12 shows the effect of TSC on the MPU. TSC must have its transitions at t_{TSE} (three-state enable) while holding $\phi1$ high and $\phi2$ low as shown. The Address Bus and R/W line will reach the high impedance state at t_{TSD} (three-state delay), with VMA being forced low. In this example, the Data Bus is also in the high impedance state while $\phi2$ is being held low since DBE = $\phi2$. At this point in time, a DMA transfer could occur on cycles #3 and #4. When TSC is returned low, the MPU Address and R/W lines return to the bus. Because it is too late in cycle #5 to access memory, this cycle is dead and used for synchronization. Program execution resumes in cycle #6.

Valid Memory Address (VMA) — This output indicates to peripheral devices that there is a valid address on the address bus. In normal operation, this signal should be utilized for enabling peripheral interfaces such as the PIA and ACIA. This signal is not three-state. One standard TTL load and 90 pF may be directly driven by this active high signal.

Halt — When this input is in the low state, all activity in the machine will be halted. This input is level sensitive.

The Halt line provides an input to the MPU to allow control of program execution by an outside source. If Halt is high, the MPU will execute the instructions; if it is low, the MPU will go to a halted or idle mode. A response signal, Bus Available (BA) provides an indication of the current MPU status. When BA is low, the MPU is in the process of executing the control program; if BA is high, the MPU has halted and all internal activity has stopped.

When BA is high, the Address Bus, Data Bus, and R/W line will be in a high impedance state, effectively removing the MPU from the system bus. VMA is forced low so that the floating system bus will not activate any device on the bus that is enabled by VMA.

FIGURE 10 – MPU FLOW CHART

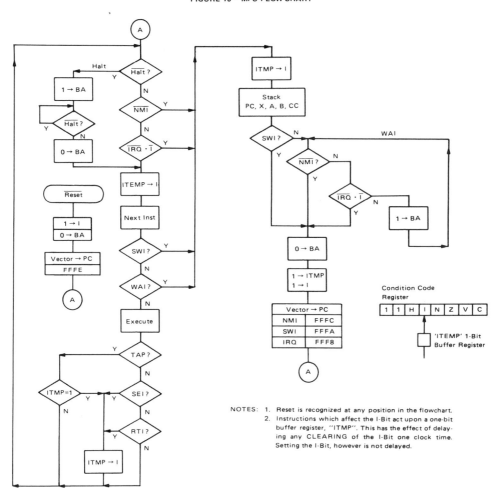

NOTES: 1. Reset is recognized at any position in the flowchart.
        2. Instructions which affect the I-Bit act upon a one-bit
            buffer register, "ITMP". This has the effect of delay-
            ing any CLEARING of the I-Bit one clock time.
            Setting the I-Bit, however is not delayed.

While the MPU is halted, all program activity is stopped, and if either an $\overline{\text{NMI}}$ or $\overline{\text{IRQ}}$ interrupt occurs, it will be latched into the MPU and acted on as soon as the MPU is taken out of the halted mode. If a $\overline{\text{Reset}}$ command occurs while the MPU is halted, the following states occur: VMA = low, BA = low, Data Bus = high impedance, R/$\overline{\text{W}}$ = high (read state), and the Address Bus will contain address FFFE as long as $\overline{\text{Reset}}$ is low. As soon as the Halt line goes high, the MPU will go to locations FFFE and FFFF for the address of the reset routine.

Figure 13 shows the timing relationships involved when halting the MPU. The instruction illustrated is a one byte, 2 cycle instruction such as CLRA. When $\overline{\text{Halt}}$ goes low, the MPU will halt after completing execution of the current instruction. The transition of $\overline{\text{Halt}}$ must occur t_{PCS} before the trailing edge of $\phi1$ of the last cycle of an instruction (point A of Figure 13). $\overline{\text{Halt}}$ must not go low any time later than the minimum t_{PCS} specified.

The fetch of the OP code by the MPU is the first cycle of the instruction. If $\overline{\text{Halt}}$ had not been low at Point A but went low during $\phi2$ of that cycle, the MPU would have halted after completion of the following instruction. BA will go high by time t_{BA} (bus available delay time) after the last instruction cycle. At this point in time, VMA is low and R/$\overline{\text{W}}$, Address Bus, and the Data Bus are in the high impedance state.

To debug programs it is advantageous to step through programs instruction by instruction. To do this, $\overline{\text{Halt}}$ must be brought high for one MPU cycle and then returned low as shown at point B of Figure 13. Again, the transitions of $\overline{\text{Halt}}$ must occur t_{PCS} before the trailing edge of $\phi1$. BA will go low at t_{BA} after the leading edge of the next $\phi1$, indicating that the Address Bus, Data Bus, VMA and R/$\overline{\text{W}}$ lines are back on the bus. A single byte, 2 cycle instruction such as LSR is used for this example also. During the first cycle, the instruction Y is fetched from address M + 1. BA returns high at t_{BA} on the last cycle of the instruction indicating the MPU is off the bus. If instruction Y had been three cycles, the width of the BA low time would have been increased by one cycle.

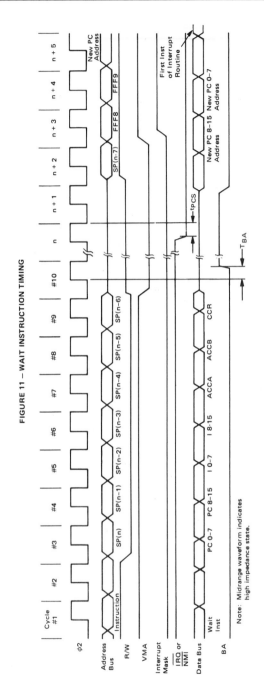

FIGURE 11 – WAIT INSTRUCTION TIMING

FIGURE 12 — THREE STATE CONTROL TIMING

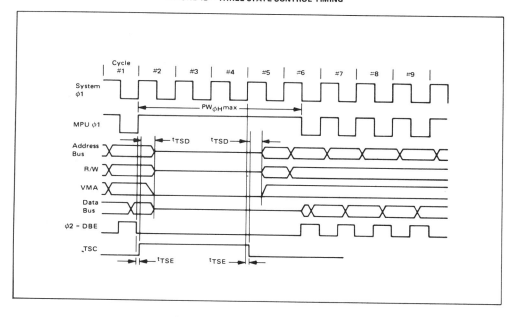

FIGURE 13 — $\overline{\text{HALT}}$ AND SINGLE INSTRUCTION EXECUTION FOR SYSTEM DEBUG

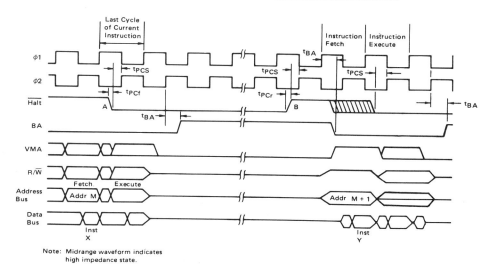

Note: Midrange waveform indicates
high impedance state.

MPU REGISTERS

The MPU has three 16-bit registers and three 8-bit registers available for use by the programmer (Figure 14).

Program Counter — The program counter is a two byte (16 bits) register that points to the current program address.

Stack Pointer — The stack pointer is a two byte register that contains the address of the next available location in an external push-down/pop-up stack. This stack is normally a random access Read/Write memory that may have any location (address) that is convenient. In those applications that require storage of information in the stack when power is lost, the stack must be nonvolatile.

Index Register — The index register is a two byte register that is used to store data or a sixteen bit memory address for the Indexed mode of memory addressing.

Accumulators — The MPU contains two 8-bit accumulators that are used to hold operands and results from an arithmetic logic unit (ALU).

Condition Code Register — The condition code register indicates the results of an Arithmetic Logic Unit operation: Negative (N), Zero (Z), Overflow (V), Carry from bit 7 (C), and half carry from bit 3 (H). These bits of the Condition Code Register are used as testable conditions for the conditional branch instructions. Bit 4 is the interrupt mask bit (I). The unused bits of the Condition Code Register (b6 and b7) are ones.

FIGURE 14 – PROGRAMMING MODEL OF THE MICROPROCESSING UNIT

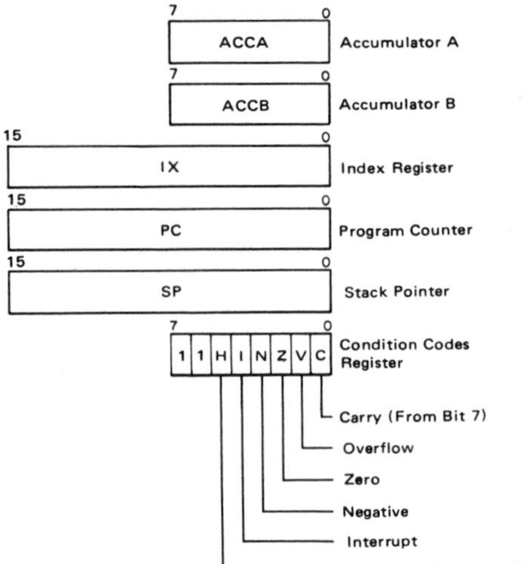

MPU INSTRUCTION SET

The MC6800 instructions are described in detail in the M6800 Programming Manual. This Section will provide a brief introduction and discuss their use in developing MC6800 control programs. The MC6800 has a set of 72 different executable source instructions. Included are binary and decimal arithmetic, logical, shift, rotate, load, store, conditional or unconditional branch, interrupt and stack manipulation instructions.

Each of the 72 executable instructions of the source language assembles into 1 to 3 bytes of machine code. The number of bytes depends on the particular instruction and on the addressing mode. (The addressing modes which are available for use with the various executive instructions are discussed later.)

The coding of the first (or only) byte corresponding to an executable instruction is sufficient to identify the instruction and the addressing mode. The hexadecimal equivalents of the binary codes, which result from the translation of the 72 instructions in all valid modes of addressing, are shown in Table 6. There are 197 valid machine codes, 59 of the 256 possible codes being unassigned.

When an instruction translates into two or three bytes of code, the second byte, or the second and third bytes contain(s) an operand, an address, or information from which an address is obtained during execution.

Microprocessor instructions are often divided into three general classifications: (1) memory reference, so called because they operate on specific memory locations; (2) operating instructions that function without needing a memory reference; (3) I/O instructions for transferring data between the microprocessor and peripheral devices.

In many instances, the MC6800 performs the same operation on both its internal accumulators and the external memory locations. In additon, the MC6800 interfaces adapters (PIA and ACIA) allow the MPU to treat peripheral devices exactly like other memory locations, hence, no I/O instructions as such are required. Because of these features, other classifications are more suitable for introducing the MC6800's instruction set: (1) Accumulator and memory operations; (2) Program control operations; (3) Condition Code Register operations.

TABLE 6 — HEXADECIMAL VALUES OF MACHINE CODES

Code	Op	Acc	Mode	Code	Op	Acc	Mode	Code	Op	Acc	Mode	Code	Op	Acc	Mode
00	*			40	NEG	A		80	SUB	A	IMM	C0	SUB	B	IMM
01	NOP			41	*			81	CMP	A	IMM	C1	CMP	B	IMM
02	*			42	*			82	SBC	A	IMM	C2	SBC	B	IMM
03	*			43	COM	A		83	*			C3	*		
04	*			44	LSR	A		84	AND	A	IMM	C4	AND	B	IMM
05	*			45	*			85	BIT	A	IMM	C5	BIT	B	IMM
06	TAP			46	ROR	A		86	LDA	A	IMM	C6	LDA	B	IMM
07	TPA			47	ASR	A		87	*			C7	*		
08	INX			48	ASL	A		88	EOR	A	IMM	C8	EOR	B	IMM
09	DEX			49	ROL	A		89	ADC	A	IMM	C9	ADC	B	IMM
0A	CLV			4A	DEC	A		8A	ORA	A	IMM	CA	ORA	B	IMM
0B	SEV			4B	*			8B	ADD	A	IMM	CB	ADD	B	IMM
0C	CLC			4C	INC	A		8C	CPX	A	IMM	CC	*		
0D	SEC			4D	TST	A		8D	BSR		REL	CD	*		
0E	CLI			4E	*			8E	LDS		IMM	CE	LDX		IMM
0F	SEI			4F	CLR	A		8F	*			CF	*		
10	SBA			50	NEG	B		90	SUB	A	DIR	D0	SUB	B	DIR
11	CBA			51	*			91	CMP	A	DIR	D1	CMP	B	DIR
12	*			52	*			92	SBC	A	DIR	D2	SBC	B	DIR
13	*			53	COM	B		93	*			D3	*		
14	*			54	LSR	B		94	AND	A	DIR	D4	AND	B	DIR
15	*			55	*			95	BIT	A	DIR	D5	BIT	B	DIR
16	TAB			56	ROR	B		96	LDA	A	DIR	D6	LDA	B	DIR
17	TBA			57	ASR	B		97	STA	A	DIR	D7	STA	B	DIR
18	*			58	ASL	B		98	EOR	A	DIR	D8	EOR	B	DIR
19	DAA			59	ROL	B		99	ADC	A	DIR	D9	ADC	B	DIR
1A	*			5A	DEC	B		9A	ORA	A	DIR	DA	ORA	B	DIR
1B	ABA			5B	*			9B	ADD	A	DIR	DB	ADD	B	DIR
1C	*			5C	INC	B		9C	CPX		DIR	DC	*		
1D	*			5D	TST	B		9D	*			DD	*		
1E	*			5E	*			9E	LDS		DIR	DE	LDX		DIR
1F	*			5F	CLR	B		9F	STS		DIR	DF	STX		DIR
20	BRA		REL	60	NEG		IND	A0	SUB	A	IND	E0	SUB	B	IND
21	*			61	*			A1	CMP	A	IND	E1	CMP	B	IND
22	BHI		REL	62	*			A2	SBC	A	IND	E2	SBC	B	IND
23	BLS		REL	63	COM		IND	A3	*			E3	*		
24	BCC		REL	64	LSR		IND	A4	AND	A	IND	E4	AND	B	IND
25	BCS		REL	65	*			A5	BIT	A	IND	E5	BIT	B	IND
26	BNE		REL	66	ROR		IND	A6	LDA	A	IND	E6	LDA	B	IND
27	BEQ		REL	67	ASR		IND	A7	STA	A	IND	E7	STA	B	IND
28	BVC		REL	68	ASL		IND	A8	EOR	A	IND	E8	EOR	B	IND
29	BVS		REL	69	ROL		IND	A9	ADC	A	IND	E9	ADC	B	IND
2A	BPL		REL	6A	DEC		IND	AA	ORA	A	IND	EA	ORA	B	IND
2B	BMI		REL	6B	*			AB	ADD	A	IND	EB	ADD	B	IND
2C	BGE		REL	6C	INC		IND	AC	CPX		IND	EC	*		
2D	BLT		REL	6D	TST		IND	AD	JSR		IND	ED	*		
2E	BGT		REL	6E	JMP		IND	AE	LDS		IND	EE	LDX		IND
2F	BLE		REL	6F	CLR		IND	AF	STS		IND	EF	STX		IND
30	TSX			70	NEG		EXT	B0	SUB	A	EXT	F0	SUB	B	EXT
31	INS			71	*			B1	CMP	A	EXT	F1	CMP	B	EXT
32	PUL	A		72	*			B2	SBC	A	EXT	F2	SBC	B	EXT
33	PUL	B		73	COM		EXT	B3	*			F3	*		
34	DES			74	LSR		EXT	B4	AND	A	EXT	F4	AND	B	EXT
35	TXS			75	*			B5	BIT	A	EXT	F5	BIT	B	EXT
36	PSH	A		76	ROR		EXT	B6	LDA	A	EXT	F6	LDA	B	EXT
37	PSH	B		77	ASR		EXT	B7	STA	A	EXT	F7	STA	B	EXT
38	*			78	ASL		EXT	B8	EOR	A	EXT	F8	ADC	B	EXT
39	RTS			79	ROL		EXT	B9	ADC	A	EXT	F9	ADC	B	EXT
3A	*			7A	DEC		EXT	BA	ORA	A	EXT	FA	ORA	B	EXT
3B	RTI			7B	*			BB	ADD	A	EXT	FB	ADD	B	EXT
3C	*			7C	INC		EXT	BC	CPX		EXT	FC	*		
3D	*			7D	TST		EXT	BD	JSR		EXT	FD	*		
3E	WAI			7E	JMP		EXT	BE	LDS		EXT	FE	LDX		EXT
3F	SWI			7F	CLR		EXT	BF	STS		EXT	FF	STX		EXT

Notes: 1. Addressing Modes: A = Accumulator A   IMM = Immediate
                                B = Accumulator B   DIR = Direct
                                REL = Relative
                                IND = Indexed
        2. Unassigned code indicated by "*"

TABLE 7 – ACCUMULATOR AND MEMORY OPERATIONS

The accumulator and memory operations and their effect on the CCR are shown in Table 7.
Included are Arithmetic Logic, Data Test and Data Handling instructions.

OPERATIONS	MNEMONIC	IMMED OP	~	#	DIRECT OP	~	#	INDEX OP	~	#	EXTND OP	~	#	IMPLIED OP	~	#	BOOLEAN/ARITHMETIC OPERATION (All register labels refer to contents)	H	I	N	Z	V	C
Add	ADDA	8B	2	2	9B	3	2	AB	5	2	BB	4	3				$A + M \rightarrow A$	↕	•	↕	↕	↕	↕
	ADDB	CB	2	2	DB	3	2	EB	5	2	FB	4	3				$B + M \rightarrow B$	↕	•	↕	↕	↕	↕
Add Acmltrs	ABA													1B	2	1	$A + B \rightarrow A$	↕	•	↕	↕	↕	↕
Add with Carry	ADCA	89	2	2	99	3	2	A9	5	2	B9	4	3				$A + M + C \rightarrow A$	↕	•	↕	↕	↕	↕
	ADCB	C9	2	2	D9	3	2	E9	5	2	F9	4	3				$B + M + C \rightarrow B$	↕	•	↕	↕	↕	↕
And	ANDA	84	2	2	94	3	2	A4	5	2	B4	4	3				$A \cdot M \rightarrow A$	•	•	↕	↕	R	•
	ANDB	C4	2	2	D4	3	2	E4	5	2	F4	4	3				$B \cdot M \rightarrow B$	•	•	↕	↕	R	•
Bit Test	BITA	85	2	2	95	3	2	A5	5	2	B5	4	3				$A \cdot M$	•	•	↕	↕	R	•
	BITB	C5	2	2	D5	3	2	E5	5	2	F5	4	3				$B \cdot M$	•	•	↕	↕	R	•
Clear	CLR							6F	7	2	7F	6	3				$00 \rightarrow M$	•	•	R	S	R	R
	CLRA													4F	2	1	$00 \rightarrow A$	•	•	R	S	R	R
	CLRB													5F	2	1	$00 \rightarrow B$	•	•	R	S	R	R
Compare	CMPA	81	2	2	91	3	2	A1	5	2	B1	4	3				$A - M$	•	•	↕	↕	↕	↕
	CMPB	C1	2	2	D1	3	2	E1	5	2	F1	4	3				$B - M$	•	•	↕	↕	↕	↕
Compare Acmltrs	CBA													11	2	1	$A - B$	•	•	↕	↕	↕	↕
Complement, 1's	COM							63	7	2	73	6	3				$\overline{M} \rightarrow M$	•	•	↕	↕	R	S
	COMA													43	2	1	$\overline{A} \rightarrow A$	•	•	↕	↕	R	S
	COMB													53	2	1	$\overline{B} \rightarrow B$	•	•	↕	↕	R	S
Complement, 2's	NEG							60	7	2	70	6	3				$00 - M \rightarrow M$	•	•	↕	↕	①	②
(Negate)	NEGA													40	2	1	$00 - A \rightarrow A$	•	•	↕	↕	①	②
	NEGB													50	2	1	$00 - B \rightarrow B$	•	•	↕	↕	①	②
Decimal Adjust, A	DAA													19	2	1	Converts Binary Add. of BCD Characters into BCD Format	•	•	↕	↕	↕	③
Decrement	DEC							6A	7	2	7A	6	3				$M - 1 \rightarrow M$	•	•	↕	↕	④	•
	DECA													4A	2	1	$A - 1 \rightarrow A$	•	•	↕	↕	④	•
	DECB													5A	2	1	$B - 1 \rightarrow B$	•	•	↕	↕	④	•
Exclusive OR	EORA	88	2	2	98	3	2	A8	5	2	B8	4	3				$A \oplus M \rightarrow A$	•	•	↕	↕	R	•
	EORB	C8	2	2	D8	3	2	E8	5	2	F8	4	3				$B \oplus M \rightarrow B$	•	•	↕	↕	R	•
Increment	INC							6C	7	2	7C	6	3				$M + 1 \rightarrow M$	•	•	↕	↕	⑤	•
	INCA													4C	2	1	$A + 1 \rightarrow A$	•	•	↕	↕	⑤	•
	INCB													5C	2	1	$B + 1 \cdot B$	•	•	↕	↕	⑤	•
Load Acmltr	LDAA	86	2	2	96	3	2	A6	5	2	B6	4	3				$M \rightarrow A$	•	•	↕	↕	R	•
	LDAB	C6	2	2	D6	3	2	E6	5	2	F6	4	3				$M \rightarrow B$	•	•	↕	↕	R	•
Or, Inclusive	ORAA	8A	2	2	9A	3	2	AA	5	2	BA	4	3				$A + M \rightarrow A$	•	•	↕	↕	R	•
	ORAB	CA	2	2	DA	3	2	EA	5	2	FA	4	3				$B + M \rightarrow B$	•	•	↕	↕	R	•
Push Data	PSHA													36	4	1	$A \rightarrow M_{SP}, SP - 1 \rightarrow SP$	•	•	•	•	•	•
	PSHB													37	4	1	$B \rightarrow M_{SP}, SP - 1 \rightarrow SP$	•	•	•	•	•	•
Pull Data	PULA													32	4	1	$SP + 1 \rightarrow SP, M_{SP} \rightarrow A$	•	•	•	•	•	•
	PULB													33	4	1	$SP + 1 \rightarrow SP, M_{SP} \rightarrow B$	•	•	•	•	•	•
Rotate Left	ROL							69	7	2	79	6	3				M	•	•	↕	↕	⑥	↕
	ROLA													49	2	1	A	•	•	↕	↕	⑥	↕
	ROLB													59	2	1	B	•	•	↕	↕	⑥	↕
Rotate Right	ROR							66	7	2	76	6	3				M	•	•	↕	↕	⑥	↕
	RORA													46	2	1	A	•	•	↕	↕	⑥	↕
	RORB													56	2	1	B	•	•	↕	↕	⑥	↕
Shift Left, Arithmetic	ASL							68	7	2	78	6	3				M	•	•	↕	↕	⑥	↕
	ASLA													48	2	1	A	•	•	↕	↕	⑥	↕
	ASLB													58	2	1	B	•	•	↕	↕	⑥	↕
Shift Right, Arithmetic	ASR							67	7	2	77	6	3				M	•	•	↕	↕	⑥	↕
	ASRA													47	2	1	A	•	•	↕	↕	⑥	↕
	ASRB													57	2	1	B	•	•	↕	↕	⑥	↕
Shift Right, Logic	LSR							64	7	2	74	6	3				M	•	•	R	↕	⑥	↕
	LSRA													44	2	1	A	•	•	R	↕	⑥	↕
	LSRB													54	2	1	B	•	•	R	↕	⑥	↕
Store Acmltr.	STAA				97	4	2	A7	6	2	B7	5	3				$A \rightarrow M$	•	•	↕	↕	R	•
	STAB				D7	4	2	E7	6	2	F7	5	3				$B \rightarrow M$	•	•	↕	↕	R	•
Subtract	SUBA	80	2	2	90	3	2	A0	5	2	B0	4	3				$A - M \rightarrow A$	•	•	↕	↕	↕	↕
	SUBB	C0	2	2	D0	3	2	E0	5	2	F0	4	3				$B - M \rightarrow B$	•	•	↕	↕	↕	↕
Subtract Acmltrs.	SBA													10	2	1	$A - B \rightarrow A$	•	•	↕	↕	↕	↕
Subtr. with Carry	SBCA	82	2	2	92	3	2	A2	5	2	B2	4	3				$A - M - C \rightarrow A$	•	•	↕	↕	↕	↕
	SBCB	C2	2	2	D2	3	2	E2	5	2	F2	4	3				$B - M - C \rightarrow B$	•	•	↕	↕	↕	↕
Transfer Acmltrs	TAB													16	2	1	$A \rightarrow B$	•	•	↕	↕	R	•
	TBA													17	2	1	$B \rightarrow A$	•	•	↕	↕	R	•
Test, Zero or Minus	TST							6D	7	2	7D	6	3				$M - 00$	•	•	↕	↕	R	R
	TSTA													4D	2	1	$A - 00$	•	•	↕	↕	R	R
	TSTB													5D	2	1	$B - 00$	•	•	↕	↕	R	R

Condition code register bottom labels: H I N Z V C

LEGEND:

OP   Operation Code (Hexadecimal);
~   Number of MPU Cycles;
#   Number of Program Bytes;
+   Arithmetic Plus;
−   Arithmetic Minus;
·   Boolean AND;
M_{SP} Contents of memory location pointed to be Stack Pointer;

+   Boolean Inclusive OR;
⊕   Boolean Exclusive OR;
M   Complement of M;
→   Transfer Into;
0   Bit = Zero;
00   Byte = Zero;

CONDITION CODE SYMBOLS:

H   Half-carry from bit 3;
I   Interrupt mask
N   Negative (sign bit)
Z   Zero (byte)
V   Overflow, 2's complement
C   Carry from bit 7
R   Reset Always
S   Set Always
↕   Test and set if true, cleared otherwise
•   Not Affected

Note − Accumulator addressing mode instructions are included in the column for IMPLIED addressing

TABLE 7 – CONTINUED

CONDITION CODE REGISTER NOTES: (Bit set if test is true and cleared otherwise)

1	(Bit V)	Test: Result = 10000000?
2	(Bit C)	Test: Result = 00000000?
3	(Bit C)	Test: Decimal value of most significant BCD Character greater than nine? (Not cleared if previously set.)
4	(Bit V)	Test: Operand = 10000000 prior to execution?
5	(Bit V)	Test: Operand = 01111111 prior to execution?
6	(Bit V)	Test: Set equal to result of N⊕C after shift has occurred.

PROGRAM CONTROL OPERATIONS

Program Control operation can be subdivided into two categories: (1) Index Register/Stack Pointer instructions; (2) Jump and Branch operations.

Index Register/Stack Pointer Operations

The instructions for direct operation on the MPU's Index Register and Stack Pointer are summarized in Table 8. Decrement (DEX, DES), increment (INX, INS), load (LDX, LDS), and store (STX, STS) instructions are provided for both. The Compare instruction, CPX, can be used to compare the Index Register to a 16-bit value and update the Condition Code Register accordingly.

The TSX instruction causes the Index Register to be loaded with the address of the last data byte put onto the "stack". The TXS instruction loads the Stack Pointer with a value equal to one less than the current contents of the Index Register. This causes the next byte to be pulled from the "stack" to come from the location indicated by the Index Register. The utility of these two instructions can be clarified by describing the "stack" concept relative to the M6800 system.

The "stack" can be thought of as a sequential list of data stored in the MPU's read/write memory. The Stack Pointer contains a 16-bit memory address that is used to access the list from one end on a last-in-first-out (LIFO) basis in contrast to the random access mode used by the MPU's other addressing modes.

The M6800 instruction set and interrupt structure allow extensive use of the stack concept for efficient handling of data movement, subroutines and interrupts. The instructions can be used to establish one or more "stacks" anywhere in read/write memory. Stack length is limited only by the amount of memory that is made available.

TABLE 8 – INDEX REGISTER AND STACK POINTER INSTRUCTIONS

		IMMED			DIRECT			INDEX			EXTND			IMPLIED				5	4	3	2	1	0
POINTER OPERATIONS	MNEMONIC	OP	~	#	OP	~	#	OP	~	#	OP	~	#	OP	~	#	BOOLEAN/ARITHMETIC OPERATION	H	I	N	Z	V	C
Compare Index Reg	CPX	8C	3	3	9C	4	2	AC	6	2	BC	5	3				$X_H - M, X_L - (M + 1)$	●	●	①	↕	②	●
Decrement Index Reg	DEX													09	4	1	$X - 1 \rightarrow X$	●	●	●	↕	●	●
Decrement Stack Pntr	DES													34	4	1	$SP - 1 \rightarrow SP$	●	●	●	●	●	●
Increment Index Reg	INX													08	4	1	$X + 1 \rightarrow X$	●	●	●	↕	●	●
Increment Stack Pntr	INS													31	4	1	$SP + 1 \rightarrow SP$	●	●	●	●	●	●
Load Index Reg	LDX	CE	3	3	DE	4	2	EE	6	2	FE	5	3				$M \rightarrow X_H, (M + 1) \rightarrow X_L$	●	●	③	↕	R	●
Load Stack Pntr	LDS	8E	3	3	9E	4	2	AE	6	2	BE	5	3				$M \rightarrow SP_H, (M + 1) \rightarrow SP_L$	●	●	③	↕	R	●
Store Index Reg	STX				DF	5	2	EF	7	2	FF	6	3				$X_H \rightarrow M, X_L \rightarrow (M + 1)$	●	●	③	↕	R	●
Store Stack Pntr	STS				9F	5	2	AF	7	2	BF	6	3				$SP_H \rightarrow M, SP_L \rightarrow (M + 1)$	●	●	③	↕	R	●
Indx Reg → Stack Pntr	TXS													35	4	1	$X - 1 \rightarrow SP$	●	●	●	●	●	●
Stack Pntr → Indx Reg	TSX													30	4	1	$SP + 1 \rightarrow X$	●	●	●	●	●	●

COND. CODE REG.

① (Bit N) Test: Sign bit of most significant (MS) byte of result = 1?
② (Bit V) Test: 2's complement overflow from subtraction of ms bytes?
③ (Bit N) Test: Result less than zero? (Bit 15 = 1)

FIGURE 15 – STACK OPERATION, PUSH INSTRUCTION

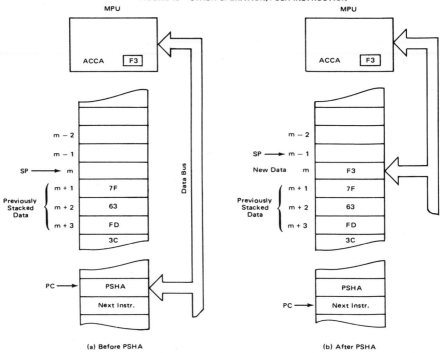

(a) Before PSHA (b) After PSHA

FIGURE 16 – STACK OPERATION, PULL INSTRUCTION

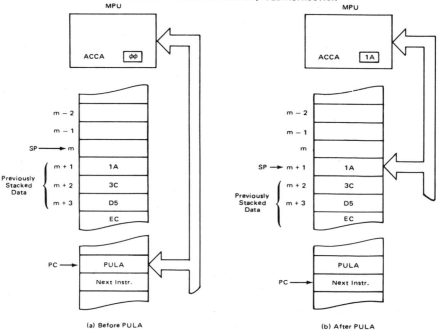

(a) Before PULA (b) After PULA

Operation of the Stack Pointer with the Push and Pull instructions is illustrated in Figures 15 and 16. The Push instruction (PSHA) causes the contents of the indicated accumulator (A in this example) to be stored in memory at the location indicated by the Stack Pointer. The Stack Pointer is automatically decremented by one following the storage operation and is "pointing" to the next empty stack location. The Pull instruction (PULA or PULB) causes the last byte stacked to be loaded into the appropriate accumulator. The Stack Pointer is automatically incremented by one just prior to the data transfer so that it will point to the last byte stacked rather than the next empty location. Note that the PULL instruction does not "remove" the data from memory; in the example, 1A is still in location (m + 1) following execution of PULA. A subsequent PUSH instruction would overwrite that location with the new "pushed" data.

Execution of the Branch to Subroutine (BSR) and Jump to Subroutine (JSR) instructions cause a return address to be saved on the stack as shown in Figures 18 through 20. The stack is decremented after each byte of the return address is pushed onto the stack. For both of these instructions, the return address is the memory location following the bytes of code that correspond to the BSR and JSR instruction. The code required for BSR or JSR may be either two or three bytes, depending on whether the JSR is in the indexed (two bytes) or the extended (three bytes) addressing mode. Before it is stacked, the Program Counter is automatically incremented the correct number of times to be pointing at the location of the next instruction. The Return from Subroutine instruction, RTS, causes the return address to be retrieved and loaded into the Program Counter as shown in Figure 21.

There are several operations that cause the status of the MPU to be saved on the stack. The Software Interrupt (SWI) and Wait for Interrupt (WAI) instructions as well as the maskable ($\overline{IRQ}$) and non-maskable ($\overline{NMI}$) hardware interrupts all cause the MPU's internal registers (except for the Stack Pointer itself) to be stacked as shown in Figure 23. MPU status is restored by the Return from Interrupt, RTI, as shown in Figure 22.

Jump and Branch Operation

The Jump and Branch instructions are summarized in Table 9. These instructions are used to control the transfer of operation from one point to another in the control program.

The No Operation instruction, NOP, while included here, is a jump operation in a very limited sense. Its only effect is to increment the Program Counter by one. It is useful during program development as a "stand-in" for some other instruction that is to be determined during debug. It is also used for equalizing the execution time through alternate paths in a control program.

TABLE 9 — JUMP AND BRANCH INSTRUCTIONS

OPERATIONS	MNEMONIC	RELATIVE			INDEX			EXTND			IMPLIED			BRANCH TEST	COND. CODE REG.					
		OP	~	#	OP	~	#	OP	~	#	OP	~	#		5 H	4 I	3 N	2 Z	1 V	0 C
Branch Always	BRA	20	4	2										None	•	•	•	•	•	•
Branch If Carry Clear	BCC	24	4	2										C = 0	•	•	•	•	•	•
Branch If Carry Set	BCS	25	4	2										C = 1	•	•	•	•	•	•
Branch If = Zero	BEQ	27	4	2										Z = 1	•	•	•	•	•	•
Branch If ≥ Zero	BGE	2C	4	2										N ⊕ V = 0	•	•	•	•	•	•
Branch If > Zero	BGT	2E	4	2										Z + (N ⊕ V) = 0	•	•	•	•	•	•
Branch If Higher	BHI	22	4	2										C + Z = 0	•	•	•	•	•	•
Branch If ≤ Zero	BLE	2F	4	2										Z + (N ⊕ V) = 1	•	•	•	•	•	•
Branch If Lower Or Same	BLS	23	4	2										C + Z = 1	•	•	•	•	•	•
Branch If < Zero	BLT	2D	4	2										N ⊕ V = 1	•	•	•	•	•	•
Branch If Minus	BMI	2B	4	2										N = 1	•	•	•	•	•	•
Branch If Not Equal Zero	BNE	26	4	2										Z = 0	•	•	•	•	•	•
Branch If Overflow Clear	BVC	28	4	2										V = 0	•	•	•	•	•	•
Branch If Overflow Set	BVS	29	4	2										V = 1	•	•	•	•	•	•
Branch If Plus	BPL	2A	4	2										N = 0	•	•	•	•	•	•
Branch To Subroutine	BSR	8D	8	2											•	•	•	•	•	•
Jump	JMP				6E	4	2	7E	3	3				See Special Operations	•	•	•	•	•	•
Jump To Subroutine	JSR				AD	8	2	BD	9	3					•	•	•	•	•	•
No Operation	NOP										01	2	1	Advances Prog. Cntr. Only	•	•	•	•	•	•
Return From Interrupt	RTI										3B	10	1		①					
Return From Subroutine	RTS										39	5	1		•	•	•	•	•	•
Software Interrupt	SWI										3F	12	1	See Special Operations	•	•	•	•	•	•
Wait for Interrupt*	WAI										3E	9	1		•	②	•	•	•	•

*WAI puts Address Bus, R/W, and Data Bus in the three-state mode while VMA is held low.

① (All) Load Condition Code Register from Stack. (See Special Operations)
② (Bit 1) Set when interrupt occurs. If previously set, a Non-Maskable Interrupt is required to exit the wait state.

Execution of the Jump Instruction, JMP, and Branch Always, BRA, affects program flow as shown in Figure 17. When the MPU encounters the Jump (Indexed) instruction, it adds the offset to the value in the Index Register and uses the result as the address of the next instruction to be executed. In the extended addressing mode, the address of the next instruction to be executed is fetched from the two locations immediately following the JMP instruction. The Branch Always (BRA) instruction is similar to the JMP (extended) instruction except that the relative addressing mode applies and the branch is limited to the range within −125 or +127 bytes of the branch instruction itself. The opcode for the BRA instruction requires one less byte than JMP (extended) but takes one more cycle to execute.

The effect on program flow for the Jump to Subroutine (JSR) and Branch to Subroutine (BSR) is shown in Figures 18 through 20. Note that the Program Counter is properly incremented to be pointing at the correct return address before it is stacked. Operation of the Branch to Subroutine and Jump to Subroutine (extended) instruction is similar except for the range. The BSR instruction requires less opcode than JSR (2 bytes versus 3 bytes)

and also executes one cycle faster than JSR. The Return from Subroutine, RTS, is used at the end of a subroutine to return to the main program as indicated in Figure 21.

The effect of executing the Software Interrupt, SWI, and the Wait for Interrupt, WAI, and their relationship to the hardware interrupts is shown in Figure 22. SWI causes the MPU contents to be stacked and then fetches the starting address of the interrupt routine from the memory locations that respond to the addresses FFFA and FFFB. Note that as in the case of the subroutine instructions, the Program Counter is incremented to point at the correct return address before being stacked. The Return from Interrupt instruction, RTI, (Figure 22) is used at the end of an interrupt routine to restore control to the main program. The SWI instruction is useful for inserting break points in the control program, that is, it can be used to stop operation and put the MPU registers in memory where they can be examined. The WAI instruction is used to decrease the time required to service a hardware interrupt; it stacks the MPU contents and then waits for the interrupt to occur, effectively removing the stacking time from a hardware interrupt sequence.

FIGURE 17 – PROGRAM FLOW FOR JUMP AND BRANCH INSTRUCTIONS

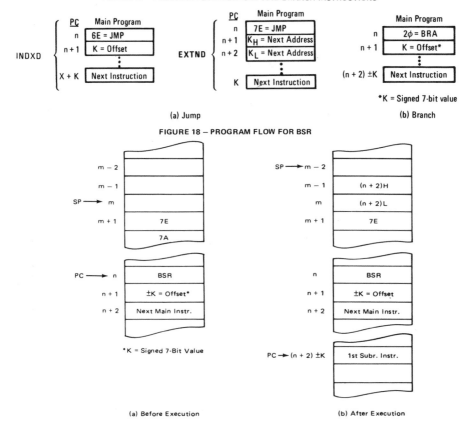

(a) Jump

(b) Branch

*K = Signed 7-bit value

FIGURE 18 – PROGRAM FLOW FOR BSR

(a) Before Execution

(b) After Execution

FIGURE 19 – PROGRAM FLOW FOR JSR (EXTENDED)

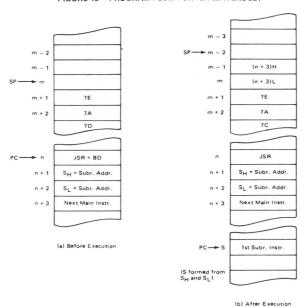

(a) Before Execution

(b) After Execution

FIGURE 20 – PROGRAM FLOW FOR JSR (INDEXED)

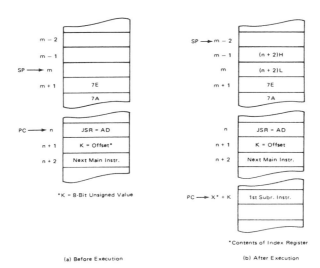

(a) Before Execution

(b) After Execution

FIGURE 21 – PROGRAM FLOW FOR RTS

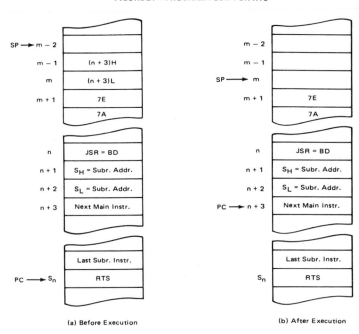

(a) Before Execution

(b) After Execution

FIGURE 22 – PROGRAM FLOW FOR RTI

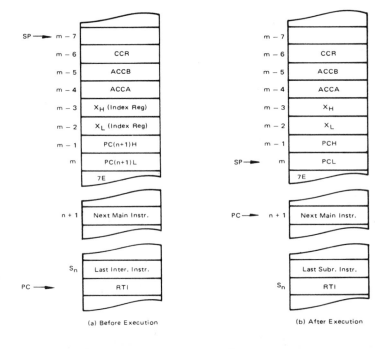

(a) Before Execution

(b) After Execution

FIGURE 23 – PROGRAM FLOW FOR INTERRUPTS

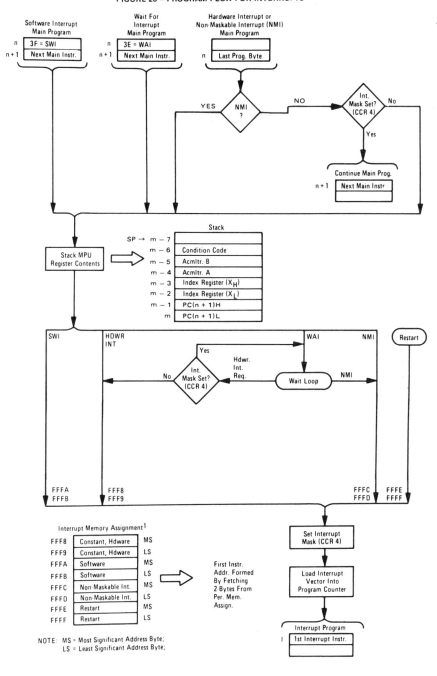

NOTE: MS = Most Significant Address Byte;
LS = Least Significant Address Byte;

FIGURE 24 – CONDITIONAL BRANCH INSTRUCTIONS

BMI :	$N = 1$;	BEQ :	$Z = 1$;
BPL :	$N = \phi$;	BNE :	$Z = \phi$;
BVC :	$V = \phi$;	BCC :	$C = \phi$;
BVS :	$V = 1$;	BCS :	$C = 1$;
BHI :	$C + Z = \phi$;	BLT :	$N \oplus V = 1$;
BLS :	$C + Z = 1$;	BGE :	$N \oplus V = \phi$;

BLE :	$Z + (N \oplus V) = 1$;
BGT :	$Z + (N \oplus V) = \phi$;

The conditional branch instructions, Figure 24, consists of seven pairs of complementary instructions. They are used to test the results of the preceding operation and either continue with the next instruction in sequence (test fails) or cause a branch to another point in the program (test succeeds).

Four of the pairs are used for simple tests of status bits N, Z, V, and C:

1. Branch on Minus (BMI) and Branch On Plus (BPL) tests the sign bit, N, to determine if the previous result was negative or positive, respectively.

2. Branch On Equal (BEQ) and Branch On Not Equal (BNE) are used to test the zero status bit, Z, to determine whether or not the result of the previous operation was equal to zero. These two instructions are useful following a Compare (CMP) instruction to test for equality between an accumulator and the operand. They are also used following the Bit Test (BIT) to determine whether or not the same bit positions are set in an accumulator and the operand.

3. Branch On Overflow Clear (BVC) and Branch On Overflow Set (BVS) tests the state of the V bit to determine if the previous operation caused an arithmetic overflow.

4. Branch On Carry Clear (BCC) and Branch On Carry Set (BCS) tests the state of the C bit to determine if the previous operation caused a carry to occur. BCC and BCS are useful for testing relative magnitude when the values being tested are regarded as unsigned binary numbers, that

is, the values are in the range 00 (lowest) to FF (highest). BCC following a comparison (CMP) will cause a branch if the (unsigned) value in the accumulator is higher than or the same as the value of the operand. Conversely, BCS will cause a branch if the accumulator value is lower than the operand.

The fifth complementary pair, Branch On Higher (BHI) and Branch On Lower or Same (BLS) are in a sense complements to BCC and BCS. BHI tests for both C and Z = 0; if used following a CMP, it will cause a branch if the value in the accumulator is higher than the operand. Conversely, BLS will cause a branch if the unsigned binary value in the accumulator is lower than or the same as the operand.

The remaining two pairs are useful in testing results of operations in which the values are regarded as signed two's complement numbers. This differs from the unsigned binary case in the following sense: In unsigned, the orientation is higher or lower; in signed two's complement, the comparison is between larger or smaller where the range of values is between – 128 and + 127.

Branch On Less Than Zero (BLT) and Branch On Greater Than Or Equal Zero (BGE) test the status bits for $N \oplus V = 1$ and $N \oplus V = 0$, respectively. BLT will always cause a branch following an operation in which two negative numbers were added. In addition, it will cause a branch following a CMP in which the value in the accumulator was negative and the operand was positive. BLT will never cause a branch following a CMP in which the accumulator value was positive and the operand negative. BGE, the complement to BLT, will cause a branch following operations in which two positive values were added or in which the result was zero.

The last pair, Branch On Less Than Or Equal Zero (BLE) and Branch On Greater Than Zero (BGT) test the status bits for $Z \oplus (N + V) = 1$ and $Z \oplus (N + V) = 0$, respectively. The action of BLE is identical to that for BLT except that a branch will also occur if the result of the previous result was zero. Conversely, BGT is similar to BGE except that no branch will occur following a zero result.

CONDITION CODE REGISTER OPERATIONS

The Condition Code Register (CCR) is a 6-bit register within the MPU that is useful in controlling program flow during system operation. The bits are defined in Figure 25.

The instructions shown in Table 10 are available to the user for direct manipulation of the CCR. In addition, the MPU automatically sets or clears the appropriate status bits as many of the other instructions on the condition code register was indicated as they were introduced.

A CLI-WAI instruction sequence operated properly with early M6800 processors only if the preceding instruction was odd. (Least Significant Bit = 1.) Similarly it was advisable to precede any SEI instruction with an odd opcode—such as NOP. These precautions are not necessary for M6800 processors indicating manufacture in November, 1977 or later.

Systems which require an interrupt window to be opened under program control should use a CLI-NOP-SEI sequence rather than CLI-SEI.

FIGURE 25 — CONDITION CODE REGISTER BIT DEFINITION

b_5 b_4 b_3 b_2 b_1 b_0

H	I	N	Z	V	C

H = Half-carry; set whenever a carry from b_3 to b_4 of the result is generated by ADD, ABA, ADC; cleared if no b_3 to b_4 carry; not affected by other instructions.

I = Interrupt Mask; set by hardware or software interrupt or SEI instruction; cleared by CLI instruction. (Normally not used in arithmetic operations.) Restored to a zero as a result of an RT1 instruction if I_m stored on the stacked is low.

N = Negative; set if high order bit (b_7) of result is set; cleared otherwise

Z = Zero; set if result = 0; cleared otherwise.

V = Overlow; set if there was arithmetic overflow as a result of the operation; cleared otherwise.

C = Carry; set if there was a carry from the most significant bit (b_7) of the result; cleared otherwise.

TABLE 10 — CONDITION CODE REGISTER INSTRUCTIONS

OPERATIONS	MNEMONIC	IMPLIED			BOOLEAN OPERATION	COND. CODE REG.					
		OP	~	#		5 H	4 I	3 N	2 Z	1 V	0 C
Clear Carry	CLC	0C	2	1	$0 \rightarrow C$	•	•	•	•	•	R
Clear Interrupt Mask	CLI	0E	2	1	$0 \rightarrow I$	•	R	•	•	•	•
Clear Overflow	CLV	0A	2	1	$0 \rightarrow V$	•	•	•	•	R	•
Set Carry	SEC	0D	2	1	$1 \rightarrow C$	•	•	•	•	•	S
Set Interrupt Mask	SEI	0F	2	1	$1 \rightarrow I$	•	S	•	•	•	•
Set Overflow	SEV	0B	2	1	$1 \rightarrow V$	•	•	•	•	S	•
Acmltr A → CCR	TAP	06	2	1	$A \rightarrow CCR$			(1)			
CCR → Acmltr A	TPA	07	2	1	$CCR \rightarrow A$	•	•	•	•	•	•

R = Reset
S = Set
• = Not affected
① (ALL) Set according to the contents of Accumulator A.

ADDRESSING MODES

The MPU operates on 8-bit binary numbers presented to it via the Data Bus. A given number (byte) may represent either data or an instruction to be executed, depending on where it is encountered in the control program. The M6800 has 72 unique instructions, however, it recognizes and takes action on 197 of the 256 possibilities that can occur using an 8-bit word length. This larger number of instructions results from the fact that many of the executive instructions have more than one addressing mode.

These addressing modes refer to the manner in which the program causes the MPU to obtain its instructions and data. The programmer must have a method for addressing the MPU's internal registers and all of the external memory locations.

Selection of the desired addressing mode is made by the user as the source statements are written. Translation into appropriate opcode then depends on the method used. If manual translation is used, the addressing mode is inherent in the opcode. For example, the Immediate,

Direct, Indexed, and Extended modes may all be used with the ADD instruction. The proper mode is determined by selecting (hexidecimal notation) 8B, 9B, AB, or BB, respectively.

The source statement format includes adequate information for the selection if an assembler program is used to generate the opcode. For instance, the Immediate mode is selected by the Assembler whenever it encounters the "≠" symbol in the operand field. Similarly, an "X" in the operand field causes the Indexed mode to be selected. Only the Relative mode applies to the branch instructions, therefore, the mnemonic instruction itself is enough for the Assembler to determine addressing mode.

For the instructions that use both Direct and Extended modes, the Assembler selects the Direct mode if the operand value is in the range 0–255 and Extended otherwise. There are a number of instructions for which the Extended mode is valid but the Direct is not. For these instructions, the Assembler automatically selects the Extended mode even if the operand is in the 0–255 range. The addressing modes are summarized in Figure 26.

FIGURE 26 – ADDRESSING MODE SUMMARY

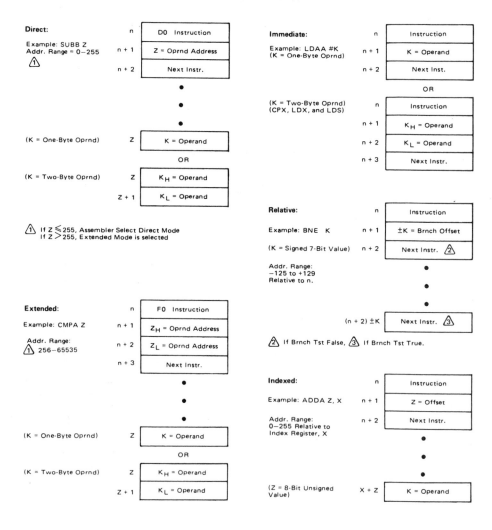

Inherent (Includes "Accumulator Addressing" Mode)

The successive fields in a statement are normally separated by one or more spaces. An exception to this rule occurs for instructions that use dual addressing in the operand field and for instructions that must distinguish between the two accumulators. In these cases, A and B are "operands" but the space between them and the operator may be omitted. This is commonly done, resulting in apparent four character mnemonics for those instructions.

The addition instruction, ADD, provides an example of dual addressing in the operand field:

	Operator	Operand	Comment
	ADDA	MEM12	ADD CONTENTS OF MEM12 TO ACCA
or	ADDB	MEM12	ADD CONTENTS OF MEM12 TO ACCB

The example used earlier for the test instruction, TST, also applies to the accumulators and uses the "accumulator addressing mode" to designate which of the two accumulators is being tested:

	Operator	Comment
	TSTB	TEST CONTENTS OF ACCB
or	TSTA	TEST CONTENTS OF ACCA

A number of the instructions either alone or together with an accumulator operand contain all of the address information that is required, that is, "inherent" in the instruction itself. For instance, the instruction ABA causes the MPU to add the contents of accumulators A and B together and place the result in accumulator A. The instruction INCB, another example of "accumulator addressing", causes the contents of accumulator B to be increased by one. Similarly, INX, increment the Index Register, causes the contents of the Index Register to be increased by one.

Program flow for instructions fo this type is illustrated in Figures 27 and 28. In these figures, the general case is shown on the left and a specific example is shown on the right. Numerical examples are in decimal notation. Instructions of this type require only one byte of opcode. Cycle-by-cycle operation of the inehrent mode is shown in Table 11.

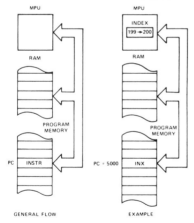

FIGURE 27 — INHERENT ADDRESSING

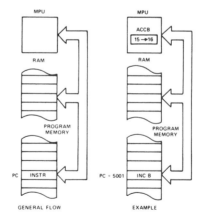

FIGURE 28 — ACCUMULATOR ADDRESSING

TABLE 11 — INHERENT MODE CYCLE BY CYCLE OPERATION

Address Mode and Instructions	Cycles	Cycle #	VMA Line	Address Bus	R/W Line	Data Bus
ABA DAA SEC ASL DEC SEI ASR INC SEV CBA LSR TAB CLC NEG TAP CLI NOP TBA CLR ROL TPA CLV ROR TST COM SBA	2	1	1	Op Code Address	1	Op Code
		2	1	Op Code Address + 1	1	Op Code of Next Instruction
DES DEX INS INX	4	1	1	Op Code Address	1	Op Code
		2	1	Op Code Address + 1	1	Op Code of Next Instruction
		3	0	Previous Register Contents	1	Irrelevant Data (Note 1)
		4	0	New Register Contents	1	Irrelevant Data (Note 1)
PSH	4	1	1	Op Code Address	1	Op Code
		2	1	Op Code Address + 1	1	Op Code of Next Instruction
		3	1	Stack Pointer	0	Accumulator Data
		4	0	Stack Pointer − 1	1	Accumulator Data
PUL	4	1	1	Op Code Address	1	Op Code
		2	1	Op Code Address + 1	1	Op Code of Next Instruction
		3	0	Stack Pointer	1	Irrelevant Data (Note 1)
		4	1	Stack Pointer + 1	1	Operand Data from Stack
TSX	4	1	1	Op Code Address	1	Op Code
		2	1	Op Code Address + 1	1	Op Code of Next Instruction
		3	0	Stack Pointer	1	Irrelevant Data (Note 1)
		4	0	New Index Register	1	Irrelevant Data (Note 1)
TXS	4	1	1	Op Code Address	1	Op Code
		2	1	Op Code Address + 1	1	Op Code of Next Instruction
		3	0	Index Register	1	Irrelevant Data
		4	0	New Stack Pointer	1	Irrelevant Data
RTS	5	1	1	Op Code Address	1	Op Code
		2	1	Op Code Address + 1	1	Irrelevant Data (Note 2)
		3	0	Stack Pointer	1	Irrelevant Data (Note 1)
		4	1	Stack Pointer + 1	1	Address of Next Instruction (High Order Byte)
		5	1	Stack Pointer + 2	1	Address of Next Instruction (Low Order Byte)

TABLE 11 — INHERENT MODE CYCLE BY CYCLE OPERATION (Continued)

Address Mode and Instructions	Cycles	Cycle #	VMA Line	Address Bus	R/W Line	Data Bus
WAI	9	1	1	Op Code Address	1	Op Code
		2	1	Op Code Address + 1	1	Op Code of Next Instruction
		3	1	Stack Pointer	0	Return Address (Low Order Byte)
		4	1	Stack Pointer − 1	0	Return Address (High Order Byte)
		5	1	Stack Pointer − 2	0	Index Register (Low Order Byte)
		6	1	Stack Pointer − 3	0	Index Register (High Order Byte)
		7	1	Stack Pointer − 4	0	Contents of Accumulator A
		8	1	Stack Pointer − 5	0	Contents of Accumulator B
		9	1	Stack Pointer − 6 (Note 3)	1	Contents of Cond. Code Register
RTI	10	1	1	Op Code Address	1	Op Code
		2	1	Op Code Address + 1	1	Irrelevant Data (Note 2)
		3	0	Stack Pointer	1	Irrelevant Data (Note 1)
		4	1	Stack Pointer + 1	1	Contents of Cond. Code Register from Stack
		5	1	Stack Pointer + 2	1	Contents of Accumulator B from Stack
		6	1	Stack Pointer + 3	1	Contents of Accumulator A from Stack
		7	1	Stack Pointer + 4	1	Index Register from Stack (High Order Byte)
		8	1	Stack Pointer + 5	1	Index Register from Stack (Low Order Byte)
		9	1	Stack Pointer + 6	1	Next Instruction Address from Stack (High Order Byte)
		10	1	Stack Pointer + 7	1	Next Instruction Address from Stack (Low Order Byte)
SWI	12	1	1	Op Code Address	1	Op Code
		2	1	Op Code Address + 1	1	Irrelevant Data (Note 1)
		3	1	Stack Pointer	0	Return Address (Low Order Byte)
		4	1	Stack Pointer − 1	0	Return Address (High Order Byte)
		5	1	Stack Pointer − 2	0	Index Register (Low Order Byte)
		6	1	Stack Pointer − 3	0	Index Register (High Order Byte)
		7	1	Stack Pointer − 4	0	Contents of Accumulator A
		8	1	Stack Pointer − 5	0	Contents of Accumulator B
		9	1	Stack Pointer − 6	0	Contents of Cond. Code Register
		10	0	Stack Pointer − 7	1	Irrelevant Data (Note 1)
		11	1	Vector Address FFFA (Hex)	1	Address of Subroutine (High Order Byte)
		12	1	Vector Address FFFB (Hex)	1	Address of Subroutine (Low Order Byte)

Note 1. If device which is addressed during this cycle uses VMA, then the Data Bus will go to the high impedance three-state condition. Depending on bus capacitance, data from the previous cycle may be retained on the Data Bus.

Note 2. Data is ignored by the MPU.

Note 3. While the MPU is waiting for the interrupt, Bus Available will go high indicating the following states of the control lines: VMA is low; Address Bus, R/W, and Data Bus are all in the high impedance state.

Immediate Addressing Mode — In the Immediate addressing mode, the operand is the value that is to be operated on. For instance, the instruction

Operator	Operand	Comment
LDAA	=25	LOAD 25 INTO ACCA

causes the MPU to "immediately load accumulator A with the value 25"; no further address reference is required. The Immediate mode is selected by preceding the operand value with the "#" symbol. Program flow for this addressing mode is illustrated in Figure 29.

The operand format allows either properly defined symbols or numerical values. Except for the instructions CPX, LDX, and LDS, the operand may be any value in the range 0 to 255. Since Compare Index Register (CPX), Load Index Register (LDX), and Load Stack Pointer (LDS), require 16-bit values, the immediate mode for

these three instructions require two-byte operands. In the Immediate addressing mode, the "address" of the operand is effectively the memory location immediately following the instruction itself. Table 12 shows the cycle-by-cycle operation for the immediate addressing mode.

Direct and Extended Addressing Modes — In the Direct and Extended modes of addressing, the operand field of the source statement is the *address* of the value that is to be operated on. The Direct and Extended modes differ only in the range of memory locations to which they can direct the MPU. Direct addressing generates a single 8-bit operand and, hence, can address only memory locations 0 through 255; a two byte operand is generated for Extended addressing, enabling the MPU to reach the remaining memory locations, 256 through 65535. An example of Direct addressing and its effect on program flow is illustrated in Figure 30.

FIGURE 29 — IMMEDIATE ADDRESSING MODE

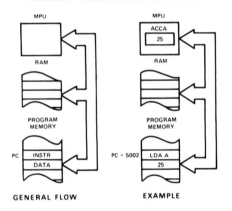

FIGURE 30 — DIRECT ADDRESSING MODE

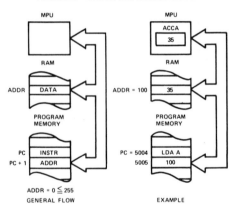

TABLE 12 — IMMEDIATE MODE CYCLE BY CYCLE OPERATION

Address Mode and Instructions	Cycles	Cycle #	VMA Line	Address Bus	R/W Line	Data Bus
ADC EOR ADD LDA AND ORA BIT SBC CMP SUB	2	1	1	Op Code Address	1	Op Code
		2	1	Op Code Address + 1	1	Operand Data
CPX LDS LDX	3	1	1	Op Code Address	1	Op Code
		2	1	Op Code Address + 1	1	Operand Data (High Order Byte)
		3	1	Op Code Address + 2	1	Operand Data (Low Order Byte)

The MPU, after encountering the opcode for the instruction LDAA (Direct) at memory location 5004 (Program Counter = 5004), looks in the next location, 5005, for the address of the operand. It then sets the program counter equal to the value found there (100 in the example) and fetches the operand, in this case a value to be loaded into accumulator A, from that location. For instructions requiring a two-byte operand such as LDX (load the Index Register), the operand bytes would be retrieved from locations 100 and 101. Table 13 shows the cycle-by-cycle operation for the direct mode of addressing.

Extended addressing, Figure 31, is similar except that a two-byte address is obtained from locations 5007 and 5008 after the LDAB (Extended) opcode shows up in location 5006. Extended addressing can be thought of as the "standard" addressing mode, that is, it is a method of reaching anyplace in memory. Direct addressing, since only one address byte is required, provides a faster method of processing data and generates fewer bytes of control code. In most applications, the direct addressing range, memory locations 0-255, are reserved for RAM. They are used for data buffering and temporary storage of system variables, the area in which faster addressing is of most value. Cycle-by-cycle operation is shown in Table 14 for Extended Addressing.

TABLE 13 — DIRECT MODE CYCLE BY CYCLE OPERATION

Address Mode and Instructions	Cycles	Cycle #	VMA Line	Address Bus	R/W̄ Line	Data Bus
ADC EOR ADD LDA AND ORA BIT SBC CMP SUB	3	1	1	Op Code Address	1	Op Code
		2	1	Op Code Address + 1	1	Address of Operand
		3	1	Address of Operand	1	Operand Data
CPX LDS LDX	4	1	1	Op Code Address	1	Op Code
		2	1	Op Code Address + 1	1	Address of Operand
		3	1	Address of Operand	1	Operand Data (High Order Byte)
		4	1	Operand Address + 1	1	Operand Data (Low Order Byte)
STA	4	1	1	Op Code Address	1	Op Code
		2	1	Op Code Address + 1	1	Destination Address
		3	0	Destination Address	1	Irrelevant Data (Note 1)
		4	1	Destination Address	0	Data from Accumulator
STS STX	5	1	1	Op Code Address	1	Op Code
		2	1	Op Code Address + 1	1	Address of Operand
		3	0	Address of Operand	1	Irrelevant Data (Note 1)
		4	1	Address of Operand	0	Register Data (High Order Byte)
		5	1	Address of Operand + 1	0	Register Data (Low Order Byte)

Note 1. If device which is address during this cycle uses VMA, then the Data Bus will go to the high impedance three-state condition. Depending on bus capacitance, data from the previous cycle may be retained on the Data Bus.

FIGURE 31 — EXTENDED ADDRESSING MODE

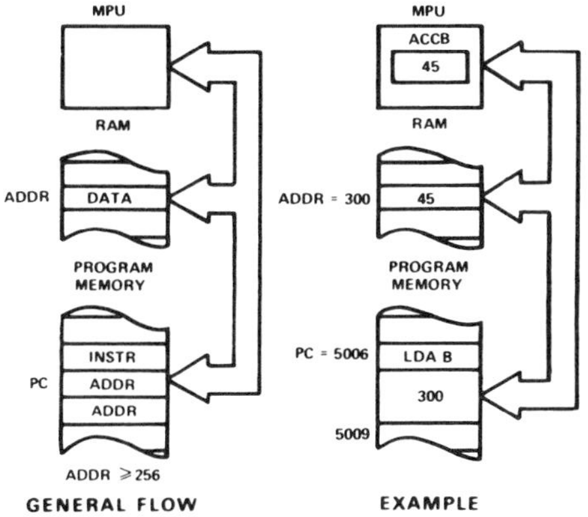

GENERAL FLOW   EXAMPLE

TABLE 14 — EXTENDED MODE CYCLE BY CYCLE

Address Mode and Instructions	Cycles	Cycle #	VMA Line	Address Bus	R/W Line	Data Bus
STS STX	6	1	1	Op Code Address	1	Op Code
		2	1	Op Code Address + 1	1	Address of Operand (High Order Byte)
		3	1	Op Code Address + 2	1	Address of Operand (Low Order Byte)
		4	0	Address of Operand	1	Irrelevant Data (Note 1)
		5	1	Address of Operand	0	Operand Data (High Order Byte)
		6	1	Address of Operand + 1	0	Operand Data (Low Order Byte)
JSR	9	1	1	Op Code Address	1	Op Code
		2	1	Op Code Address + 1	1	Address of Subroutine (High Order Byte)
		3	1	Op Code Address + 2	1	Address of Subroutine (Low Order Byte)
		4	1	Subroutine Starting Address	1	Op Code of Next Instruction
		5	1	Stack Pointer	0	Return Address (Low Order Byte)
		6	1	Stack Pointer − 1	0	Return Address (High Order Byte)
		7	0	Stack Pointer − 2	1	Irrelevant Data (Note 1)
		8	0	Op Code Address + 2	1	Irrelevant Data (Note 1)
		9	1	Op Code Address + 2	1	Address of Subroutine (Low Order Byte)
JMP	3	1	1	Op Code Address	1	Op Code
		2	1	Op Code Address + 1	1	Jump Address (High Order Byte)
		3	1	Op Code Address + 2	1	Jump Address (Low Order Byte)
ADC EOR ADD LDA AND ORA BIT SBC CMP SUB	4	1	1	Op Code Address	1	Op Code
		2	1	Op Code Address + 1	1	Address of Operand (High Order Byte)
		3	1	Op Code Address + 2	1	Address of Operand (Low Order Byte)
		4	1	Address of Operand	1	Operand Data
CPX LDS LDX	5	1	1	Op Code Address	1	Op Code
		2	1	Op Code Address + 1	1	Address of Operand (High Order Byte)
		3	1	Op Code Address + 2	1	Address of Operand (Low Order Byte)
		4	1	Address of Operand	1	Operand Data (High Order Byte)
		5	1	Address of Operand + 1	1	Operand Data (Low Order Byte)
STA A STA B	5	1	1	Op Code Address	1	Op Code
		2	1	Op Code Address + 1	1	Destination Address (High Order Byte)
		3	1	Op Code Address + 2	1	Destination Address (Low Order Byte)
		4	0	Operand Destination Address	1	Irrelevant Data (Note 1)
		5	1	Operand Destination Address	0	Data from Accumulator
ASL LSR ASR NEG CLR ROL COM ROR DEC TST INC	6	1	1	Op Code Address	1	Op Code
		2	1	Op Code Address + 1	1	Address of Operand (High Order Byte)
		3	1	Op Code Address + 2	1	Address of Operand (Low Order Byte)
		4	1	Address of Operand	1	Current Operand Data
		5	0	Address of Operand	1	Irrelevant Data (Note 1)
		6	1/0 (Note 2)	Address of Operand	0	New Operand Data (Note 2)

Note 1. If device which is addressed during this cycle uses VMA, then the Data Bus will go to the high impedance three-state condition. Depending on bus capacitance, data from the previous cycle may be retained on the Data Bus.

Note 2. For TST, VMA = 0 and Operand data does not change.

Relative Address Mode — In both the Direct and Extended modes, the address obtained by the MPU is an absolute numerical address. The Relative addressing mode, implemented for the MPU's branch instructions, specifies a memory location relative to the Program Counter's current location. Branch instructions generate two bytes of machine code, one for the instruction opcode and one for the "relative" address (see Figure 32). Since it is desirable to be able to branch in either direction, the 8-bit address byte is interpreted as a signed 7-bit value; the 8th bit of the operand is treated as a sign bit, "0" = plus and "1" = minus. The remaining seven bits represent the numerical value. This results in a relative addressing range of ± 127 with respect to the location of the branch instruction itself. However, the branch range is computed with respect to the next instruction that would be executed if the branch conditions are not satisfied. Since two bytes are generated, the next instruction is located at PC + 2. If D is defined as the address of the branch destination, the range is then:

$$(PC + 2) - 127 \leqslant D \leqslant (PC + 2) + 127$$

or

$$PC - 125 \leqslant D \leqslant PC + 129$$

that is, the destination of the branch instruction must be within -125 to $+129$ memory locations of the branch instruction itself. For transferring control beyond this range, the unconditional jump (JMP), jump to subroutine (JSR), and return from subroutine (RTS) are used.

In Figure 32, when the MPU encounters the opcode for BEQ (Branch if result of last instruction was zero), it tests the Zero bit in the Condition Code Register. If that bit is "0", indicating a non-zero result, the MPU continues execution with the next instruction (in location 5010 in Figure 32). If the previous result was zero, the branch condition is satisfied and the MPU adds the offset, 15 in this case, to PC + 2 and branches to location 5025 for the next instruction.

The branch instructions allow the programmer to efficiently direct the MPU to one point or another in the control program depending on the outcome of test results. Since the control program is normally in read-only memory and cannot be changed, the relative address used in execution of branch instructions is a constant numerical value. Cycle-by-cycle operation is shown in Table 15 for relative addressing.

TABLE 15 — RELATIVE MODE CYCLE-BY-CYCLE OPERATION

Address Mode and Instructions	Cycles	Cycle #	VMA Line	Address Bus	R/W Line	Data Bus
BCC BHI BNE BCS BLE BPL BEQ BLS BRA BGE BLT BVC BGT BMI BVS	4	1	1	Op Code Address	1	Op Code
		2	1	Op Code Address + 1	1	Branch Offset
		3	0	Op Code Address + 2	1	Irrelevant Data (Note 1)
		4	0	Branch Address	1	Irrelevant Data (Note 1)
BSR	8	1	1	Op Code Address	1	Op Code
		2	1	Op Code Address + 1	1	Branch Offset
		3	0	Return Address of Main Program	1	Irrelevant Data (Note 1)
		4	1	Stack Pointer	0	Return Address (Low Order Byte)
		5	1	Stack Pointer − 1	0	Return Address (High Order Byte)
		6	0	Stack Pointer − 2	1	Irrelevant Data (Note 1)
		7	0	Return Address of Main Program	1	Irrelevant Data (Note 1)
		8	0	Subroutine Address	1	Irrelevant Data (Note 1)

Note 1.   If device which is addressed during this cycle uses VMA, then the Data Bus will go to the high impedance three-state condition. Depending on bus capacitance, data from the previous cycle may be retained on the Data Bus.

FIGURE 32 – RELATIVE ADDRESSING MODE

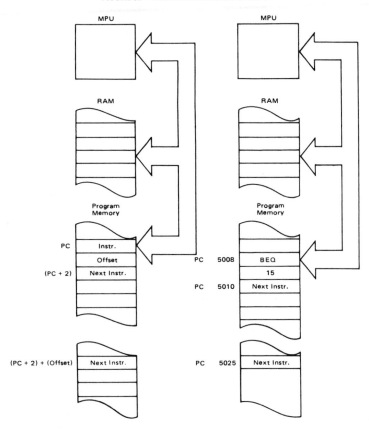

Indexed Addressing Mode — With Indexed addressing, the numerical address is variable and depend on the current contents of the Index Register. A source statement such as

Operator	Operand	Comment
STAA	X	PUT A IN INDEXED LOCATION

causes the MPU to store the contents of accumulator A in the memory location specified by the contents of the Index Register (recall that the label "X" is reserved to designate the Index Register). Since there are instructions for manipulating X during program execution (LDX, INX, DEX, etc.), the Indexed addressing mode provides a dynamic "on the fly" way to modify program activity.

The operand field can also contain a numerical value that will be automatically added to X during execution. This format is illustrated in Figure 33.

When the MPU encounters the LDAB (Indexed) opcode in location 5006, it looks in the next memory location for the value to be added to X (5 in the example) and calculates the required address by adding 5 to the present Index Register value of 400. In the operand format, the offset may be represented by a label or a numerical value in the range 0–255 as in the example. In the earlier example, STAA X, the operand is equivalent to 0,X, that is, the 0 may be omitted when the desired address is equal to X. Table 16 shows the cycle-by-cycle operation for the Indexed Mode of Addressing.

FIGURE 33 — INDEXED ADDRESSING MODE

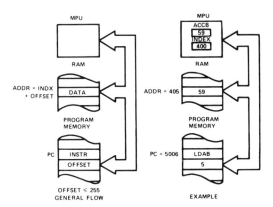

TABLE 16 — INDEXED MODE CYCLE BY CYCLE

Address Mode and Instructions	Cycles	Cycle #	VMA Line	Address Bus	R/W Line	Data Bus
INDEXED						
JMP	4	1	1	Op Code Address	1	Op Code
		2	1	Op Code Address + 1	1	Offset
		3	0	Index Register	1	Irrelevant Data (Note 1)
		4	0	Index Register Plus Offset (w/o Carry)	1	Irrelevant Data (Note 1)
ADC EOR ADD LDA AND ORA BIT SBC CMP SUB	5	1	1	Op Code Address	1	Op Code
		2	1	Op Code Address + 1	1	Offset
		3	0	Index Register	1	Irrelevant Data (Note 1)
		4	0	Index Register Plus Offset (w/o Carry)	1	Irrelevant Data (Note 1)
		5	1	Index Register Plus Offset	1	Operand Data
CPX LDS LDX	6	1	1	Op Code Address	1	Op Code
		2	1	Op Code Address + 1	1	Offset
		3	0	Index Register	1	Irrelevant Data (Note 1)
		4	0	Index Register Plus Offset (w/o Carry)	1	Irrelevant Data (Note 1)
		5	1	Index Register Plus Offset	1	Operand Data (High Order Byte)
		6	1	Index Register Plus Offset + 1	1	Operand Data (Low Order Byte)
STA	6	1	1	Op Code Address	1	Op Code
		2	1	Op Code Address + 1	1	Offset
		3	0	Index Register	1	Irrelevant Data (Note 1)
		4	0	Index Register Plus Offset (w/o Carry)	1	Irrelevant Data (Note 1)
		5	0	Index Register Plus Offset	1	Irrelevant Data (Note 1)
		6	1	Index Register Plus Offset	0	Operand Data
ASL LSR ASR NEG CLR ROL COM ROR DEC TST INC	7	1	1	Op Code Address	1	Op Code
		2	1	Op Code Address + 1	1	Offset
		3	0	Index Register	1	Irrelevant Data (Note 1)
		4	0	Index Register Plus Offset (w/o Carry)	1	Irrelevant Data (Note 1)
		5	1	Index Register Plus Offset	1	Current Operand Data
		6	0	Index Register Plus Offset	1	Irrelevant Data (Note 1)
		7	1/0 (Note 2)	Index Register Plus Offset	0	New Operand Data (Note 2)
STS STX	7	1	1	Op Code Address	1	Op Code
		2	1	Op Code Address + 1	1	Offset
		3	0	Index Register	1	Irrelevant Data (Note 1)
		4	0	Index Register Plus Offset (w/o Carry)	1	Irrelevant Data (Note 1)
		5	0	Index Register Plus Offset	1	Irrelevant Data (Note 1)
		6	1	Index Register Plus Offset	0	Operand Data (High Order Byte)
		7	1	Index Register Plus Offset + 1	0	Operand Data (Low Order Byte)
JSR	8	1	1	Op Code Address	1	Op Code
		2	1	Op Code Address + 1	1	Offset
		3	0	Index Register	1	Irrelevant Data (Note 1)
		4	1	Stack Pointer	0	Return Address (Low Order Byte)
		5	1	Stack Pointer − 1	0	Return Address (High Order Byte)
		6	0	Stack Pointer − 2	1	Irrelevant Data (Note 1)
		7	0	Index Register	1	Irrelevant Data (Note 1)
		8	0	Index Register Plus Offset (w/o Carry)	1	Irrelevant Data (Note 1)

Note 1.   If device which is addressed during this cycle uses VMA, then the Data Bus will go to the high impedance three-state condition. Depending on bus capacitance, data from the previous cycle may be retained on the Data Bus.

Note 2.   For TST, VMA = 0 and Operand data does not change.

PACKAGE DIMENSIONS

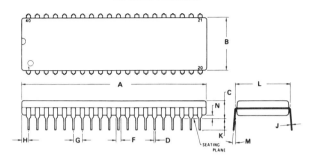

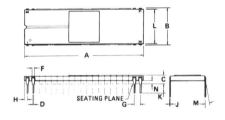

NOTES:
1. LEADS TRUE POSITIONED WITHIN 0.25 mm (0.010) DIA AT SEATING PLANE AT MAXIMUM MATERIAL CONDITION (DIM "D").
2. DIM "L" TO CENTER OF LEADS WHEN FORMED PARALLEL.

DIM	MILLIMETERS		INCHES	
	MIN	MAX	MIN	MAX
A	51.82	52.32	2.040	2.060
B	13.72	14.22	0.540	0.560
C	4.57	5.08	0.180	0.200
D	0.36	0.51	0.014	0.020
F	1.02	1.52	0.040	0.060
G	2.54 BSC		0.100 BSC	
H	1.65	2.16	0.065	0.085
J	0.20	0.30	0.008	0.012
K	3.05	3.56	0.120	0.140
L	15.24 BSC		0.600 BSC	
M	0°	10°	0°	10°
N	0.51	1.02	0.020	0.040

CASE 711-02
(PLASTIC)

DIM	MILLIMETERS		INCHES	
	MIN	MAX	MIN	MAX
A	50.29	51.31	1.980	2.020
B	14.86	15.62	0.585	0.615
C	2.54	4.19	0.130	0.165
D	0.38	0.53	0.015	0.021
F	0.76	1.40	0.030	0.055
G	2.54 BSC		0.100 BSC	
H	0.76	1.78	0.030	0.070
J	0.20	0.33	0.008	0.013
K	2.54	4.19	0.100	0.165
L	14.60	15.37	0.575	0.605
M	0°	10°	0°	10°
N	0.51	1.52	0.020	0.060

NOTE:
1. LEADS, TRUE POSITIONED WITHIN 0.25 mm (0.010) DIA (AT SEATING PLANE), AT MAX. MAT'L CONDITION.

CASE 715-02
(CERAMIC)

MC6802

<table>
<tr><td>

Advance Information

MICROPROCESSOR WITH CLOCK AND RAM

The MC6802 is a monolithic 8-bit microprocessor that contains all the registers and accumulators of the present MC6800 plus an internal clock oscillator and driver on the same chip. In addition, the MC6802 has 128 bytes of RAM on board located at hex addresses 0000 to 007F. The first 32 bytes of RAM, at hex addresses 0000 to 001F, may be retained in a low power mode by utilizing V_{CC} standby, thus facilitating memory retention during a power-down situation.

The MC6802 is completely software compatible with the MC6800 as well as the entire M6800 family of parts. Hence, the MC6802 is expandable to 65K words.

- On-Chip Clock Circuit
- 128 x 8 Bit On-Chip RAM
- 32 Bytes of RAM Are Retainable
- Software-Compatible with the MC6800
- Expandable to 65K words
- Standard TTL-Compatible Inputs and Outputs
- 8 Bit Word Size
- 16 Bit Memory Addressing
- Interrupt Capability

</td><td>

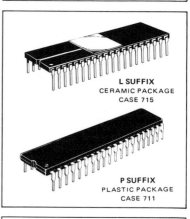

MOS

(N-CHANNEL, SILICON-GATE, DEPLETION LOAD)

MICROPROCESSOR WITH CLOCK AND RAM

L SUFFIX
CERAMIC PACKAGE
CASE 715

P SUFFIX
PLASTIC PACKAGE
CASE 711

</td></tr>
</table>

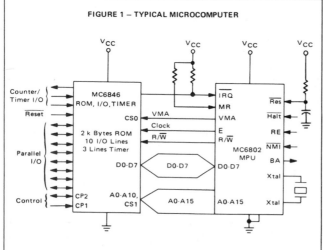

FIGURE 1 – TYPICAL MICROCOMPUTER

Figure 1 is a block diagram of a typical cost effective microcomputer. The MPU is the center of the microcomputer system and is shown in a minimum system interfacing with a ROM combination chip. It is not intended that this system be limited to this function but that it be expandable with other parts in the M6800 Microcomputer family.

PIN ASSIGNMENT

1	V_{SS}	Reset	40
2	Halt	Xtal	39
3	MR	EXtal	38
4	IRQ	E	37
5	VMA	RE	36
6	NMI	V_{CC} Standby	35
7	BA	R/W	34
8	V_{CC}	D0	33
9	A0	D1	32
10	A1	D2	31
11	A2	D3	30
12	A3	D4	29
13	A4	D5	28
14	A5	D6	27
15	A6	D7	26
16	A7	A15	25
17	A8	A14	24
18	A9	A13	23
19	A10	A12	22
20	A11	V_{SS}	21

MAXIMUM RATINGS

Rating	Symbol	Value	Unit
Supply Voltage	V_{CC}	–0.3 to +7.0	Vdc
Input Voltage	V_{in}	–0.3 to +7.0	Vdc
Operating Temperature Range	T_A	0 to +70	°C
Storage Temperature Range	T_{stg}	–55 to +150	°C
Thermal Resistance	θ_{JA}	70	°C/W

This device contains circuitry to protect the inputs against damage due to high static voltages or electric fields; however, it is advised that normal precautions be taken to avoid application of any voltage higher than maximum rated voltages to this high impedance circuit.

ELECTRICAL CHARACTERISTICS (V_{CC} = 5.0 V ± 5%, V_{SS} = 0, T_A = 0 to 70°C unless otherwise noted.)

Characteristic		Symbol	Min	Typ	Max	Unit
Input High Voltage	Logic, EXtal	V_{IH}	V_{SS} + 2.0	–	V_{CC}	Vdc
	$\overline{Reset}$		V_{SS} + 4.0	–	V_{CC}	
Input Low Voltage	Logic, EXtal, $\overline{Reset}$	V_{IL}	V_{SS} – 0.3	–	V_{SS} + 0.8	Vdc
Input Leakage Current (V_{in} = 0 to 5.25 V, V_{CC} = max)	Logic*	I_{in}	–	1.0	2.5	µAdc
Output High Voltage		V_{OH}				Vdc
(I_{Load} = –205 µAdc, V_{CC} = min)	D0-D7		V_{SS} + 2.4	–	–	
(I_{Load} = –145 µAdc, V_{CC} = min)	A0-A15, R/$\overline{W}$, VMA, E		V_{SS} + 2.4	–	–	
(I_{Load} = –100 µAdc, V_{CC} = min)	BA		V_{SS} + 2.4	–	–	
Output Low Voltage (I_{Load} = 1.6 mAdc, V_{CC} = min)		V_{OL}	–	–	V_{SS} + 0.4	Vdc
Power Dissipation		P_D**	–	0.600	1.2	W
Capacitance # (V_{in} = 0, T_A = 25°C, f = 1.0 MHz)		C_{in}				pF
	D0-D7		–	10	12.5	
	Logic Inputs, EXtal		–	6.5	10	
	A0-A15, R/$\overline{W}$, VMA	C_{out}	–	–	12	pF
Frequency of Operation (Input Clock ÷4)		f	0.1	–	1.0	MHz
(Crystal Frequency)		f_{Xtal}	1.0	–	4.0	
Clock Timing						
Cycle Time		t_{cyc}	1.0	–	10	µs
Clock Pulse Width (Measured at 2.4 V)		$PW_{\phi H}$s $PW_{\phi L}$	450	–	4500	ns
Fall Time (Measured between V_{SS} + 0.4 V and V_{SS} – 2.4 V)		t_ϕ	–	–	25	ns

*Except $\overline{IRQ}$ and $\overline{NMI}$, which require 3 kΩ pullup load resistors for wire-OR capability at optimum operation. Does not include EXtal and Xtal, which are crystal inputs.

**In power-down mode, maximum power dissipation is less than 40 mW.

#Capacitances are periodically sampled rather than 100% tested.

READ/WRITE TIMING (Figures 2 through 6; Load Circuit of Figure 4.)

Characteristic	Symbol	Min	Typ	Max	Unit
Address Delay	t_{AD}	–	–	270	ns
Peripheral Read Access Time $t_{acc} = t_{ut} - (t_{AD} + t_{DSR})$	t_{acc}	–	–	530	ns
Data Setup Time (Read)	t_{DSR}	100	–	–	ns
Input Data Hold Time	t_H	10	–	–	ns
Output Data Hold Time	t_H	20	–	–	ns
Address Hold Time (Address, R/$\overline{W}$, VMA)	t_{AH}	20	–	–	ns
Data Delay Time (Write)	t_{DDW}	–	165	225	ns
Processor Controls					
Processor Control Setup Time	t_{PCS}	200	–	–	ns
Processor Control Rise and Fall Time (Measured between 0.8 V and 2.0 V)	t_{PCr}, t_{PCf}	–	–	100	ns

FIGURE 2 — READ DATA FROM MEMORY OR PERIPHERALS

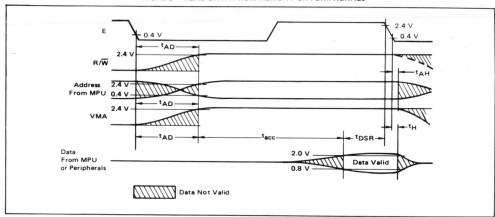

FIGURE 3 — WRITE DATA IN MEMORY OR PERIPHERALS

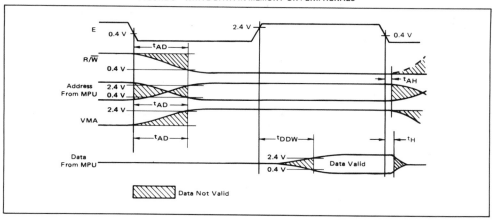

FIGURE 4 — BUS TIMING TEST LOAD

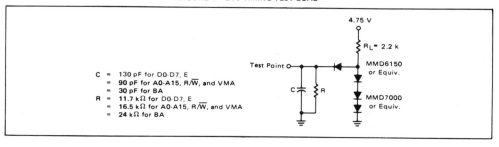

**FIGURE 5 — TYPICAL DATA BUS OUTPUT DELAY
versus CAPACITIVE LOADING**

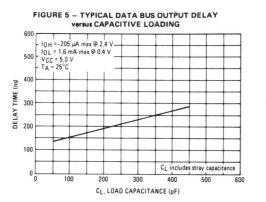

**FIGURE 6 — TYPICAL READ/WRITE, VMA, AND
ADDRESS OUTPUT DELAY versus CAPACITIVE LOADING**

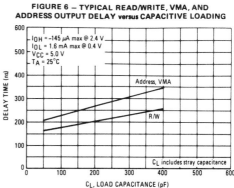

FIGURE 7 — MC6802 EXPANDED BLOCK DIAGRAM

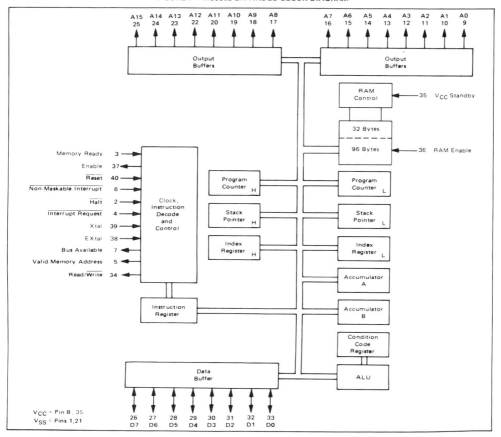

MPU REGISTERS

A general block diagram of the MC6802 is shown in Figure 7. As shown, the number and configuration of the registers are the same as for the MC6800. The 128 x 8 bit RAM has been added to the basic MPU. The first 32 bytes may be operated in a low power mode via a V_{CC} standby. These 32 bytes can be retained during power-up and power-down conditions via the RE signal.

The MPU has three 16-bit registers and three 8-bit registers available for use by the programmer (Figure 8).

Program Counter — The program counter is a two byte (16-bits) register that points to the current program address.

Stack Pointer — The stack pointer is a two byte register that contains the address of the next available location in an external push-down/pop-up stack. This stack is normally a random access Read/Write memory that may have any location (address) that is convenient. In those applications that require storage of information in the stack when power is lost, the stack must be non-volatile.

Index Register — The index register is a two byte register that is used to store data or a sixteen bit memory address for the Indexed mode of memory addressing.

Accumulators — The MPU contains two 8-bit accumulators that are used to hold operands and results from an arithmetic logic unit (ALU).

Condition Code Register — The condition code register indicates the results of an Arithmetic Logic Unit operation: Negative (N), Zero (Z), Overflow (V), Carry from bit 7 (C), and half carry from bit 3 (H). These bits of the Condition Code Register are used as testable conditions for the conditional branch instructions. Bit 4 is the interrupt mask bit (I). The used bits of the Condition Code Register (b6 and b7) are ones.

Figure 9 shows the order of saving the microprocessor status within the stack.

FIGURE 8 — PROGRAMMING MODEL OF THE MICROPROCESSING UNIT

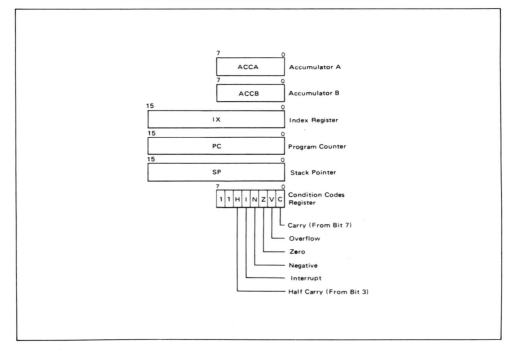

FIGURE 9 — SAVING THE STATUS OF THE MICROPROCESSOR IN THE STACK

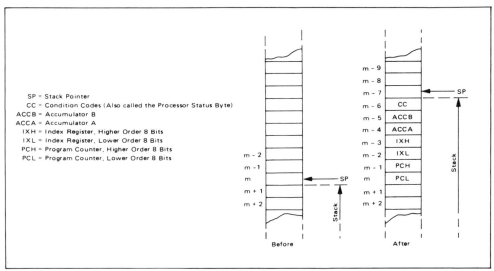

SP = Stack Pointer
CC = Condition Codes (Also called the Processor Status Byte)
ACCB = Accumulator B
ACCA = Accumulator A
IXH = Index Register, Higher Order 8 Bits
IXL = Index Register, Lower Order 8 Bits
PCH = Program Counter, Higher Order 8 Bits
PCL = Program Counter, Lower Order 8 Bits

MC6802 MPU SIGNAL DESCRIPTION

Proper operation of the MPU requires that certain control and timing signals be provided to accomplish specific functions and that other signal lines be monitored to determine the state of the processor. These control and timing signals for the MC6802 are identical to those of the MC6800 except that TSC, DBE, $\phi1$, $\phi2$ input, and two unused pins have been eliminated, and the following signal and timing lines have been added:

RAM Enable (RE)
Crystal Connections EXtal and Xtal
Memory Ready (MR)
V_{CC} Standby
Enable $\phi2$ Output (E)

The following is a summary of the MC6802 MPU signals:

Address Bus (A0-A15) — Sixteen pins are used for the address bus. The outputs are capable of driving one standard TTL load and 130 pF.

Data Bus (D0-D7) — Eight pins are used for the data bus. It is bidirectional, transferring data to and from the memory and peripheral devices. It also has three-state output buffers capable of driving one standard TTL load and 130 pF.

Halt — When this input is in the low state, all activity in the machine will be halted. This input is level sensitive. In the halt mode, the machine will stop at the end of an instruction, Bus Available will be at a high state, Valid Memory Address will be at a low state, and all other three-state lines will be in the three-state mode. The address bus will display the address of the next instruction.

To insure single instruction operation, transition of the Halt line must not occur during the last 250 ns of E and the Halt line must go high for one Clock cycle.

Read/Write (R/W) — This TTL compatible output signals the peripherals and memory devices whether the MPU is in a Read (high) or Write (low) state. The normal standby state of this signal is Read (high). When the processor is halted, it will be in the logical one state. This output is capable of driving one standard TTL load and 90 pF.

Valid Memory Address (VMA) — This output indicates to peripheral devices that there is a valid address on the address bus. In normal operation, this signal should be utilized for enabling peripheral interfaces such as the PIA and ACIA. This signal is not three-state. One standard TTL load and 90 pF may be directly driven by this active high signal.

Bus Available (BA) — The Bus Available signal will normally be in the low state; when activated, it will go to the high state indicating that the microprocessor has stopped and that the address bus is available. This will occur if the $\overline{\text{Halt}}$ line is in the low state or the processor is in the WAIT state as a result of the execution of a WAIT instruction. At such time, all three-state output drivers will go to their off state and other outputs to their normally inactive level. The processor is removed from the WAIT state by the occurrence of a maskable (mask bit I = 0) or nonmaskable interrupt. This output is capable of driving one standard TTL load and 30 pF.

Interrupt Request ($\overline{\text{IRQ}}$) — This level sensitive input requests that an interrupt sequence be generated within the machine. The processor will wait until it completes the current instruction that is being executed before it recognizes the request. At that time, if the interrupt mask bit in the Condition Code Register is not set, the machine will begin an interrupt sequence. The Index Register, Program Counter, Accumulators, and Condition Code Register are stored away on the stack. Next the MPU will respond to the interrupt request by setting the interrupt mask bit high so that no further interrupts may occur. At the end of the cycle, a 16-bit address will be loaded that points to a vectoring address which is located in memory locations FFF8 and FFF9. An address loaded at these locations causes the MPU to branch to an interrupt routine in memory.

The $\overline{\text{Halt}}$ line must be in the high state for interrupts to be serviced. Interrupts will be latched internally while $\overline{\text{Halt}}$ is low.

The $\overline{\text{IRQ}}$ has a high impedance pullup device internal to the chip; however a 3 kΩ external resistor to V_{CC} should be used for wire-OR and optimum control of interrupts.

Reset — This input is used to reset and start the MPU from a power down condition, resulting from a power failure or an initial start-up of the processor. When this line is low, the MPU is inactive and the information in the registers will be lost. If a high level is detected on the input, this will signal the MPU to begin the restart sequence. This will start execution of a routine to initialize the processor from its reset condition. All the higher order address lines will be forced high. For the restart, the last two (FFFE, FFFF) locations in memory will be used to load the program that is addressed by the program counter. During the restart routine, the interrupt mask bit is set and must be reset before the MPU can be interrupted by $\overline{\text{IRQ}}$. Power-up and reset timing and power-down sequences are shown in Figures 10 and 11, respectively.

FIGURE 10 — POWER-UP AND RESET TIMING

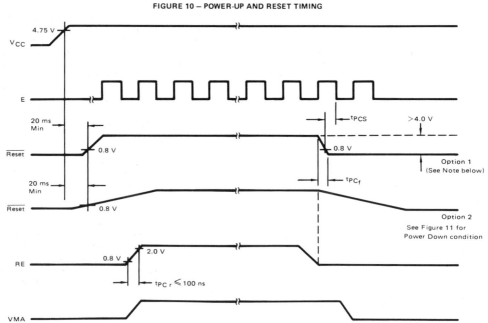

NOTE: If option 1 is chosen, $\overline{\text{Reset}}$ and RE pins can be tied together.

FIGURE 11 – POWER-DOWN SEQUENCE

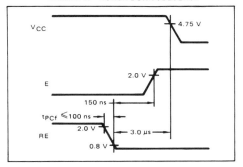

Figure 12 is a flow chart describing the major decision paths and interrupt vectors of the microprocessor. Table 1 gives the memory map for interrupt vectors.

RAM Enable (RE) — A TTL-compatible RAM enable input controls the on-chip RAM of the MC6802. When placed in the high state, the on-chip memory is enabled to respond to the MPU controls. In the low state, RAM is disabled. This pin may also be utilized to disable reading and writing the on-chip RAM during a power-down situation. RAM enable must be low three μs before V_{CC} goes below 4.75 V during power-down.

EXtal and Xtal — The MC6802 has an internal oscillator that may be crystal controlled. These connections are for a series resonant fundamental crystal. (AT cut.) A divide-by-four circuit has been added to the MC6802 so that a 4 MHz crystal may be used in lieu of a 1 MHz crystal for a more cost effective system. Pin 38 of the MC6802 may be driven externally by a TTL input signal if a separate clock is required. Pin 39 is to be left open in this mode.

Memory Ready (MR) — MR is a TTL compatible input control signal which allows stretching of E. When RM is high, E will be in normal operation. When MR is low, E may be stretched integral multiples of half periods, thus allowing interface to slow memories. Memory Ready timing is shown in Figure 13.

Enable (E) — This pin supplies the clock for the MPU and the rest of the system. This is a single phase, TTL compatible clock. This clock may be conditioned by a Memory Ready Signal. This is equivalent to $\phi 2$ on the MC6800.

V_{CC} Standby — This pin supplies the dc voltage to the first 32 bytes of RAM as well as the RAM Enable (RE) control logic. Thus retention of data in this portion of the RAM on a power-up, power-down, or standby condition is guaranteed. Maximum current drain at 5.25 V is 8 mA.

Non-Maskable Interrupt (NMI) — A low-going edge on this input requests that a non-mask-interrupt sequence be generated within the processor. As with the $\overline{\text{Interrupt}}$ $\overline{\text{Request}}$ signal, the processor will complete the current instruction that is being executed before it recognizes the $\overline{\text{NMI}}$ signal. The interrupt mask bit in the Condition Code Register has no effect on $\overline{\text{NMI}}$.

The index Register, Program Counter, Accumulators, and Condition Code Register are stored away on the stack. At the end of the cycle, a 16-bit address will be loaded that points to a vectoring address which is located in memory locations FFFC and FFFD. An address loaded at these locations caused the MPU to branch to a non-maskable interrupt routine in memory.

$\overline{\text{NMI}}$ has a high impedance pullup resistor internal to the chip; however a 3 kΩ external resistor to V_{CC} should be used for wire-OR and optimum control of interrupts.

Inputs $\overline{\text{IRQ}}$ and $\overline{\text{NMI}}$ are hardware interrupt lines that are sampled when E is high and will start the interrupt routine on a low E following the completion of an instruction.

TABLE 1 – MEMORY MAP FOR INTERRUPT VECTORS

Vector		Description
MS	LS	
FFFE	FFFF	Restart
FFFC	FFFD	Non-maskable Interrupt
FFFA	FFFB	Software Interrupt
FFF8	FFF9	Interrupt Request

FIGURE 12 – MPU FLOW CHART

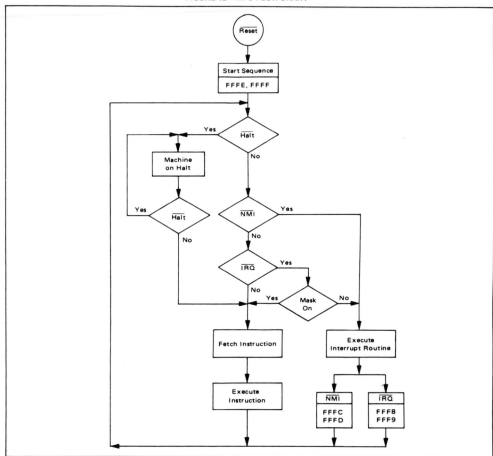

FIGURE 13 – MEMORY READY CONTROL FUNCTION

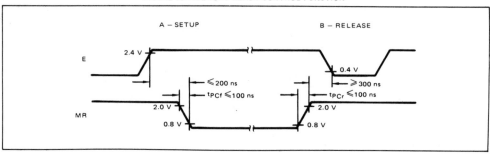

MPU INSTRUCTION SET

The MC6802 has a set of 72 different instructions. Included are binary and decimal arithmetic, logical, shift, rotate, load, store, conditional or unconditional branch, interrupt and stack manipulation instructions (Tables 2 thru 6). This instruction set is the same as that for the MC6800.

MPU ADDRESSING MODES

The MC6802 eight-bit microprocessing unit has seven address modes that can be used by a programmer, with the addressing mode a function of both the type of instruction and the coding within the instruction. A summary of the addressing modes for a particular instruction can be found in Table 7 along with the associated instruction execution time that is given in machine cycles. With a clock frequency of 1 MHz, these times would be microseconds.

Accumulator (ACCX) Addressing — In accumulator only addressing, either accumulator A or accumulator B is specified. These are one-byte instructions.

Immediate Addressing — In immediate addressing, the operand is contained in the second byte of the instruction except LDS and LDX which have the operand in the second and third bytes of the instruction. The MPU addresses this location when it fetches the immediate instruction for execution. These are two or three-byte instructions.

Direct Addressing — In direct addressing, the address of the operand is contained in the second byte of the instruction. Direct addressing allows the user to directly address the lowest 256 bytes in the machine i.e., locations zero through 255. Enhanced execution times are achieved by storing data in these locations. In most configurations, it should be a random access memory. These are two-byte instructions.

Extended Addressing — In extended addressing, the address contained in the second byte of the instruction is used as the higher eight-bits of the address of the operand. The third byte of the instruction is used as the lower eight-bits of the address for the operand. This is an absolute address in memory. These are three-byte instructions.

Indexed Addressing — In indexed addressing, the address contained in the second byte of the instruction is added to the index register's lowest eight bits in the MPU. The carry is then added to the higher order eight bits of the index register. This result is then used to address memory. The modified address is held in a temporary address register so there is no change to the index register. These are two-byte instructions.

Implied Addressing — In the implied addressing mode the instruction gives the address (i.e., stack pointer, index register, etc.). These are one-byte instructions.

Relative Addressing — In relative addressing, the address contained in the second byte of the instruction is added to the program counter's lowest eight bits plus two. The carry or borrow is then added to the high eight bits. This allows the user to address data within a range of –125 to +129 bytes of the present instruction. These are two-byte instructions.

TABLE 2 – MICROPROCESSOR INSTRUCTION SET – ALPHABETIC SEQUENCE

ABA	Add Accumulators	CLR	Clear	PUL	Pull Data
ADC	Add with Carry	CLV	Clear Overflow	ROL	Rotate Left
ADD	Add	CMP	Compare	ROR	Rotate Right
AND	Logical And	COM	Complement	RTI	Return from Interrupt
ASL	Arithmetic Shift Left	CPX	Compare Index Register	RTS	Return from Subroutine
ASR	Arithmetic Shift Right	DAA	Decimal Adjust		
BCC	Branch if Carry Clear	DEC	Decrement	SBA	Subtract Accumulators
BCS	Branch if Carry Set	DES	Decrement Stack Pointer	SBC	Subtract with Carry
BEQ	Branch if Equal to Zero	DEX	Decrement Index Register	SEC	Set Carry
BGE	Branch if Greater or Equal Zero	EOR	Exclusive OR	SEI	Set Interrupt Mask
BGT	Branch if Greater than Zero			SEV	Set Overflow
BHI	Branch if Higher	INC	Increment	STA	Store Accumulator
BIT	Bit Test	INS	Increment Stack Pointer	STS	Store Stack Register
BLE	Branch if Less or Equal	INX	Increment Index Register	STX	Store Index Register
BLS	Branch if Lower or Same			SUB	Subtract
BLT	Branch if Less than Zero	JMP	Jump	SWI	Software Interrupt
BMI	Branch if Minus	JSR	Jump to Subroutine	TAB	Transfer Accumulators
BNE	Branch if Not Equal to Zero	LDA	Load Accumulator	TAP	Transfer Accumulators to Condition Code Reg.
BPL	Branch if Plus	LDS	Load Stack Pointer	TBA	Transfer Accumulators
BRA	Branch Always	LDX	Load Index Register	TPA	Transfer Condition Code Reg. to Accumulator
BSR	Branch to Subroutine	LSR	Logical Shift Right	TST	Test
BVC	Branch if Overflow Clear	NEG	Negate	TSX	Transfer Stack Pointer to Index Register
BVS	Branch if Overflow Set	NOP	No Operation	TXS	Transfer Index Register to Stack Pointer
CBA	Compare Accumulators	ORA	Inclusive OR Accumulator	WAI	Wait for Interrupt
CLC	Clear Carry	PSH	Push Data		
CLI	Clear Interrupt Mask				

TABLE 3 – ACCUMULATOR AND MEMORY INSTRUCTIONS

OPERATIONS	MNEMONIC	IMMED OP	~	#	DIRECT OP	~	#	INDEX OP	~	#	EXTND OP	~	#	IMPLIED OP	~	#	BOOLEAN/ARITHMETIC OPERATION (All register labels refer to contents)	H	I	N	Z	V	C
Add	ADDA	8B	2	2	9B	3	2	AB	5	2	BB	4	3				A + M → A	↕	●	↕	↕	↕	↕
	ADDB	CB	2	2	DB	3	2	EB	5	2	FB	4	3				B + M → B	↕	●	↕	↕	↕	↕
Add Acmltrs	ABA													1B	2	1	A + B → A	↕	●	↕	↕	↕	↕
Add with Carry	ADCA	89	2	2	99	3	2	A9	5	2	B9	4	3				A + M + C → A	↕	●	↕	↕	↕	↕
	ADCB	C9	2	2	D9	3	2	E9	5	2	F9	4	3				B + M + C → B	↕	●	↕	↕	↕	↕
And	ANDA	84	2	2	94	3	2	A4	5	2	B4	4	3				A · M → A	●	●	↕	↕	R	●
	ANDB	C4	2	2	D4	3	2	E4	5	2	F4	4	3				B · M → B	●	●	↕	↕	R	●
Bit Test	BITA	85	2	2	95	3	2	A5	5	2	B5	4	3				A · M	●	●	↕	↕	R	●
	BITB	C5	2	2	D5	3	2	E5	5	2	F5	4	3				B · M	●	●	↕	↕	R	●
Clear	CLR							6F	7	2	7F	6	3				00 → M	●	●	R	S	R	R
	CLRA													4F	2	1	00 → A	●	●	R	S	R	R
	CLRB													5F	2	1	00 → B	●	●	R	S	R	R
Compare	CMPA	81	2	2	91	3	2	A1	5	2	B1	4	3				A − M	●	●	↕	↕	↕	↕
	CMPB	C1	2	2	D1	3	2	E1	5	2	F1	4	3				B − M	●	●	↕	↕	↕	↕
Compare Acmltrs	CBA													11	2	1	A − B	●	●	↕	↕	↕	↕
Complement, 1's	COM							63	7	2	73	6	3				$\overline{M}$ → M	●	●	↕	↕	R	S
	COMA													43	2	1	$\overline{A}$ → A	●	●	↕	↕	R	S
	COMB													53	2	1	$\overline{B}$ → B	●	●	↕	↕	R	S
Complement, 2's	NEG							60	7	2	70	6	3				00 − M → M	●	●	↕	↕	①	②
(Negate)	NEGA													40	2	1	00 − A → A	●	●	↕	↕	①	②
	NEGB													50	2	1	00 − B → B	●	●	↕	↕	①	②
Decimal Adjust, A	DAA													19	2	1	Converts Binary Add. of BCD Characters into BCD Format	●	●	↕	↕	↕	③
Decrement	DEC							6A	7	2	7A	6	3				M − 1 → M	●	●	↕	↕	④	●
	DECA													4A	2	1	A − 1 → A	●	●	↕	↕	④	●
	DECB													5A	2	1	B − 1 → B	●	●	↕	↕	④	●
Exclusive OR	EORA	88	2	2	98	3	2	A8	5	2	B8	4	3				A ⊙ M → A	●	●	↕	↕	R	●
	EORB	C8	2	2	D8	3	2	E8	5	2	F8	4	3				B ⊙ M → B	●	●	↕	↕	R	●
Increment	INC							6C	7	2	7C	6	3				M + 1 → M	●	●	↕	↕	⑤	●
	INCA													4C	2	1	A + 1 → A	●	●	↕	↕	⑤	●
	INCB													5C	2	1	B + 1 → B	●	●	↕	↕	⑤	●
Load Acmltr	LDAA	86	2	2	96	3	2	A6	5	2	B6	4	3				M → A	●	●	↕	↕	R	●
	LDAB	C6	2	2	D6	3	2	E6	5	2	F6	4	3				M → B	●	●	↕	↕	R	●
Or, Inclusive	ORAA	8A	2	2	9A	3	2	AA	5	2	BA	4	3				A + M → A	●	●	↕	↕	R	●
	ORAB	CA	2	2	DA	3	2	EA	5	2	FA	4	3				B + M → B	●	●	↕	↕	R	●
Push Data	PSHA													36	4	1	A → M$_{SP}$, SP − 1 → SP	●	●	●	●	●	●
	PSHB													37	4	1	B → M$_{SP}$, SP − 1 → SP	●	●	●	●	●	●
Pull Data	PULA													32	4	1	SP + 1 → SP, M$_{SP}$ → A	●	●	●	●	●	●
	PULB													33	4	1	SP + 1 → SP, M$_{SP}$ → B	●	●	●	●	●	●
Rotate Left	ROL							69	7	2	79	6	3				M	●	●	↕	↕	⑥	↕
	ROLA													49	2	1	A	●	●	↕	↕	⑥	↕
	ROLB													59	2	1	B	●	●	↕	↕	⑥	↕
Rotate Right	ROR							66	7	2	76	6	3				M	●	●	↕	↕	⑥	↕
	RORA													46	2	1	A	●	●	↕	↕	⑥	↕
	RORB													56	2	1	B	●	●	↕	↕	⑥	↕
Shift Left, Arithmetic	ASL							68	7	2	78	6	3				M	●	●	↕	↕	⑥	↕
	ASLA													48	2	1	A	●	●	↕	↕	⑥	↕
	ASLB													58	2	1	B	●	●	↕	↕	⑥	↕
Shift Right, Arithmetic	ASR							67	7	2	77	6	3				M	●	●	↕	↕	⑥	↕
	ASRA													47	2	1	A	●	●	↕	↕	⑥	↕
	ASRB													57	2	1	B	●	●	↕	↕	⑥	↕
Shift Right, Logic	LSR							64	7	2	74	6	3				M	●	●	R	↕	⑥	↕
	LSRA													44	2	1	A	●	●	R	↕	⑥	↕
	LSRB													54	2	1	B	●	●	R	↕	⑥	↕
Store Acmltr.	STAA				97	4	2	A7	6	2	B7	5	3				A → M	●	●	↕	↕	R	●
	STAB				D7	4	2	E7	6	2	F7	5	3				B → M	●	●	↕	↕	R	●
Subtract	SUBA	80	2	2	90	3	2	A0	5	2	B0	4	3				A − M → A	●	●	↕	↕	↕	↕
	SUBB	C0	2	2	D0	3	2	E0	5	2	F0	4	3				B − M → B	●	●	↕	↕	↕	↕
Subtract Acmltrs.	SBA													10	2	1	A − B → A	●	●	↕	↕	↕	↕
Subtr. with Carry	SBCA	82	2	2	92	3	2	A2	5	2	B2	4	3				A − M − C → A	●	●	↕	↕	↕	↕
	SBCB	C2	2	2	D2	3	2	E2	5	2	F2	4	3				B − M − C → B	●	●	↕	↕	↕	↕
Transfer Acmltrs	TAB													16	2	1	A → B	●	●	↕	↕	R	●
	TBA													17	2	1	B → A	●	●	↕	↕	R	●
Test, Zero or Minus	TST							6D	7	2	7D	6	3				M − 00	●	●	↕	↕	R	R
	TSTA													4D	2	1	A − 00	●	●	↕	↕	R	R
	TSTB													5D	2	1	B − 00	●	●	↕	↕	R	R

H	I	N	Z	V	C

LEGEND:

OP   Operation Code (Hexadecimal);
~   Number of MPU Cycles;
=   Number of Program Bytes;
+   Arithmetic Plus;
−   Arithmetic Minus;
·   Boolean AND;
M$_{SP}$ Contents of memory location pointed to be Stack Pointer;

+   Boolean Inclusive OR;
⊙   Boolean Exclusive OR;
$\overline{M}$ Complement of M;
→   Transfer Into;
0   Bit = Zero;
00   Byte = Zero;

CONDITION CODE SYMBOLS:

H   Half-carry from bit 3;
I   Interrupt mask
N   Negative (sign bit)
Z   Zero (byte)
V   Overflow, 2's complement
C   Carry from bit 7
R   Reset Always
S   Set Always
↕   Test and set if true, cleared otherwise
●   Not Affected

Note – Accumulator addressing mode instructions are included in the column for IMPLIED addressing

TABLE 4 – INDEX REGISTER AND STACK MANIPULATION INSTRUCTIONS

POINTER OPERATIONS	MNEMONIC	IMMED OP	~	#	DIRECT OP	~	#	INDEX OP	~	#	EXTND OP	~	#	IMPLIED OP	~	#	BOOLEAN/ARITHMETIC OPERATION	H	I	N	Z	V	C
Compare Index Reg	CPX	8C	3	3	9C	4	2	AC	6	2	BC	5	3				$X_H - M$, $X_L - (M + 1)$	•	•	⑦	↕	⑧	•
Decrement Index Reg	DEX													09	4	1	$X - 1 \rightarrow X$	•	•	•	↕	•	•
Decrement Stack Pntr	DES													34	4	1	$SP - 1 \rightarrow SP$	•	•	•	•	•	•
Increment Index Reg	INX													08	4	1	$X + 1 \rightarrow X$	•	•	•	↕	•	•
Increment Stack Pntr	INS													31	4	1	$SP + 1 \rightarrow SP$	•	•	•	•	•	•
Load Index Reg	LDX	CE	3	3	DE	4	2	EE	6	2	FE	5	3				$M \rightarrow X_H$, $(M + 1) \rightarrow X_L$	•	•	⑨	↕	R	•
Load Stack Pntr	LDS	8E	3	3	9E	4	2	AE	6	2	BE	5	3				$M \rightarrow SP_H$, $(M + 1) \rightarrow SP_L$	•	•	⑨	↕	R	•
Store Index Reg	STX				DF	5	2	EF	7	2	FF	6	3				$X_H \rightarrow M$, $X_L \rightarrow (M + 1)$	•	•	⑨	↕	R	•
Store Stack Pntr	STS				9F	5	2	AF	7	2	BF	6	3				$SP_H \rightarrow M$, $SP_L \rightarrow (M + 1)$	•	•	⑨	↕	R	•
Indx Reg → Stack Pntr	TXS													35	4	1	$X - 1 \rightarrow SP$	•	•	•	•	•	•
Stack Pntr → Indx Reg	TSX													30	4	1	$SP + 1 \rightarrow X$	•	•	•	•	•	•

COND. CODE REG. columns: 5 H, 4 I, 3 N, 2 Z, 1 V, 0 C

TABLE 5 – JUMP AND BRANCH INSTRUCTIONS

OPERATIONS	MNEMONIC	RELATIVE OP	~	#	INDEX OP	~	#	EXTND OP	~	#	IMPLIED OP	~	#	BRANCH TEST	H	I	N	Z	V	C
Branch Always	BRA	20	4	2										None	•	•	•	•	•	•
Branch If Carry Clear	BCC	24	4	2										C = 0	•	•	•	•	•	•
Branch If Carry Set	BCS	25	4	2										C = 1	•	•	•	•	•	•
Branch If = Zero	BEQ	27	4	2										Z = 1	•	•	•	•	•	•
Branch If ≥ Zero	BGE	2C	4	2										$N \oplus V = 0$	•	•	•	•	•	•
Branch If > Zero	BGT	2E	4	2										$Z + (N \oplus V) = 0$	•	•	•	•	•	•
Branch If Higher	BHI	22	4	2										C + Z = 0	•	•	•	•	•	•
Branch If ≤ Zero	BLE	2F	4	2										$Z + (N \oplus V) = 1$	•	•	•	•	•	•
Branch If Lower Or Same	BLS	23	4	2										C + Z = 1	•	•	•	•	•	•
Branch If < Zero	BLT	2D	4	2										$N \oplus V = 1$	•	•	•	•	•	•
Branch If Minus	BMI	2B	4	2										N = 1	•	•	•	•	•	•
Branch If Not Equal Zero	BNE	26	4	2										Z = 0	•	•	•	•	•	•
Branch If Overflow Clear	BVC	28	4	2										V = 0	•	•	•	•	•	•
Branch If Overflow Set	BVS	29	4	2										V = 1	•	•	•	•	•	•
Branch If Plus	BPL	2A	4	2										N = 0	•	•	•	•	•	•
Branch To Subroutine	BSR	8D	8	2										⎫	•	•	•	•	•	•
Jump	JMP				6E	4	2	7E	3	3				⎬ See Special Operations	•	•	•	•	•	•
Jump To Subroutine	JSR				AD	8	2	BD	9	3				⎭	•	•	•	•	•	•
No Operation	NOP										01	2	1	Advances Prog. Cntr. Only	•	•	•	•	•	•
Return From Interrupt	RTI										3B	10	1				⑩			
Return From Subroutine	RTS										39	5	1	⎫	•	•	•	•	•	•
Software Interrupt	SWI										3F	12	1	⎬ See Special Operations	•	•	•	•	•	•
Wait for Interrupt *	WAI										3E	9	1	⎭	•	⑪	•	•	•	•

COND. CODE REG. columns: 5 H, 4 I, 3 N, 2 Z, 1 V, 0 C

*WAI puts Address Bus, R/W, and Data Bus in the three-state mode while VMA is held low.

SPECIAL OPERATIONS

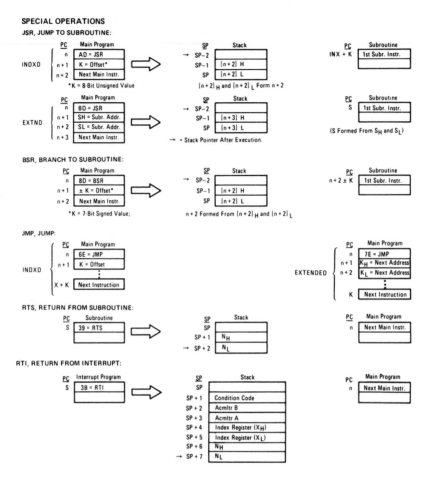

TABLE 6 – CONDITION CODE REGISTER MANIPULATION INSTRUCTIONS

| | | IMPLIED | | | | COND. CODE REG. | | | | | |
OPERATIONS	MNEMONIC	OP	~	#	BOOLEAN OPERATION	5 H	4 I	3 N	2 Z	1 V	0 C
Clear Carry	CLC	0C	2	1	$0 \rightarrow C$	●	●	●	●	●	R
Clear Interrupt Mask	CLI	0E	2	1	$0 \rightarrow I$	●	R	●	●	●	●
Clear Overflow	CLV	0A	2	1	$0 \rightarrow V$	●	●	●	●	R	●
Set Carry	SEC	0D	2	1	$1 \rightarrow C$	●	●	●	●	●	S
Set Interrupt Mask	SEI	0F	2	1	$1 \rightarrow I$	●	S	●	●	●	●
Set Overflow	SEV	0B	2	1	$1 \rightarrow V$	●	●	●	●	S	●
Acmltr A → CCR	TAP	06	2	1	$A \rightarrow CCR$			—⑫—			
CCR → Acmltr A	TPA	07	2	1	$CCR \rightarrow A$	●	●	●	●	●	●

CONDITION CODE REGISTER NOTES: (Bit set if test is true and cleared otherwise)

1	(Bit V)	Test: Result = 10000000?
2	(Bit C)	Test: Result = 00000000?
3	(Bit C)	Test: Decimal value of most significant BCD Character greater than nine? (Not cleared if previously set.)
4	(Bit V)	Test: Operand = 10000000 prior to execution?
5	(Bit V)	Test: Operand = 01111111 prior to execution?
6	(Bit V)	Test: Set equal to result of N⊕C after shift has occurred.
7	(Bit N)	Test: Sign bit of most significant (MS) byte = 1?
8	(Bit V)	Test: 2's complement overflow from subtraction of MS bytes?
9	(Bit N)	Test: Result less than zero? (Bit 15 = 1)
10	(All)	Load Condition Code Register from Stack. (See Special Operations)
11	(Bit I)	Set when interrupt occurs. If previously set, a Non-Maskable Interrupt is required to exit the wait state.
12	(All)	Set according to the contents of Accumulator A.

TABLE 7 – INSTRUCTION ADDRESSING MODES AND ASSOCIATED EXECUTION TIMES
(Times in Machine Cycles)

	(Dual Operand)	ACCX	Immediate	Direct	Extended	Indexed	Implied	Relative
ABA							2	
ADC	x		2	3	4	5		
ADD	x		2	3	4	5		
AND	x		2	3	4	5		
ASL		2			6	7		
ASR		2			6	7		
BCC								4
BCS								4
BEA								4
BGE								4
BGT								4
BHI								4
BIT	x		2	3	4	5		
BLE								4
BLS								4
BLT								4
BMI								4
BNE								4
BPL								4
BRA								4
BSR								8
BVC								4
BVS								4
CBA							2	
CLC							2	
CLI							2	
CLR		2			6	7		
CLV							2	
CMP	x		2	3	4	5		
COM		2			6	7		
CPX			3	4	5	6		
DAA							2	
DEC		2			6	7		
DES							4	
DEX							4	
EOR	x		2	3	4	5		

	(Dual Operand)	ACCX	Immediate	Direct	Extended	Indexed	Implied
INC		2			6	7	
INS							4
INX							4
JMP					3	4	
JSR					9	8	
LDA	x		2	3	4	5	
LDS			3	4	5	6	
LDX			3	4	5	6	
LSR		2			6	7	
NEG		2			6	7	
NOP							2
ORA	x		2	3	4	5	
PSH							4
PUL							4
ROL		2			6	7	
ROR		2			6	7	
RTI							10
RTS							5
SBA							2
SBC	x		2	3	4	5	
SEC							2
SEI							2
SEV							2
STA	x			4	5	6	
STS				5	6	7	
STX				5	6	7	
SUB	x		2	3	4	5	
SWI							12
TAB							2
TAP							2
TBA							2
TPA							2
TST		2			6	7	
TSX							4
TSX							4
WAI							9

NOTE: Interrupt time is 12 cycles from the end of
the instruction being executed, except following
a WAI instruction. Then it is 4 cycles.

SUMMARY OF CYCLE BY CYCLE OPERATION

Table 8 provides a detailed description of the information present on the Address Bus, Data Bus, Valid Memory Address line (VMA), and the Read/Write line (R/W) during each cycle for each instruction.

This information is useful in comparing actual with expected results during debug of both software and hardware as the control program is executed. The information is categorized in groups according to Addressing Mode and Number of Cycles per instruction. (In general, instructions with the same Addressing Mode and Number of Cycles execute in the same manner; exceptions are indicated in the table.)

TABLE 8 – OPERATION SUMMARY

Address Mode and Instructions	Cycles	Cycle #	VMA Line	Address Bus	R/W Line	Data Bus
IMMEDIATE						
ADC EOR ADD LDA AND ORA BIT SBC CMP SUB	2	1 2	1 1	Op Code Address Op Code Address + 1	1 1	Op Code Operand Data
CPX LDS LDX	3	1 2 3	1 1 1	Op Code Address Op Code Address + 1 Op Code Address + 2	1 1 1	Op Code Operand Data (High Order Byte) Operand Data (Low Order Byte)
DIRECT						
ADC EOR ADD LDA AND ORA BIT SBC CMP SUB	3	1 2 3	1 1 1	Op Code Address Op Code Address + 1 Address of Operand	1 1 1	Op Code Address of Operand Operand Data
CPX LDS LDX	4	1 2 3 4	1 1 1 1	Op Code Address Op Code Address + 1 Address of Operand Operand Address + 1	1 1 1 1	Op Code Address of Operand Operand Data (High Order Byte) Operand Data (Low Order Byte)
STA	4	1 2 3 4	1 1 0 1	Op Code Address Op Code Address + 1 Destination Address Destination Address	1 1 1 0	Op Code Destination Address Irrelevant Data (Note 1) Data from Accumulator
STS STX	5	1 2 3 4 5	1 1 0 1 1	Op Code Address Op Code Address + 1 Address of Operand Address of Operand Address of Operand + 1	1 1 1 0 0	Op Code Address of Operand Irrelevant Data (Note 1) Register Data (High Order Byte) Register Data (Low Order Byte)
INDEXED						
JMP	4	1 2 3 4	1 1 0 0	Op Code Address Op Code Address + 1 Index Register Index Register Plus Offset (w/o Carry)	1 1 1 1	Op Code Offset Irrelevant Data (Note 1) Irrelevant Data (Note 1)
ADC EOR ADD LDA AND ORA BIT SBC CMP SUB	5	1 2 3 4 5	1 1 0 0 1	Op Code Address Op Code Address + 1 Index Register Index Register Plus Offset (w/o Carry) Index Register Plus Offset	1 1 1 1 1	Op Code Offset Irrelevant Data (Note 1) Irrelevant Data (Note 1) Operand Data
CPX LDS LDX	6	1 2 3 4 5 6	1 1 0 0 1 1	Op Code Address Op Code Address + 1 Index Register Index Register Plus Offset (w/o Carry) Index Register Plus Offset Index Register Plus Offset + 1	1 1 1 1 1 1	Op Code Offset Irrelevant Data (Note 1) Irrelevant Data (Note 1) Operand Data (High Order Byte) Operand Data (Low Order Byte)

TABLE 8 – OPERATION SUMMARY (Continued)

Address Mode and Instructions	Cycles	Cycle #	VMA Line	Address Bus	R/W Line	Data Bus
INDEXED (Continued)						
STA	6	1	1	Op Code Address	1	Op Code
		2	1	Op Code Address + 1	1	Offset
		3	0	Index Register	1	Irrelevant Data (Note 1)
		4	0	Index Register Plus Offset (w/o Carry)	1	Irrelevant Data (Note 1)
		5	0	Index Register Plus Offset	1	Irrelevant Data (Note 1)
		6	1	Index Register Plus Offset	0	Operand Data
ASL LSR ASR NEG CLR ROL COM ROR DEC TST INC	7	1	1	Op Code Address	1	Op Code
		2	1	Op Code Address + 1	1	Offset
		3	0	Index Register	1	Irrelevant Data (Note 1)
		4	0	Index Register Plus Offset (w/o Carry)	1	Irrelevant Data (Note 1)
		5	1	Index Register Plus Offset	1	Current Operand Data
		6	0	Index Register Plus Offset	1	Irrelevant Data (Note 1)
		7	1/0 (Note 3)	Index Register Plus Offset	0	New Operand Data (Note 3)
STS STX	7	1	1	Op Code Address	1	Op Code
		2	1	Op Code Address + 1	1	Offset
		3	0	Index Register	1	Irrelevant Data (Note 1)
		4	0	Index Register Plus Offset (w/o Carry)	1	Irrelevant Data (Note 1)
		5	0	Index Register Plus Offset	1	Irrelevant Data (Note 1)
		6	1	Index Register Plus Offset	0	Operand Data (High Order Byte)
		7	1	Index Register Plus Offset + 1	0	Operand Data (Low Order Byte)
JSR	8	1	1	Op Code Address	1	Op Code
		2	1	Op Code Address + 1	1	Offset
		3	0	Index Register	1	Irrelevant Data (Note 1)
		4	1	Stack Pointer	0	Return Address (Low Order Byte)
		5	1	Stack Pointer − 1	0	Return Address (High Order Byte)
		6	0	Stack Pointer − 2	1	Irrelevant Data (Note 1)
		7	0	Index Register	1	Irrelevant Data (Note 1)
		8	0	Index Register Plus Offset (w/o Carry)	1	Irrelevant Data (Note 1)
EXTENDED						
JMP	3	1	1	Op Code Address	1	Op Code
		2	1	Op Code Address + 1	1	Jump Address (High Order Byte)
		3	1	Op Code Address + 2	1	Jump Address (Low Order Byte)
ADC EOR ADD LDA AND ORA BIT SBC CMP SUB	4	1	1	Op Code Address	1	Op Code
		2	1	Op Code Address + 1	1	Address of Operand (High Order Byte)
		3	1	Op Code Address + 2	1	Address of Operand (Low Order Byte)
		4	1	Address of Operand	1	Operand Data
CPX LDS LDX	5	1	1	Op Code Address	1	Op Code
		2	1	Op Code Address + 1	1	Address of Operand (High Order Byte)
		3	1	Op Code Address + 2	1	Address of Operand (Low Order Byte)
		4	1	Address of Operand	1	Operand Data (High Order Byte)
		5	1	Address of Operand + 1	1	Operand Data (Low Order Byte)
STA A STA B	5	1	1	Op Code Address	1	Op Code
		2	1	Op Code Address + 1	1	Destination Address (High Order Byte)
		3	1	Op Code Address + 2	1	Destination Address (Low Order Byte)
		4	0	Operand Destination Address	1	Irrelevant Data (Note 1)
		5	1	Operand Destination Address	0	Data from Accumulator
ASL LSR ASR NEG CLR ROL COM ROR DEC TST INC	6	1	1	Op Code Address	1	Op Code
		2	1	Op Code Address + 1	1	Address of Operand (High Order Byte)
		3	1	Op Code Address + 2	1	Address of Operand (Low Order Byte)
		4	1	Address of Operand	1	Current Operand Data
		5	0	Address of Operand	1	Irrelevant Data (Note 1)
		6	1/0 (Note 3)	Address of Operand	0	New Operand Data (Note 3)

TABLE 8 — OPERATION SUMMARY (Continued)

Address Mode and Instructions	Cycles	Cycle #	VMA Line	Address Bus	R/W Line	Data Bus
EXTENDED (Continued)						
STS STX	6	1	1	Op Code Address	1	Op Code
		2	1	Op Code Address + 1	1	Address of Operand (High Order Byte)
		3	1	Op Code Address + 2	1	Address of Operand (Low Order Byte)
		4	0	Address of Operand	1	Irrelevant Data (Note 1)
		5	1	Address of Operand	0	Operand Data (High Order Byte)
		6	1	Address of Operand + 1	0	Operand Data (Low Order Byte)
JSR	9	1	1	Op Code Address	1	Op Code
		2	1	Op Code Address + 1	1	Address of Subroutine (High Order Byte)
		3	1	Op Code Address + 2	1	Address of Subroutine (Low Order Byte)
		4	1	Subroutine Starting Address	1	Op Code of Next Instruction
		5	1	Stack Pointer	0	Return Address (Low Order Byte)
		6	1	Stack Pointer − 1	0	Return Address (High Order Byte)
		7	0	Stack Pointer − 2	1	Irrelevant Data (Note 1)
		8	0	Op Code Address + 2	1	Irrelevant Data (Note 1)
		9	1	Op Code Address + 2	1	Address of Subroutine (Low Order Byte)
INHERENT						
ABA DAA SEC ASL DEC SEI ASR INC SEV CBA LSR TAB CLC NEG TAP CLI NOP TBA CLR ROL TPA CLV ROR TST COM SBA	2	1	1	Op Code Address	1	Op Code
		2	1	Op Code Address + 1	1	Op Code of Next Instruction
DES DEX INS INX	4	1	1	Op Code Address	1	Op Code
		2	1	Op Code Address + 1	1	Op Code of Next Instruction
		3	0	Previous Register Contents	1	Irrelevant Data (Note 1)
		4	0	New Register Contents	1	Irrelevant Data (Note 1)
PSH	4	1	1	Op Code Address	1	Op Code
		2	1	Op Code Address + 1	1	Op Code of Next Instruction
		3	1	Stack Pointer	0	Accumulator Data
		4	0	Stack Pointer − 1	1	Accumulator Data
PUL	4	1	1	Op Code Address	1	Op Code
		2	1	Op Code Address + 1	1	Op Code of Next Instruction
		3	0	Stack Pointer	1	Irrelevant Data (Note 1)
		4	1	Stack Pointer + 1	1	Operand Data from Stack
TSX	4	1	1	Op Code Address	1	Op Code
		2	1	Op Code Address + 1	1	Op Code of Next Instruction
		3	0	Stack Pointer	1	Irrelevant Data (Note 1)
		4	0	New Index Register	1	Irrelevant Data (Note 1)
TXS	4	1	1	Op Code Address	1	Op Code
		2	1	Op Code Address + 1	1	Op Code of Next Instruction
		3	0	Index Register	1	Irrelevant Data
		4	0	New Stack Pointer	1	Irrelevant Data
RTS	5	1	1	Op Code Address	1	Op Code
		2	1	Op Code Address + 1	1	Irrelevant Data (Note 2)
		3	0	Stack Pointer	1	Irrelevant Data (Note 1)
		4	1	Stack Pointer + 1	1	Address of Next Instruction (High Order Byte)
		5	1	Stack Pointer + 2	1	Address of Next Instruction (Low Order Byte)

TABLE 8 – OPERATION SUMMARY (Continued)

Address Mode and Instructions	Cycles	Cycle #	VMA Line	Address Bus	R/W Line	Data Bus
INHERENT (Continued)						
WAI		1	1	Op Code Address	1	Op Code
		2	1	Op Code Address + 1	1	Op Code of Next Instruction
		3	1	Stack Pointer	0	Return Address (Low Order Byte)
		4	1	Stack Pointer − 1	0	Return Address (High Order Byte)
	9	5	1	Stack Pointer − 2	0	Index Register (Low Order Byte)
		6	1	Stack Pointer − 3	0	Index Register (High Order Byte)
		7	1	Stack Pointer − 4	0	Contents of Accumulator A
		8	1	Stack Pointer − 5	0	Contents of Accumulator B
		9	1	Stack Pointer − 6 (Note 4)	1	Contents of Cond. Code Register
RTI		1	1	Op Code Address	1	Op Code
		2	1	Op Code Address + 1	1	Irrelevant Data (Note 2)
		3	0	Stack Pointer	1	Irrelevant Data (Note 1)
		4	1	Stack Pointer + 1	1	Contents of Cond. Code Register from Stack
	10	5	1	Stack Pointer + 2	1	Contents of Accumulator B from Stack
		6	1	Stack Pointer + 3	1	Contents of Accumulator A from Stack
		7	1	Stack Pointer + 4	1	Index Register from Stack (High Order Byte)
		8	1	Stack Pointer + 5	1	Index Register from Stack (Low Order Byte)
		9	1	Stack Pointer + 6	1	Next Instruction Address from Stack (High Order Byte)
		10	1	Stack Pointer + 7	1	Next Instruction Address from Stack (Low Order Byte)
SWI		1	1	Op Code Address	1	Op Code
		2	1	Op Code Address + 1	1	Irrelevant Data (Note 1)
		3	1	Stack Pointer	0	Return Address (Low Order Byte)
		4	1	Stack Pointer − 1	0	Return Address (High Order Byte)
		5	1	Stack Pointer − 2	0	Index Register (Low Order Byte)
	12	6	1	Stack Pointer − 3	0	Index Register (High Order Byte)
		7	1	Stack Pointer − 4	0	Contents of Accumulator A
		8	1	Stack Pointer − 5	0	Contents of Accumulator B
		9	1	Stack Pointer − 6	0	Contents of Cond. Code Register
		10	0	Stack Pointer − 7	1	Irrelevant Data (Note 1)
		11	1	Vector Address FFFA (Hex)	1	Address of Subroutine (High Order Byte)
		12	1	Vector Address FFFB (Hex)	1	Address of Subroutine (Low Order Byte)
RELATIVE						
BCC BHI BNE BCS BLE BPL BEQ BLS BRA BGE BLT BVC BGT BMI BVS	4	1	1	Op Code Address	1	Op Code
		2	1	Op Code Address + 1	1	Branch Offset
		3	0	Op Code Address + 2	1	Irrelevant Data (Note 1)
		4	0	Branch Address	1	Irrelevant Data (Note 1)
BSR		1	1	Op Code Address	1	Op Code
		2	1	Op Code Address + 1	1	Branch Offset
		3	0	Return Address of Main Program	1	Irrelevant Data (Note 1)
	8	4	1	Stack Pointer	0	Return Address (Low Order Byte)
		5	1	Stack Pointer − 1	0	Return Address (High Order Byte)
		6	0	Stack Pointer − 2	1	Irrelevant Data (Note 1)
		7	0	Return Address of Main Program	1	Irrelevant Data (Note 1)
		8	0	Subroutine Address	1	Irrelevant Data (Note 1)

Note 1. If device which is addressed during this cycle uses VMA, then the Data Bus will go to the high impedance three-state condition. Depending on bus capacitance, data from the previous cycle may be retained on the Data Bus.
Note 2. Data is ignored by the MPU.
Note 3. For TST, VMA = 0 and Operand data does not change.
Note 4. While the MPU is waiting for the interrupt, Bus Available will go high indicating the following states of the control lines: VMA is low; Address Bus, R/W, and Data Bus are all in the high impedance state.

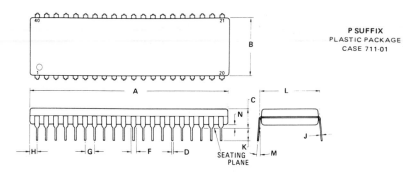

P SUFFIX
PLASTIC PACKAGE
CASE 711-01

DIM	MILLIMETERS		INCHES	
	MIN	MAX	MIN	MAX
A	51.82	52.32	2.040	2.060
B	13.72	14.22	0.540	0.560
C	4.57	5.08	0.180	0.200
D	0.36	0.51	0.014	0.020
F	1.02	1.52	0.040	0.060
G	2.41	2.67	0.095	0.105
H	1.65	2.16	0.065	0.085
J	0.20	0.30	0.008	0.012
K	3.68	4.19	0.145	0.165
L	14.99	15.49	0.590	0.610
M	0°	10°	0°	10°
N	0.51	1.02	0.020	0.040

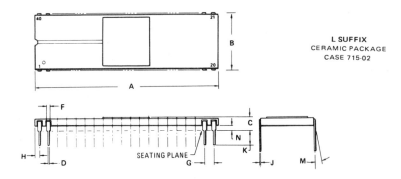

L SUFFIX
CERAMIC PACKAGE
CASE 715-02

DIM	MILLIMETERS		INCHES	
	MIN	MAX	MIN	MAX
A	50.29	51.31	1.980	2.020
B	14.86	15.62	0.585	0.615
C	2.54	4.19	0.100	0.165
D	0.38	0.53	0.015	0.021
F	0.76	1.40	0.030	0.055
G	2.54 BSC		0.100 BSC	
H	0.76	1.78	0.030	0.070
J	0.20	0.33	0.008	0.013
K	2.54	4.19	0.100	0.165
M	0°	10°	0°	10°
N	0.51	1.52	0.020	0.060

NOTE:
1. LEADS, TRUE POSITIONED WITHIN
0.25 mm (0.010) DIA (AT SEATING
PLANE), AT MAX. MAT'L
CONDITION.

MCM6810   MCM68A10   MCM68B10
1.0 MHz   1.5 MHz   2.0 MHz

128 X 8-BIT STATIC RANDOM ACCESS MEMORY

The MCM6810 is a byte-organized memory designed for use in bus-organized systems. It is fabricated with N-channel silicon-gate technology. For ease of use, the device operates from a single power supply, has compatibility with TTL and DTL, and needs no clocks or refreshing because of static operation.

The memory is compatible with the M6800 Microcomputer Family, providing random storage in byte increments. Memory expansion is provided through multiple Chip Select inputs.

- Organized as 128 Bytes of 8 Bits
- Static Operation
- Bidirectional Three-State Data Input/Output
- Six Chip Select Inputs (Four Active Low, Two Active High)
- Single 5-Volt Power Supply
- TTL Compatible
- Maximum Access Time = 450 ns — MCM6810
                          360 ns — MCM68A10
                          250 ns — MCM68B10

MOS
(N-CHANNEL, SILICON-GATE)

128 X 8-BIT STATIC RANDOM ACCESS MEMORY

PIN ASSIGNMENT

Pin	Signal	Signal	Pin
1	Gnd O	V_{CC}	24
2	D0	A0	23
3	D1	A1	22
4	D2	A2	21
5	D3	A3	20
6	D4	A4	19
7	D5	A5	18
8	D6	A6	17
9	D7	R/W	16
10	CS0	$\overline{CS5}$	15
11	$\overline{CS1}$	$\overline{CS4}$	14
12	$\overline{CS2}$	CS3	13

MC6821   MC68A21   MC68B21
(1.0 MHz)   (1.5 MHz)   (2.0 MHz)

PERIPHERAL INTERFACE ADAPTER (PIA)

The MC6821 Peripheral Interface Adapter provides the universal means of interfacing peripheral equipment to the MC6800 Microprocessing Unit (MPU). This device is capable of interfacing the MPU to peripherals through two 8-bit bidirectional peripheral data buses and four control lines. No external logic is required for interfacing to most peripheral devices.

The functional configuration of the PIA is programmed by the MPU during system initialization. Each of the peripheral data lines can be programmed to act as an input or output, and each of the four control/interrupt lines may be programmed for one of several control modes. This allows a high degree of flexibility in the over-all operation of the interface.

- 8-Bit Bidirectional Data Bus for Communication with the MPU
- Two Bidirectional 8-Bit Buses for Interface to Peripherals
- Two Programmable Control Registers
- Two Programmable Data Direction Registers
- Four Individually-Controlled Interrupt Input Lines; Two Usable as Peripheral Control Outputs
- Handshake Control Logic for Input and Output Peripheral Operation
- High-Impedance 3-State and Direct Transistor Drive Peripheral Lines
- Program Controlled Interrupt and Interrupt Disable Capability
- CMOS Drive Capability on Side A Peripheral Lines
- Two TTL Drive Capability on All A and B Side Buffers
- TTL-Compatible
- Static Operation

MOS

(N-CHANNEL, SILICON-GATE, DEPLETION LOAD)

PERIPHERAL INTERFACE ADAPTER

PIN ASSIGNMENT

1	V_{SS}	CA1	40
2	PA0	CA2	39
3	PA1	$\overline{IRQA}$	38
4	PA2	$\overline{IRQB}$	37
5	PA3	RS0	36
6	PA4	RS1	35
7	PA5	$\overline{Reset}$	34
8	PA6	D0	33
9	PA7	D1	32
10	PB0	D2	31
11	PB1	D3	30
12	PB2	D4	29
13	PB3	D5	28
14	PB4	D6	27
15	PB5	D7	26
16	PB6	E	25
17	PB7	CS1	24
18	CB1	$\overline{CS2}$	23
19	CB2	CS0	22
20	V_{CC}	$R/\overline{W}$	21

INTERNAL CONTROLS

There are six locations within the PIA accessible to the MPU data bus: two Peripheral Registers, two Data Direction Registers, and two Control Registers. Selection of these locations is controlled by the RS0 and RS1 inputs together with bit 2 in the Control Register, as shown in Table 1.

INITIALIZATION

A low reset line has the effect of zeroing all PIA registers. This will set PA0-PA7, PB0-PB7, CA2 and CB2 as inputs, and all interrupts disabled. The PIA must be configured during the restart program which follows the reset.

TABLE 1 – INTERNAL ADDRESSING

		Control Register Bit		
RS1	RS0	CRA-2	CRB-2	Location Selected
0	0	1	X	Peripheral Register A
0	0	0	X	Data Direction Register A
0	1	X	X	Control Register A
1	0	X	1	Peripheral Register B
1	0	X	0	Data Direction Register B
1	1	X	X	Control Register B

X = Don't Care

Details of possible configurations of the Data Direction and Control Register are as follows.

DATA DIRECTION REGISTERS (DDRA and DDRB)

The two Data Direction Registers allow the MPU to control the direction of data through each corresponding peripheral data line. A Data Direction Register bit set at "0" configures the corresponding peripheral data line as an input; a "1" results in an output.

CONTROL REGISTERS (CRA and CRB)

The two Control Registers (CRA and CRB) allow the MPU to control the operation of the four peripheral control lines CA1, CA2, CB1 and CB2. In addition they allow the MPU to enable the interrupt lines and monitor the status of the interrupt flags. Bits 0 through 5 of the two registers may be written or read by the MPU when the proper chip select and register select signals are applied. Bits 6 and 7 of the two registers are read only and are modified by external interrupts occurring on control lines CA1, CA2, CB1 or CB2. The format of the control words is shown in Table 2.

Data Direction Access Control Bit (CRA-2 and CRB-2) — Bit 2 in each Control register (CRA and CRB) allows selection of either a Peripheral Interface Register or the Data Direction Register when the proper register select signals are applied to RS0 and RS1.

Interrupt Flags (CRA-6, CRA-7, CRB-6, and CRB-7) — The four interrupt flag bits are set by active transitions of signals on the four Interrupt and Peripheral Control lines when those lines are programmed to be inputs. These bits cannot be set directly from the MPU Data Bus and are reset indirectly by a Read Peripheral Data Operation on the appropriate section.

TABLE 2 – CONTROL WORD FORMAT

	7	6	5	4	3	2	1	0
CRA	IRQA1	IRQA2	CA2 Control			DDRA Access	CA1 Control	
	7	6	5	4	3	2	1	0
CRB	IRQB1	IRQB2	CB2 Control			DDRB Access	CB1 Control	

Control of CA1 and CB1 Interrupt Input Lines (CRA-0, CRB-0, CRA-1, and CRB-1) — The two lowest order bits of the control registers are used to control the interrupt input lines CA1 and CB1. Bits CRA-0 and CRB-0 are used to enable the MPU interrupt signals $\overline{IRQA}$ and $\overline{IRQB}$, respectively. Bits CRA-1 and CRB-1 determine the active transition of the interrupt input signals CA1 and CB1 (Table 3).

TABLE 3 – CONTROL OF INTERRUPT INPUTS CA1 AND CB1

CRA-1 (CRB-1)	CRA-0 (CRB-0)	Interrupt Input CA1 (CB1)	Interrupt Flag CRA-7 (CRB-7)	MPU Interrupt Request $\overline{IRQA}$ ($\overline{IRQB}$)
0	0	↓ Active	Set high on ↓ of CA1 (CB1)	Disabled — $\overline{IRQ}$ remains high
0	1	↓ Active	Set high on ↓ of CA1 (CB1)	Goes low when the interrupt flag bit CRA-7 (CRB-7) goes high
1	0	↑ Active	Set high on ↑ of CA1 (CB1)	Disabled — $\overline{IRQ}$ remains high
1	1	↑ Active	Set high on ↑ of CA1 (CB1)	Goes low when the interrupt flag bit CRA-7 (CRB-7) goes high

Notes: 1　↑ indicates positive transition (low to high)

2　↓ indicates negative transition (high to low)

3　The Interrupt flag bit CRA-7 is cleared by an MPU Read of the A Data Register, and CRB-7 is cleared by an MPU Read of the B Data Register.

4　If CRA-0 (CRB-0) is low when an interrupt occurs (Interrupt disabled) and is later brought high, $\overline{IRQA}$ ($\overline{IRQB}$) occurs after CRA-0 (CRB-0) is written to a "one".

Control of CA2 and CB2 Peripheral Control Lines (CRA-3, CRA-4, CRA-5, CRB-3, CRB-4, and CRB-5) — Bits 3, 4, and 5 of the two control registers are used to control the CA2 and CB2 Peripheral Control lines. These bits determine if the control lines will be an interrupt input or an output control signal. If bit CRA-5 (CRB-5) is low, CA2 (CB2) is an interrupt input line similar to CA1 (CB1) (Table 4). When CRA-5 (CRB-5) is high, CA2 (CB2) becomes an output signal that may be used to control peripheral data transfers. When in the output mode, CA2 and CB2 have slightly different characteristics (Tables 5 and 6).

TABLE 4 – CONTROL OF CA2 AND CB2 AS INTERRUPT INPUTS
CRA5 (CRB5) is low

CRA-5 (CRB-5)	CRA-4 (CRB-4)	CRA-3 (CRB-3)	Interrupt Input CA2 (CB2)	Interrupt Flag CRA-6 (CRB-6)	MPU Interrupt Request $\overline{IRQA}$ ($\overline{IRQB}$)
0	0	0	↓ Active	Set high on ↓ of CA2 (CB2)	Disabled — $\overline{IRQ}$ remains high
0	0	1	↓ Active	Set high on ↓ of CA2 (CB2)	Goes low when the interrupt flag bit CRA-6 (CRB-6) goes high
0	1	0	↑ Active	Set high on ↑ of CA2 (CB2)	Disabled — $\overline{IRQ}$ remains high
0	1	1	↑ Active	Set high on ↑ of CA2 (CB2)	Goes low when the interrupt flag bit CRA-6 (CRB-6) goes high

Notes: 1. ↑ indicates positive transition (low to high)
2. ↓ indicates negative transition (high to low)
3. The Interrupt flag bit CRA-6 is cleared by an MPU Read of the A Data Register and CRB-6 is cleared by an MPU Read of the B Data Register.
4. If CRA-3 (CRB-3) is low when an interrupt occurs (Interrupt disabled) and is later brought high, IRQA (IRQB) occurs after CRA-3 (CRB-3) is written to a "one".

TABLE 5 – CONTROL OF CB2 AS AN OUTPUT
CRB-5 is high

CRB-5	CRB-4	CRB-3	CB2 Cleared	CB2 Set
1	0	0	Low on the positive transition of the first E pulse following an MPU Write "B" Data Register operation.	High when the interrupt flag bit CRB-7 is set by an active transition of the CB1 signal.
1	0	1	Low on the positive transition of the first E pulse after an MPU Write "B" Data Register operation.	High on the positive edge of the first "E" pulse following an "E" pulse which occurred while the part was deselected.
1	1	0	Low when CRB-3 goes low as a result of an MPU Write in Control Register "B".	Always low as long as CRB-3 is low. Will go high on an MPU Write in Control Register "B" that changes CRB-3 to "one".
1	1	1	Always high as long as CRB-3 is high. Will be cleared when an MPU Write Control Register "B" results in clearing CRB-3 to "zero".	High when CRB-3 goes high as a result of an MPU Write into Control Register "B".

TABLE 6 – CONTROL OF CA-2 AS AN OUTPUT
CRA-5 is high

CRA-5	CRA-4	CRA-3	CA2 Cleared	CA2 Set
1	0	0	Low on negative transition of E after an MPU Read "A" Data operation.	High when the interrupt flag bit CRA-7 is set by an active transition of the CA1 signal.
1	0	1	Low on negative transition of E after an MPU Read "A" Data operation.	High on the negative edge of the first "E" pulse which occurs during a deselect.
1	1	0	Low when CRA-3 goes low as a result of an MPU Write to Control Register "A".	Always low as long as CRA-3 is low. Will go high on an MPU Write to Control Register "A" that changes CRA-3 to "one".
1	1	1	Always high as long as CRA-3 is high. Will be cleared on an MPU Write to Control Register "A" that clears CRA-3 to a "zero".	High when CRA-3 goes high as a result of an MPU Write to Control Register "A".

MC6843

<table>
<tr><td>

Advance Information

FLOPPY DISK CONTROLLER (FDC)

The MC6843 Floppy Disk Controller performs the complex MPU/Floppy interface function. The FDC was designed to optimize the balance between the "Hardware/Software" in order to achieve integration of all key functions and maintain flexibility.

The FDC can interface a wide range of drives with a minimum of external hardware. Multiple drives can be controlled with the addition of external multiplexing rather than additional FDC's.

- Format compatible with IBM 3740
- User Programmable read/write format
- Ten powerful macro commands
- Macro End Interrupt allows parallel processing of MPU and FDC
- Controls multiple Floppies with external multiplexing
- Direct interface with MC6800
- Programmable step and settling times enable operation with a wide range of Floppy drives
- Offers both Programmed Controlled I/O (PCIO) and DMA data transfer mode
- Free-Format read or write
- Single 5-volt power supply
- All registers directly accessible

</td><td>

MOS

(N-Channel, Silicon-Gate)

FLOPPY DISK CONTROLLER

FIGURE 2 – PIN ASSIGNMENT

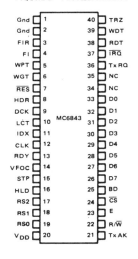

</td></tr>
</table>

FORMAT

The format used by the MC6843, shown in Figure 20, is compatible with the soft sector format of the IBM 3740.

MACRO COMMAND SET

The macro command set shown in Table 4 is discussed in the following paragraphs.

Seek Track Zero (STZ)

The STZ command causes the R/W head to be released from the suface of the disk (HLD is reset) and positioned above track 00. The FDC issues step pulses on the STP output until the TRZ input becomes a high level or until 83 pulses have been sent to the drive. When the TRZ input becomes high, the step pulses are inhibited on the STP output but the FDC remains busy until all 83 have been generated internally.

If the TRZ input remains low (logic '0') after all 83 pulses have been generated, the seek error flag (STRB bit 4) is set.

After all 83 pulses have been generated, the head is loaded (HLD becomes a '1'). After the settling time specified in the SUR has expired, the settling time

complete flag is set (ISR bit 1), Busy STRA-7 is reset, CTAR and GCR are cleared. The head remains in contact with the disk. A command such as RCR (Read CRC) may be issued following a STZ if the head must be released.

Seek (SEK)

The SEK command is used to position the R/W head over the track on which a Read/Write operation is to be performed. The contents of the GCR are taken as the destination address and the content of the CTAR is the source address; therefore, the number of pulses (N) on the STP output are given by:

$$N = |(CTAR) - (GCR)|$$

HDR is a '1' for (GCR) > (CTAR) otherwise it is a '0'.

When a SEK command is issued, Busy is set, the head is raised from the disk, HDR is set as described above, and N number of pulses appear on the STP output. After the last step pulse is used, the head is placed in contact with the disk. Once the head settling time has expired, the Settling Time Complete flag (ISR bit 1) is set, Busy is reset, and the contents of the GCR are transferred to the CTAR.

TABLE 4 – MACRO COMMAND SET

			CMR Bits				Hex
			Bit 3	Bit 2	Bit 1	Bit 0	Code
1	STZ	Seek Track Zero	0	0	1	0	2
2	SEK	Seek	0	0	1	1	3
3	SSR	Single Sector Read	0	1	0	0	4
4	SSW	Single Sector Write	0	1	0	1	5
5	RCR	Read CRC	0	1	1	0	6
6	SWD	Single Sector Write with Delete Data Mark	0	1	1	1	7
7	MSW	Multi Sector Write	1	1	0	1	D
8	MSR	Multi Sector Read	1	1	0	0	C
9	FFW	Free Format Write	1	0	1	1	B
10	FFR	Free Format Read	1	0	1	0	A

SINGLE SECTOR READ/WRITE COMMANDS

The single sector Read/Write commands (SSR, RCR, SSW, and SWD) are used to Read/Write data from a single 128 byte sector on the disk. As shown in Figure 21 these types of instructions can be divided into two sections. The first section, which is common to all instructions, is the address search operation, while the second section is unique to the requirements of each instruction.

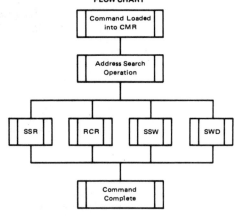

FIGURE 21 – BASIC SINGLE SECTOR COMMAND FLOW CHART

Single Sector Read (SSR)

The single sector read command follows the address search procedure as defined in the previous flowchart. If the search is successful, status sense request is set and the operation continues as described by the flowchart

Read CRC (RCR)

The RCR command is used to verify that correct data was written on a disk. The operation is the same as for the SSR command with the exception that the data transfer request (STRA bit 0) is not set. The SSR interrupt can be disabled by using the DMA mode.

Single Sector Write (SSW)

Single sector write is used to write 128 bytes of data on the disk. After the command is issued, the address search is performed. The remainder of the instruction's operation is shown in Figure 24.

Single Sector Write with Delete Data Mark (SWD)

The operation flow of SWD is exactly like that of SSW. For SWD, the data pattern of the Data Address Mark becomes F8 instead of FB. The clock pattern remains C7.

Multi-Sector Commands (MSR/MSW)

MSR is used for sequential reading of two or more sectors. If S sectors are to be read, S-1 must be written into the GCR before the command is issued.

The basic operation for the MSR and MSW is the same as that for the SSR and SSW respectively. The basic operation begins with an address search operation, which is followed by a single sector read or write operation. This completes the operation on the first sector. The SAR is incremented, the GCR is decremented, and if no overflow is detected from the GCR (i.e., GCR become negative) the sequence is repeated until S number of sectors are read or written.

The completion of an MSR or MSW is like that of an SSR or SSW command. First MCC is set, after the settling time has expired, Busy is reset, and the head is released.

If a delete data mark is detected during an MSR command, STRA bit 1 (Delete Data Mark Detected) remains set throughout the commands operation.

When a multi-sector instruction is issued, the sum of the SAR and GCR must be less than 27. If SAR + GCR > 26, an address error (STRB bit 3 set) will occur after the contents of SAR becomes greater than 26.

Free Format Write (FFW)

The FFW has two modes of operation which are selected by FWF (Free Format Write Flag) which is data bit 4 of the CMR.

When FWF = '0', the data bits of the DOR are written directly to the disk without first wrting the preamble, address mark, etc. The contents of the DOR are FM modulated with a clock pattern of all ones.

If FWF = '1' the odd bits of the DOR are used as clock bits and even bits are used for data bits. In this mode, the DOSR clock is twice a normal write operation and one byte of DOR is one nibble (four bits of data) on the disk.

The two modes of the FFW command allow formatting a disk with either the IBM3470 format or a user defined format.

After the FFW command is loaded into the CMR, WGT becomes a high level, the contents of DOR are transferred to the DOSR, data transfer request (STRA bit 0) is set, and the serial bit pattern is shifted out on the WDT line. Therefore, DOR must be loaded before the FFW command is issued. Data from the DOR is continually transferred to the DOSR and shifted out on WDT until the CMR has been written with an all zero pattern. When CMR becomes zero, WGT beocms a low level, but MCC is not set and the R/W head is left in contact with the disk.

Free Format Read (FFR)

FFR is used to input all data (including Address marks) from a disk. Once the FFR command is set into the CMR, the head is loaded and after the settling time has expired the serial data from the FDC is brought into the DISR. After 8 bits have accumulated, it is transferred to the DIR and Data Transfer Request (STRA bit 0) is set.

This operation continues until a zero pattern is stored in the CMR, terminating the FFR command. As in the case of the FFW command, MCC is not set and the head remains in contact with the disk.

The first data that enters the DISR is not necessarily the first bit of a data word since the head may be lowered at any place on the disk. To prevent the FDC from remaining unsynchronized to the data, the FFR command will synchronize to either an ID address mark (FE) or a data Address mark (FB or F8).

REGISTER DEFINITIONS

Data Output Register (DOR) — Hex address 0, write only

Bit 7	Bit 6	Bit 5	Bit 4	Bit 3	Bit 2	Bit 1	Bit 0
8 Bits of Data Used for a Disk Write Operation							

When one of the four write macro commands (SSW, SWD, MSW, and FFW) is executed, the information contained in the DOR is loaded into the DOSR, and is shifted out on the WDT line using a double frequency (FM) format.

Data Input Register (DIR) — Hex address 0, read only

Bit 7	Bit 6	Bit 5	Bit 4	Bit 3	Bit 2	Bit 1	Bit 0
8 Bits of Data Used for a Disk Read Operation							

One of the three read macro commands (SSR, MSR, FFR) executed, will cause the information on the RDT input to be clocked into the DISR. When 8 clock pulses have occurred, the 8 bits of information in the DISR are transferred to the DIR where it can be read by the bus interface.

Current Track Address (CTAR) — Hex address 1, read/write

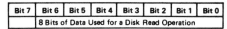

Bit 7	Bit 6	Bit 5	Bit 4	Bit 3	Bit 2	Bit 1	Bit 0
Not Used	7 Bit Track Address of Current Head Position						

The address of the track over which the R/W head is currently positioned is contained in the CTAR. At the end of a SEK command, the contents of the GCR are transferred to the CTAR. CTAR is cleared at the completion of a STZ command. CTAR is a read/write register so that the head position can be updated when several drives are connected to one FDC. Bit 7 is read as a '0'.

Command Register (CMR) — Hex address 2, write only

Bit 7	Bit 6	Bit 5	Bit 4	Bit 3*	Bit 2*	Bit 1*	Bit 0*
Function Interrupt Mask	ISR3 Interrupt Mask	DMA Flag	FWF	Macro Command			

*Bits 0-4 are cleared by R̄e̅s̅e̅t̅.

The commands that control the FDC are loaded into the lower four bits of the CMR. Information that controls the data transfer mode and interrupt conditions are loaded into bits four through seven.

Bit 0-Bit 3: Macro Command

The Macro Command to be executed by the FDC is written to bits 0-3.

MC6845

CRT CONTROLLER (CRTC)

The MC6845 CRT Controller performs the interface to raster scan CRT displays. It is intended for use in processor-based controllers for CRT terminals in stand-alone or cluster configurations.

The CRTC is optimized for hardware/software balance in order to achieve integration of all key functions and maintain flexibility. For instance, all keyboard functions, R/W, cursor movements, and editing are under processor control; whereas the CRTC provides video timing and Refresh Memory Addressing.

- Applications include "glass-teletype," smart, programmable, intelligent CRT terminals; video games; information display.
- Alphanumeric, semi-graphic, and full graphic capability.
- Fully programmable via processor data bus. Can generate timing for almost any alphanumeric screen density, e.g. 80 x 24, 72 x 64, 132 x 20, etc.
- Single +5 volt supply. TTL/6800 compatible I/O.
- Hardware scroll (paging or by line or by character)
- Compatible with CPU's and MPU's which provide a means for synchronizing external devices.
- Cursor register and compare circuitry.
- Cursor format and blink are programmable.
- Light pen register.
- Line buffer-less operation. No external DMA required. Refresh Memory is multiplexed between CRTC and MPU.
- Programmable interlace or non-interlace scan.
- 14-bit wide refresh address.

MOS

(N-Channel, Silicon-Gate)

CRT CONTROLLER (CRTC)

FIGURE 7 – PIN ASSIGNMENT

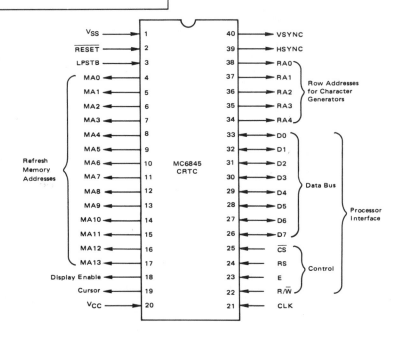

MCM6830L7 MIKBUG/MINIBUG ROM

Prepared by
Mike Wiles
Computer Systems

Andre Felix
Support Products Group

The MIKBUG/MINIBUG ROM is an MCM6830 ROM of the M6800 Family of parts. This ROM provides an asynchronous communications program, a loader program, and a diagnostic program for use with the MC6800 Microprocessing Unit.

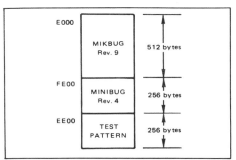

FIGURE 1-1. MIKBUG/MINIBUG ROM Memory Map

NOTE

All enables for the ROM are active high.

2.0 FEATURES

The more important features of these programs are:

MIKBUG Rev. 9
    A. Memory Loader
    B. Print Registers of Target Program
    C. Print/Punch Dump
    D. Memory Change
    E. Go to Target Program
    F. Operates with PIA for the Parallel-to-Serial Interface
    G. Restart/NMI/SWI Interrupt Vectors

MINIBUG Rev. 4
    A. Memory Loader
    B. Memory Change
    C. Print Registers of Target Program
    D. Go to Target Program
    E. Assumes a UART for the Parallel-to-Serial Interface

3.0 HARDWARE CONFIGURATION

3.1 MIKBUG Hardware

The MIKBUG/MINIBUG ROM is intended for use with the MC6800 Microprocessing Unit in an M6800 Microcomputer system. This ROM, using the MIKBUG Firmware, should be connected into the system as illustrated in Figure 3-1. As shown, all of the enable inputs are high levels and the address line A9 on pin 15 is grounded. The MIKBUG Firmware in this ROM uses addresses E000 through E1FF. The ROM should be connected into a system so that its two

top MIKBUG Firmware addresses also will respond to addresses FFFE and FFFF. This is required for the system to restart properly. There should not be any devices in the system at a higher address than this ROM's addresses. Figure 3-2 depicts a memory map for a system using the MIKBUG Firmware and Figure 3-3 depicts this system's block diagram.

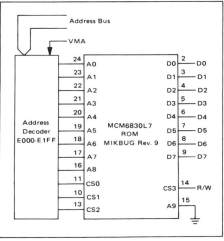

FIGURE 3-1. MCM6830L7 MIKBUG ROM Schematic

The MIKBUG Firmware operates with an MC6820 Peripheral Interface Adapter (PIA) as shown in Figure 3-4. The MC14536 device is used as the interface timer. This timer's interval is set by adjusting the 50 k ohm resistor and monitoring the output signal on pin 13 of the MC14536 device. The zero level of the timing pulse should be 9.1 ms for 10 characters per second (CPS) operation and 3.3 ms for 30 CPS operation. Also, pin 16 (PB6) of the MC6820 PIA should be connected to +5 volts for 10 CPS operation and ground for 30 CPS operation.

The MC1488 and MC1489A devices provide the system with RS-232C interface capability. If the system is to interface only with an RS-232C terminal, no other interface circuitry is required; however, a jumper should be strapped between E3 and E4. The 4N33 optical isolators and associated circuitry are required to interface with a 20 mA current loop TTY. A jumper should be connected between E1 and E2 for TTY operation.

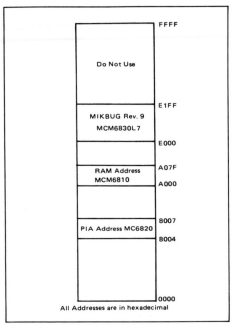

FIGURE 3-2. MIKBUG Rev. 9 Memory Map

The MIKBUG Firmware also requires random access memory for a stack and temporary memory storage. The MCM6810 RAM used for this memory should be configured for the base memory address at A000 hexadecimal.

A reset switch is required in the system to provide for restarting the MC6800 MPU and for resetting the MC6820 PIA. The function may be provided by a pushbutton switch and a cross-coupled latch flip-flop.

4.0   SOFTWARE OPERATION

4.1   MIKBUG Operation

The MIKBUG Firmware may be used to debug and evaluate a user's program. The MIKBUG Firmware enables the user to perform the following functions:

Memory Loader Function
Memory Examine and Change Function
Print/Punch Memory Function
Display Contents of MPU Registers Function
Go to User's Program Function
Interrupt Request Function
Non-Maskable Interrupt Function

The operating procedures for each of these routines as well as the Reset Function are discussed in the following paragraphs. The MIKBUG Firmware is inhibited from performing the user's program except in the Go to User's Program Function and the interrupt functions.

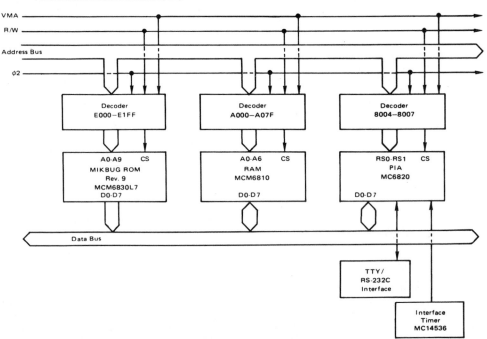

FIGURE 3-3. MIKBUG ROM Rev. 9 System Block Diagram

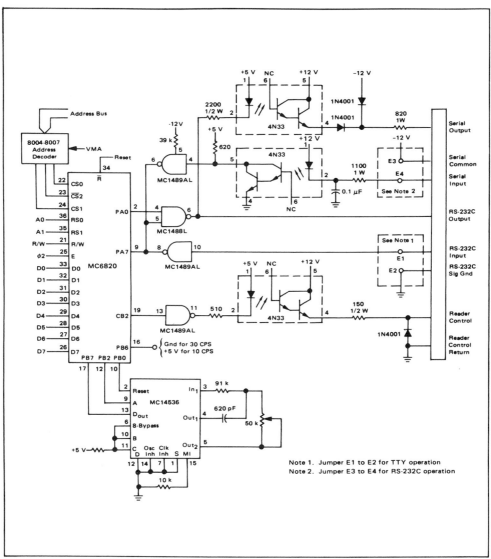

FIGURE 3-4. TTY/RS-232C Interface Used with MIKBUG ROM

4.1.1 RESET Function

Perform the RESET Function when power is first applied and any time the MIKBUG Firmware loses program control.

Press the RESET pushbutton switch. The MIKBUG Firmware should gain program control and the terminal should respond with a carriage return, a line feed and an asterisk. The MIKBUG control program is ready for an input.

4.1.2 Memory Loader Function

The Memory Loader Function of MIKBUG loads formatted binary object tapes or MIKBUG punched memory dump tapes into memory and if used, external memory modules. Figure 4-1 depicts the paper tape format. It is assumed at the start of this function that the MC6800 MPU is performing its MIKBUG control program and the last data printed by the terminal is an asterisk. Figure 4-2 illustrates a typical Memory Loader Function.

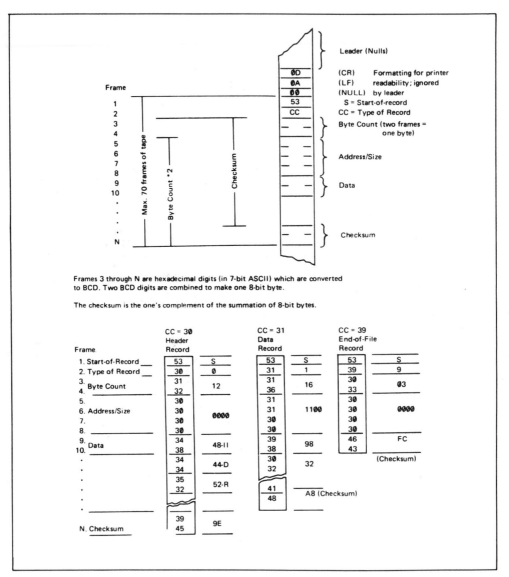

FIGURE 4-1. Paper Tape Format

FIGURE 4-2. Typical Memory Loader Function

a. Load the tape into the terminal tape reader.
b. Set the tape reader switch to AUTO.
c. Enter the character L after the asterisk. This initiates the MIKBUG loading procedure. The MIKBUG Firmware ignores all characters prior to the start-of-record on the tape.

NOTE

Tapes punched by MIKBUG do not have an end-of-file character at the end of the record; therefore, you must type in the characters S9 to exit from the memory loader function, or push the RESET pushbutton switch.

Checksum Error Detection

If, during the loading function, the MIKBUG Firmware detects a checksum error, it instructs the terminal to print a question mark and then stops the tape reader.

NOTE

Underlined characters indicate user input.

d. If a checksum error is present, perform one of the following substeps:

1) Press the RESET pushbutton switch and abort from the Memory Loader Function. The MPU will return to the MIKBUG control program and the terminal will print a carriage return, a line feed, and an asterisk.

2) Reposition the tape and enter the character L. The record causing the checksum error is reread.

3) Ignore the checksum error and enter the character L. The MIKBUG Firmware ignores the checksum error and continues the Memory Loader Function.

CAUTION

If a checksum error is in an address and the continue option in substep 3 is selected, there is no certain way of determining where the data will be loaded into the memory.

4.1.3 Memory Examine and Change Function

The MIKBUG Firmware performs this function in three steps: 1) examining the contents of the selected memory location (opening the memory location); 2) changing the contents of this location, if required; and 3) returning the contents to memory (closing the memory location). The MIKBUG Firmware, in examining a memory location, instructs the terminal to print the contents of this memory location. The MIKBUG Firmware in this function displays each of the program instructions in machine language.

It is assumed at the start of this function that the MPU is performing its MIKBUG control program and the last data printed by the terminal is an asterisk. Figure 4-3 depicts a typical Memory Examine and Change Function.

NOTE

If the memory address selected is in ROM, PROM, or protected RAM, the contents of this memory location cannot be changed and the terminal will print a question mark.

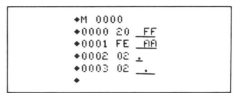

FIGURE 4-3. Typical Memory Examine and Change Function

a. Enter the character M after the asterisk to open a memory location. The terminal will insert a space after the M.

b. Enter in 4-character hexadecimal format the memory address to be opened. The terminal will print on the next line the memory address being opened and the contents of this memory location. The contents are in hexadecimal.

c. The operator must now decide whether to change the data at this memory location. If the data is to be changed, change the data in accordance with step d. If the data is not to be changed, the operator must decide whether to close this location and open the following memory location (step e) or to close this memory location and return to the MIKBUG control program (step f).

d. If the contents of this memory location are to be changed, enter a space code and then the new data (in hexadecimal format) to be stored at this location. The new contents are stored in memory and the terminal prints the following memory address and its contents. Return to step c.

e. To close the present memory and open the following memory location, enter any character except a space character after the displayed memory address contents. The contents are returned to memory and the terminal prints the following memory address and its contents. Return to step c.

f. To close the present memory location and return to the MIKBUG control program, enter a space code followed by a carriage return control character. The contents are returned to memory and the terminal prints an asterisk on the next line.

4.1.4 Print/Punch Memory Function

The Print/Punch Memory Function instructs the MIKBUG Firmware to punch an absolute formatted binary tape and to print the selected memory contents. The tape is formatted as shown in Figure 4-1 except that this tape does not contain an end-of-file control character.

The beginning address and the ending address must be entered into the memory. Memory addresses A002 and A003 are used to store the beginning address and addresses A004 and A005 are used to store the ending address.

It is assumed that the MPU is performing its MIKBUG control program and the last data printed by the terminal is an asterisk. Figure 4-4 illustrates a typical Print/Punch Memory Function.

NOTE

If you do not wish to punch a tape, turn off the terminal's tape reader.

a. Enter the character M after the asterisk to open a memory location. The terminal will insert a space code after the M.

b. Enter the address A002 after the space code. The terminal will print on the next line the memory address A002 and the contents of the address.

c. Enter a space code and the two most significant hexadecimal bytes of the beginning address after the contents of address A002. These two bytes are stored in memory and the terminal prints address A003 and its contents on the next line.

d. Enter a space code and the two least significant hexadecimal bytes of the beginning address after the contents of address A003. These two bytes are stored in memory and the terminal prints address A004 and its contents on the next line.

e. Enter a space code and the two most significant hexadecimal bytes of the ending address after the contents of address A004. These two bytes are stored in memory and the terminal prints address A005 and its contents on the next line.

f. Enter a space code and the two least significant hexadecimal bytes of the ending address after the contents of address A005. These two bytes are stored in memory and the terminal prints address A006 and its contents on the next line.

g. Enter a space code and carriage return character after the contents of address A006. The control returns to MIKBUG control program and the terminal prints an asterisk.

```
◆M A002
◆A002 F7  00
◆A003 6E  01
◆A004 99  00
◆A005 EE  10
◆A006 A0  __
◆F
S1130001AA0202020202020202020202020202020202AC79
◆
```

FIGURE 4-4. Typical Print/Punch Memory Function

h. Enter the character P after the asterisk. The MIKBUG Firmware initiates the print/punch operation. At the conclusion of the print/punch operation the terminal prints an asterisk, and returns to the MIKBUG control program.

4.1.5 Display Contents of MPU Registers Function

The Display Contents of MPU Registers Function enables the MIKBUG Firmware to display the contents of the MC6800 Microprocessing Unit registers for examination and change. It is assumed at the start of this function that the MPU is performing its MIKBUG control program and the last data printed by the terminal is an asterisk. Figure 4-5 illustrates a typical Display Contents of MPU Registers Function.

```
◆R  8A  D6  CE  87AE  CF4B  A042
◆M  A043
◆A043  8A  _
◆A044  D6  _
◆A045  CE  _
◆A046  87  _
◆A047  AE  _
◆A048  CF   00
◆A049  4B   00
◆A04A  9E  __
◆R  8A  D6  CE  87AE  0000  A042
◆
```

FIGURE 4-5. Typical Display Contents of MPU Registers Function

a. Enter the character R after the asterisk. The terminal will print the contents of the MPU registers in the following sequence: condition code register, B accumulator, A accumulator, index register, program counter, and stack pointer. On the following line the terminal prints an asterisk.

b. If the contents of any of the registers are to be changed, change the data in accordance with Paragraph 4.1.3. It should be noted that the address of the stack pointer is stored last, and it takes eight memory locations to store the contents of the MPU registers on the stack. Figure 4-5 illustrates changing the contents of the MPU registers and identifies the location of each register's data.

4.1.6 Go to User's Program Function

This function enables the MPU to perform the user's program. It is assumed at the start of this function that the MPU is performing its MIKBUG control program and the data printed by the terminal is an asterisk.

Enter the character G after the asterisk. The MC6800 MPU System will perform the user's program until one of the following conditions occurs:

1) The MPU encounters a WAI (WAIt) instruction. The MPU now waits for a non-maskable interrupt or an interrupt request.

2) The MPU encounters a SWI (Software Interrupt) instruction. The MPU stores the data in the MPU registers on the stack and jumps to the MIKBUG control program. The terminal prints the contents of the MPU registers from the stack.

3) The RESET pushbutton switch is actuated. This switch is to be actuated when the user's program blows and places the MPU under the MIKBUG control program.

4.1.7 Interrupt Request Function

This function enables the user to evaluate a maskable interrupt routine. Steps a through e prepare the firmware to process an interrupt request and step f discusses performing the interrupt routine. It should be noted that this interrupt may be initiated at any time. It is assumed in preparing the MPU to process the interrupt request that the MPU is processing its MIKBUG control program and the last data printed by the terminal is an asterisk.

a. Enter the character M after the asterisk. The terminal will insert a space code after the M.

b. Enter the address A000. The terminal will print on the next line the memory address A000 and the contents of this memory location.

c. Enter a space code and the two most significant hexadecimal bytes of the first interrupt routine's address after the contents of address A000. These two bytes are stored in memory and the terminal prints address A001 and its contents on the next line.

d. Enter a space code and the two least significant hexadecimal bytes of the first interrupt routine's address after the contents of address A001. These two bytes are stored in memory and the terminal prints address A002 and its contents on the next line.

e. Enter a space code and a carriage return character after address A002. The MPU jumps to its MIKBUG control program and the terminal prints an asterisk.

The MPU now is enabled and ready to perform a maskable interrupt routine when the interrup mask is cleared. This interrupt routine may be initiated at any time either through the PIA (if enabled) or the $\overline{\text{IRQ}}$ input to the MPU. Initiating an interrupt through the PIA is discussed in the MC6820 Peripheral Interface Adapter data sheet while initiating an interrupt through the $\overline{\text{IRQ}}$ input is discussed below.

f. Ground $\overline{\text{IRQ}}$ input. If the interrupt mask is not set, the MPU will jump to the interrupt service routine indirectly through addresses A000 and A001. This is accomplished in MIKBUG by loading the index register with the contents of addresses A000 and A001 and then jumping to the address stored in the index register.

g. Remove the ground from the IRQ input.

4.1.8 Non-Maskable Interrupt Function

This function enables the user to evaluate a non-maskable interrupt routine. Steps a through e prepare the MC6800 MPU System to process a NMI (Non-Maskable Interrupt) input and step f discusses performing the interrupt routine. It is assumed in preparing the MC6800 MPU System to process a non-maskable interrupt that the MC6800 MPU System is processing its MIKBUG control program and the last last data printed by the data terminal is an asterisk.

a. Enter the character M after the asterisk. The terminal will insert a space code after the M.

b. Enter the address A006. The terminal will print on the next line the memory address A006 and the contents of this memory location.

c. Enter a space code and the two most significant hexadecimal digits of the first interrupt routine's address after the contents of address A006. These two digits are stored in memory and the terminal prints address A007 and its contents on the next line.

d. Enter a space code and the two least significant hexadecimal digits of the first interrupt routine's address after the contents of address A007. These two digits are stored in memory and the terminal prints address A008 and its contents on the next line.

e. Enter a space code and a carriage return character after address A008. The MC6800 MPU System jumps to its MIKBUG control program and the terminal prints an asterisk.

The MC6800 MPU System now is enabled to perform a non-maskable interrupt routine. This non-maskable interrupt routine may be initiated at any time through the MC6800 MPU System $\overline{\text{NMI}}$ input.

f. Ground the $\overline{\text{NMI}}$ input P1-E. If the non-maskable interrupt is not disabled (E3 to E4), the MPU will jump to the interrupt service routine indirectly through addresses A006 and A007. This is accomplished in MIKBUG by loading the index register with the contents of addresses A006 and A007 and then jumping to the address stored in the index register.

g. Remove the ground from the $\overline{\text{NMI}}$ input P1-E.

4.2 MINIBUG Rev. 4 Operation

The MINIBUG Firmware enables the user's system using the MIKBUG/MINIBUG ROM to perform the following functions:

Memory Loader Function
Memory Examine and Change Function
Display Contents of MPU Registers Function
Go to User's Program Function

The operating procedures for each of these routines as well as the RESET Function are discussed in the following paragraphs.

4.2.1 RESET Function

Perform the RESET Function when power is first applied and any time the MINIBUG Firmware loses program control.

Press the RESET switch (or equivalent). The MINIBUG Firmware should respond with a carriage return and a line feed character. The MINIBUG program control now is ready for an input.

4.2.2 Memory Loader Function

The memory loader function of MINIBUG loads formatted binary object tapes into memory. Figure 4-1 depicts the paper tape format. It is assumed at the start of this function that the MC6800 MPU is performing its MINIBUG control program. Figure 4-6 illustrates a typical memory loader function.

a. Load the tape into the tape reader.
b. Set the tape reader switch to AUTO.
c. Enter the character L. This initiates the MINIBUG loading procedure. The MINIBUG program ignores all characters prior to the start-of-record on the tape.

Checksum Error Detection

If during the loading function, the MINIBUG Firmware detects a checksum error, it instructs the terminal to print a question mark and stops while the MPU performs the MINIBUG control program. To load the tape, the user will have to repeat the memory loader function.

4.2.3 Memory Examine and Change Function

The MINIBUG Firmware performs this function in three steps: 1) examining the contents of the selected memory location (opening the memory location); 2) changing the contents of this location, if required; and 3) returning the contents to memory (closing the memory location). The Firmware, in examining a memory location, instructs the terminal to print the contents of this memory location in hexadecimal format. The MINIBUG Firmware in this function displays each of the program instructions in machine language.

It is assumed at the start of this function that the MPU is performing its MINIBUG control program. Figure 4-7 depicts a typical Memory Examine and Change Function.

NOTE
If no memory, a ROM, or a PROM is located at the selected address, the contents of this memory address cannot be changed and the terminal will print a question mark.

```
M FF2E  00  F0
M FF2F  00  00
```

FIGURE 4-7. Typical Memory Examine and Change Function

a. Enter the character M. The terminal will insert a space code after the M.
b. Enter in 4-character hexadecimal the memory address to be opened. The terminal will print a space code and then the contents of this memory location. The contents are in hexadecimal.
c. The operator must now decide whether to change the data at this memory location. If the data is to be changed, enter the two new hexadecimal characters to be stored in this location. The new contents are stored in memory and the MPU returns to the MINIBUG control program. If

L

S113000020FE020202020202020202020202020202B2

S9

FIGURE 4-6. Typical Memory Loader Function

the data is not to be changed, enter a carriage return character; the previous contents are returned to memory and the MPU returns to the MINIBUG control program.

4.2.4 Display Contents of MPU Registers Function

The Display Contents of MPU Registers Function enables the MINIBUG Firmware to display the contents of the MC6800 Microprocessing Unit registers for examination and change. It is assumed at the start of this function that the MPU is performing the MINIBUG control program. Figure 4-8 illustrates a typical Display Contents of MPU Registers Function.

a. Enter the character P. The terminal will print the contents of the MPU registers in the following sequence:

SP	Contents	MPU Register
FF29	00	Condition Code Register
FF2A	00	B Accumulator
FF2B	00	A Accumulator
FF2C	00	Index Register High
FF2D	00	Index Register Low
FF2E	F0	Program Counter High
FF2F	00	Program Counter Low

b. Use the Memory Examine and Change Function in paragraph 4.2.3 to change the contents of a register.

4.2.5 Go to User's Program Function

This function enables the MPU to perform the user's program. It is assumed at the start of this function that the MPU is performing its MINIBUG control program. Figure 4-9 illustrates a typical Go to User's Program Function.

```
  CC B  A  XH XL PH PL SH SL
P 00 00 00 00 00 F0 00 FF 29
```

FIGURE 4-8. Typical Contents of MPU Register Function

```
P 00 00 00 00 00 00 00 FF 29
M 0000 FF 7E
M 0001 00
M 0002 00
G
```

FIGURE 4-9. Typical Go to User's Program Function

Enter the character G. The MPU will load the MPU registers with the contents identified in Paragraph 4.2.4 and then start running the user's program at the address in the program counter (locations FF2E and FF2F). The program counter may be changed using the Memory Examine and Change Function in Paragraph 4.2.3.

5.0 MIKBUG REV. 9 PROGRAM LISTING

```
00100                         NAM     MIKBUG
00200                 *       REV 009
00300                 *       COPYRIGHT 1974 BY MOTOROLA INC

00500                 *       MIKBUG (TM)

00700                 *       L   LOAD
00800                 *       G   GO TO TARGET PROGRAM
00900                 *       M   MEMORY CHANGE
01000                 *       P   PRINT/PUNCH DUMP
01100                 *       R   DISPLAY CONTENTS OF TARGET STACK
01200                 *               CC   B    A    X    P    S

01400        8007     PIASB   EQU     $8007
01500        8006     PIADB   EQU     $8006        B DATA
01600        8005     PIAS    EQU     $8005        PIA STATUS
01700        8004     PIAD    EQU     $8004        PIA DATA
01800                         OPT     MEMORY
01900 E000                    ORG     $E000

02100                 *       I/O INTERRUPT SEQUENCE
02200 E000 FE A000 IO        LDX     IOV
02300 E003 6E 00              JMP     X

 500                 * NMI SEQUENCE
02600 E005 FE A006 POWDWN LDX     NIO          GET NMI VECTOR
02700 E008 6E 00              JMP     X


03000        E00A     LOAD    EQU     *
03100 E00A 86 3C              LDA A   #$3C
03200 E00C B7 8007            STA A   PIASB        READER RELAY ON
03300 E00F 86 11              LDA A   #@21
03400 E011 8D 62              BSR     OUTCH        OUTPUT CHAR

03600 E013 8D 63  LOAD3       BSR     INCH
03700 E015 81 53              CMP A   #'S
03800 E017 26 FA              BNE     LOAD3        1ST CHAR NOT (S)
03900 E019 8D 5D              BSR     INCH         READ CHAR
04000 E01B 81 39              CMP A   #'9
04100 E01D 27 25              BEQ     LOAD21
04200 E01F 81 31              CMP A   #'1
04300 E021 26 F0              BNE     LOAD3        2ND CHAR NOT (1)
04400 E023 7F A00A            CLR     CKSM         ZERO CHECKSUM
04500 E026 8D 2D              BSR     BYTE         READ BYTE
04600 E028 80 02              SUB A   #2
04700 E02A B7 A00B            STA A   BYTECT       BYTE COUNT
04800                 * BUILD ADDRESS
04900 E02D 8D 18              BSR     BADDR
05000                 * STORE DATA
05100 E02F 8D 24  LOAD11      BSR     BYTE
```

MIKBUG REV. 9 PROGRAM LISTING (continued)

```
05200 E031 7A A00B          DEC     BYTECT
05300 E034 27 05            BEQ     LOAD15      ZERO BYTE COUNT
05400 E036 A7 00            STA A   X           STORE DATA
05500 E038 08               INX
05600 E039 20 F4            BRA     LOAD11

05800 E03B 7C A00A LOAD15   INC     CKSM
05900 E03E 27 D3            BEQ     LOAD3
06000 E040 86 3F   LOAD19   LDA A   #'?         PRINT QUESTION MARK
06100 E042 8D 31            BSR     OUTCH
06200      E044   LOAD21   EQU     *
06300 E044 7E E0E3 C1       JMP     CONTRL


06500              * BUILD ADDRESS
06600 E047 8D 0C   BADDR    BSR     BYTE        READ 2 FRAMES
06700 E049 B7 A00C          STA A   XHI
06800 E04C 8D 07            BSR     BYTE
06900 E04E B7 A00D          STA A   XLOW
07000 E051 FE A00C          LDX     XHI         (X) ADDRESS WE BUILT
07100 E054 39               RTS


07300              * INPUT BYTE (TWO FRAMES)
07400 E055 8D 53   BYTE     BSR     INHEX       GET HEX CHAR
07500 E057 48               ASL A
07600 E058 48               ASL A
07700 E059 48               ASL A
07800 E05A 48               ASL A
07900 E05B 16               TAB
08000 E05C 8D 4C            BSR     INHEX
08100 E05E 1B               ABA
08200 E05F 16               TAB
08300 E060 FB A00A          ADD B   CKSM
08400 E063 F7 A00A          STA B   CKSM
08500 E066 39               RTS

08700 E067 44      OUTHL    LSR A               OUT HEX LEFT BCD DIGIT
08800 E068 44               LSR A
08900 E069 44               LSR A
09000 E06A 44               LSR A


09300 E06B 84 0F   OUTHR    AND A   #$F         OUT HEX RIGHT BCD DIGIT
09400 E06D 8B 30            ADD A   #$30
09500 E06F 81 39            CMP A   #$39
09600 E071 23 02            BLS     OUTCH
09700 E073 8B 07            ADD A   #$7

09900              * OUTPUT ONE CHAR
10000 E075 7E E1D1 OUTCH    JMP     OUTEEE
10100 E078 7E E1AC INCH     JMP     INEEE
```

MIKBUG REV. 9 PROGRAM LISTING (continued)

```
10200                         * PRINT DATA POINTED AT BY X-REG
10300 E07B 8D F8   PDATA2 BSR      OUTCH
10400 E07D 08             INX
10500 E07E A6 00   PDATA1 LDA A    X
10600 E080 81 04          CMP A    #4
10700 E082 26 F7          BNE      PDATA2
10800 E084 39             RTS               STOP ON EOT

11000                         * CHANGE MEMORY (M AAAA DD NN)
11100 E085 8D C0   CHANGE BSR      BADDR     BUILD ADDRESS
11200 E087 CE E19D CHA51  LDX      #MCL
11300 E08A 8D F2          BSR      PDATA1    C/R L/F
11400 E08C CE A00C        LDX      #XHI
11500 E08F 8D 37          BSR      OUT4HS    PRINT ADDRESS
11600 E091 FE A00C        LDX      XHI
11700 E094 8D 34          BSR      OUT2HS    PRINT DATA (OLD)
11800 E096 FF A00C        STX      XHI       SAVE DATA ADDRESS
11900 E099 8D DD          BSR      INCH      INPUT ONE CHAR
12000 E09B 81 20          CMP A    #$20
12100 E09D 26 E8          BNE      CHA51     NOT SPACE
12200 E09F 8D B4          BSR      BYTE      INPUT NEW DATA
12300 E0A1 09             DEX
12400 E0A2 A7 00          STA A    X         CHANGE MEMORY
12500 E0A4 A1 00          CMP A    X
12600 E0A6 27 DF          BEQ      CHA51     DID CHANGE
12700 E0A8 20 96          BRA      LOAD19    NOT CHANGED


13100                         * INPUT HEX CHAR
13200 E0AA 8D CC   INHEX  BSR      INCH
13300 E0AC 80 30          SUB A    #$30
13400 E0AE 2B 94          BMI      C1        NOT HEX
13500 E0B0 81 09          CMP A    #$09
13600 E0B2 2F 0A          BLE      IN1HG
13700 E0B4 81 11          CMP A    #$11
13800 E0B6 2B 8C          BMI      C1        NOT HEX
13900 E0B8 81 16          CMP A    #$16
14000 E0BA 2E 88          BGT      C1        NOT HEX
14100 E0BC 80 07          SUB A    #7
14200 E0BE 39     IN1HG  RTS


14500 E0BF A6 00   OUT2H  LDA A    0,X       OUTPUT 2 HEX CHAR
14600 E0C1 8D A4   OUT2HA BSR      OUTHL     OUT LEFT HEX CHAR
14700 E0C3 A6 00          LDA A    0,X
14800 E0C5 08             INX
14900 E0C6 20 A3          BRA      OUTHR     OUTPUT RIGHT HEX CHAR AND R

15100 E0C8 8D F5   OUT4HS BSR      OUT2H     OUTPUT 4 HEX CHAR + SPACE
15200 E0CA 8D F3   OUT2HS BSR      OUT2H     OUTPUT 2 HEX CHAR + SPACE
```

MIKBUG REV. 9 PROGRAM LISTING (continued)

```
15300 EOCC 86 20    OUTS    LDA A   #$20      SPACE
15400 EOCE 20 A5            BRA     OUTCH     (BSR & RTS)

15600                 * ENTER POWER ON SEQUENCE
15700        EODO    START   EQU     *
15800 EODO 8E A042           LDS     #STACK
15900 EOD3 BF A008           STS     SP        INZ TARGET'S STACK PNTR
16000                 * INZ PIA
16100 EOD6 CE 8004           LDX     #PIAD     (X) POINTER TO.DEVICE PIA
16200 EOD9 6C 00             INC     0,X       SET DATA DIR PIAD
16300 EODB 86 07             LDA A   #$7
16400 EODD A7 01             STA A   1,X       INIT CON PIAS
16500 EODF 6C 00             INC     0,X       MARK COM LINE
16600 EOE1 A7 02             STA A   2,X       SET DATA DIR PIADB
16700 EOE3 86 34    CONTRL   LDA A   #$34
16800 EOE5 B7 8007           STA A   PIASB     SET CONTROL PIASB TURN READ
16900 EOE8 B7 8006           STA A   PIADB     SET TIMER INTERVAL
17000 EOEB 8E A042           LDS     #STACK    SET CONTRL STACK POINTER
17100 EOEE CE E19C           LDX     #MCLOFF

17300 EOF1 8D 8B             BSR     PDATA1    PRINT DATA STRING

17500 EOF3 8D 83             BSR     INCH      READ CHARACTER
17600 EOF5 16               TAB
17700 EOF6 8D D4             BSR     OUTS      PRINT SPACE
17800 EOF8 C1 4C             CMP B   #'L
17900 EOFA 26 03             BNE     *+5
18000 EOFC 7E EODA           JMP     LOAD
18100 EOFF C1 4D             CMP B   #'M
18200 E101 27 82             BEQ     CHANGE
18300 E103 C1 52             CMP B   #'R
18400 E105 27 18             BEQ     PRINT     STACK
18500 E107 C1 50             CMP B   #'P
18600 E109 27 32             BEQ     PUNCH     PRINT/PUNCH
18700 E10B C1 47             CMP B   #'G
18800 E10D 26 D4             BNE     CONTRL
18900 E10F BE A008           LDS     SP        RESTORE PGM'S STACK PTR
19000 E112 3B               RTI               GO

19200                 * ENTER FROM SOFTWARE INTERRUPT
19300        E113    SFE     EQU     *
19400 E113 BF A008           STS     SP        SAVE TARGET'S STACK POINTER
19500                 * DECREMENT P-COUNTER
19600 E116 30               TSX
19700 E117 6D 06             TST     6,X
19800 E119 26 02             BNE     *+4
19900 E11B 6A 05             DEC     5,X
20000 E11D 6A 06             DEC     6,X

20200                 * PRINT CONTENTS OF STACK
20300 E11F FE A008   PRINT   LDX     SP
20400 E122 08               INX
```

MIKBUG REV. 9 PROGRAM LISTING (continued)

```
20500 E123 8D A5          BSR   OUT2HS   CONDITION CODES
20600 E125 8D A3          BSR   OUT2HS   ACC-B
20700 E127 8D A1          BSR   OUT2HS   ACC-A
20800 E129 8D 9D          BSR   OUT4HS   X-REG
20900 E12B 8D 9B          BSR   OUT4HS   P-COUNTER
21000 E12D CE A008        LDX   #SP
21100 E130 8D 96          BSR   OUT4HS   STACK POINTER
21200 E132 20 AF    C2    BRA   CONTRL


21400            *     PUNCH DUMP
21500            *     PUNCH FROM BEGINING ADDRESS (BEGA) THRU ENDI
21600            *     ADDRESS (ENDA)
21700            *

21900 E134 0D    MTAPE1 FCB   $D,$A,0,0,0,0,'S','1',4   PUNCH FORMAT
      E135 0A
      E136 00
      E137 00
      E138 00
      E139 00
      E13A 53
      E13B 31
      E13C 04


22100      E13D   PUNCH   EQU   *

22300 E13D 86 12          LDA A  #$12     TURN TTY PUNCH ON
22400 E13F BD E075        JSR    OUTCH    OUT CHAR

22600 E142 FE A002        LDX    BEGA
22700 E145 FF A00F        STX    TW       TEMP BEGINING ADDRESS
22800 E148 B6 A005 PUN11  LDA A  ENDA+1
22900 E14B B0 A010        SUB A  TW+1
23000 E14E F6 A004        LDA B  ENDA
23100 E151 F2 A00F        SBC B  TW
23200 E154 26 04          BNE    PUN22
23300 E156 81 10          CMP A  #16
23400 E158 25 02          BCS    PUN23
23500 E15A 86 0F   PUN22  LDA A  #15
23600 E15C 8B 04   PUN23  ADD A  #4
23700 E15E B7 A011        STA A  MCONT    FRAME COUNT THIS RECORD
23800 E161 80 03          SUB A  #3
23900 E163 B7 A00E        STA A  TEMP     BYTE COUNT THIS RECORD
24000            *     PUNCH C/R,L/F,NULL,S,1
24100 E166 CE E134        LDX    #MTAPE1
24200 E169 BD E07E        JSR    PDATA1
24300 E16C 5F             CLR B           ZERO CHECKSUM
24400            *     PUNCH FRAME COUNT
24500 E16D CE A011        LDX    #MCONT
24600 E170 8D 25          BSR    PUNT2    PUNCH 2 HEX CHAR
24700            *     PUNCH ADDRESS
```

MIKBUG REV. 9 PROGRAM LISTING (continued)

```
24800 E172 CE A00F        LDX    #TW
24900 E175 8D 20          BSR    PUNT2
25000 E177 8D 1E          BSR    PUNT2
25100              *    PUNCH DATA
25200 E179 FE A00F        LDX    TW
25300 E17C 8D 19   PUN32  BSR    PUNT2    PUNCH ONE BYTE (2 FRAMES)
25400 E17E 7A A00E        DEC    TEMP     DEC BYTE COUNT
25500 E181 26 F9          BNE    PUN32
25600 E183 FF A00F        STX    TW
25700 E186 53             COM B
25800 E187 37             PSH B
25900 E188 30             TSX
26000 E189 8D 0C          BSR    PUNT2    PUNCH CHECKSUM
26100 E18B 33             PUL B           RESTORE STACK
26200 E18C FE A00F        LDX    TW
26300 E18F 09             DEX
26400 E190 BC A004        CPX    ENDA
26500 E193 26 B3          BNE    PUN11
26600 E195 20 9B          BRA    C2       JMP TO CONTRL


26800              *    PUNCH 2 HEX CHAR, UPDATE CHECKSUM
26900 E197 EB 00   PUNT2  ADD B  0,X      UPDATE CHECKSUM
27000 E199 7E E0BF        JMP    OUT2H    OUTPUT TWO HEX CHAR AND RTS


27020 E19C 13      MCLOFF FCB    $13      READER OFF
27100 E19D 00      MCL    FCB    $D,$A,$14,0,0,0,'*,4   C/R,L/F,PUNCH
      E19E 0A
      E19F 14
      E1A0 00
      E1A1 00
      E1A2 00
      E1A3 2A
      E1A4 04
27200              *
27300 E1A5 FF A012 SAV    STX    XTEMP
27400 E1A8 CE 8004        LDX    #PIAD
27500 E1AB 39             RTS
27600              * INPUT ONE CHAR INTO A-REGISTER
27700 E1AC 37      INEEE  PSH B           SAVE ACC-B
27800 E1AD 8D F6          BSR    SAV      SAV XR
27900 E1AF A6 00   IN1    LDA A  0,X      LOOK FOR START BIT
28000 E1B1 2B FC          BMI    IN1
28100 E1B3 6F 02          CLR    2,X      SET COUNTER FOR HALF BIT TI
28200 E1B5 8D 3C          BSR    DE       START TIMER
28300 E1B7 8D 36          BSR    DEL      DELAY HALF BIT TIME
28400 E1B9 C6 04          LDA B  #4       SET DEL FOR FULL BIT TIME
28500 E1BB E7 02          STA B  2,X
28600 E1BD 58             ASL B           SET UP CNTR WITH 8
```

MIKBUG REV. 9 PROGRAM LISTING (continued)

```
28700 E1BE 8D 2F    IN3    BSR    DEL        WAIT ONE CHAR TIME
28800 E1C0 0D               SEC               MARK COM LINE
28900 E1C1 69 00            ROL    0,X        GET BIT INTO CFF
29000 E1C3 46               ROR A             CFF TO AR
29100 E1C4 5A               DEC B
29200 E1C5 26 F7            BNE    IN3
29300 E1C7 8D 26            BSR    DEL        WAIT FOR STOP BIT
29400 E1C9 84 7F            AND A  #$7F       RESET PARITY BIT
29500 E1CB 81 7F            CMP A  #$7F
29600 E1CD 27 E0            BEQ    IN1        IF RUBOUT,GET NEXT CHAR
29700 E1CF 20 12            BRA    IOUT2      GO RESTORE REG


29900                * OUTPUT ONE CHAR
30000 E1D1 37    OUTEEE PSH B                 SAV BR
30100 E1D2 8D D1            BSR    SAV        SAV XR
30200 E1D4 C6 0A    IOUT   LDA B  #$A        SET UP COUNTER
30300 E1D6 6A 00            DEC    0,X        SET START BIT
30400 E1D8 8D 19            BSR    DE         START TIMER
30500             *
30600 E1DA 8D 13    OUT1   BSR    DEL        DELAY ONE BIT TIME
30700 E1DC A7 00            STA A  0,X        PUT OUT ONE DATA BIT
30800 E1DE 0D               SEC               SET CARRY BIT
30900 E1DF 46               ROR A             SHIFT IN NEXT BIT
31000 E1E0 5A               DEC B             DECREMENT COUNTER
31100 E1E1 26 F7            BNE    OUT1       TEST FOR 0
31200 E1E3 E6 02    IOUT2  LDA B  2,X        TEST FOR STOP BITS
31300 E1E5 58               ASL B             SHIFT BIT TO SIGN
31400 E1E6 2A 02            BPL    IOS        BRANCH FOR 1 STOP BIT
31500 E1E8 8D 05            BSR    DEL        DELAY FOR STOP BITS
31600 E1EA FE A012 IOS     LDX    XTEMP      RES XR
31700 E1ED 33               PUL B             RESTORE BR
31800 E1EE 39               RTS
31900             *
32000 E1EF 6D 02    DEL    TST    2,X        IS TIME UP
32100 E1F1 2A FC            BPL    DEL
32200 E1F3 6C 02    DE     INC    2,X        RESET TIMER
32300 E1F5 6A 02            DEC    2,X
32400 E1F7 39               RTS


32600 E1F8 E000            FDB    IO
32700 E1FA E113            FDB    $FE
32800 E1FC E005            FDB    POWDWN
32900 E1FE E0D0            FDB    START
33000 A000                 ORG    $A000
33100 A000 0002    IOV     RMB    2          IO INTERRUPT POINTER
33200 A002 0002    BEGA    RMB    2          BEGINING ADDR PRINT/PUNCH
33300 A004 0002    ENDA    RMB    2          ENDING ADDR PRINT/PUNCH
33400 A006 0002    NIO     RMB    2          NMI INTERRUPT POINTER
33500 A008 0001    SP      RMB    1          S-HIGH
33600 A009 0001            RMB    1          S-LOW
33700 A00A 0001    CKSM    RMB    1          CHECKSUM
```

MIKBUG REV. 9 PROGRAM LISTING (continued)

```
33800 A00B 0001    BYTECT  RMB   1      BYTE COUNT
33900 A00C 0001    XHI     RMB   1      XREG HIGH
34000 A00D 0001    XLOW    RMB   1      XREG LOW
34100 A00E 0001    TEMP    RMB   1      CHAR COUNT (INADD)
34200 A00F 0002    TW      RMB   2      TEMP/
34300 A011 0001    MCONT   RMB   1      TEMP
34400 A012 0002    XTEMP   RMB   2      X-REG TEMP STORAGE
34500 A014 002E            RMB   46
34600 A042 0001    STACK   RMB   1      STACK POINTER


35000                      END


SYMBOL TABLE


PIASB  8007   PIADB  8006   PIAS   8005   PIAD   8004   IO     E000
POWDWN E005   LOAD   E00A   LOAD3  E013   LOAD11 E02F   LOAD15 E03B
LOAD19 E040   LOAD21 E044   C1     E044   BADDR  E047   BYTE   E055
OUTHL  E067   OUTHR  E06B   OUTCH  E075   INCH   E078   PDATA2 E07B
PDATA1 E07E   CHANGE E085   CHA51  E087   INHEX  E0AA   IN1HG  E0BE
OUT2H  E0BF   OUT2HA E0C1   OUT4HS E0C8   OUT2HS E0CA   OUTS   E0CC
START  E0DD   CONTRL E0E3   SFE    E113   PRINT  E11F   C2     E132
MTAPE1 E134   PUNCH  E13D   PUN11  E148   PUN22  E15A   PUN23  E15C
PUN32  E17C   PUNT2  E197   MCLOFF E19C   MCL    E19D   SAV    E1A5
INEEE  E1AC   IN1    E1AF   IN3    E1BE   OUTEEE E1D1   IOUT   E1D4
OUT1   E1DA   IOUT2  E1E3   IOS    E1EA   DEL    E1EF   DE     E1F3
IOV    A000   BEGA   A002   ENDA   A004   NIO    A006   SP     A008
CKSM   A00A   BYTECT A00B   XHI    A00C   XLOW   A00D   TEMP   A00E
TW     A00F   MCONT  A011   XTEMP  A012   STACK  A042
```

Index